Involving Children and Young People in Health and Social Care Research

Led by both children's rights perspectives and methodological arguments, there is a growing emphasis on children's and young people's participation in health and social care research by researchers, policy makers and funding bodies – with many now considering the active involvement of children and young people a requirement. However, although increasingly important, there is little exploration of how to address and overcome the many challenges arising from their participation.

Divided into five parts, this practical book begins by considering what research with young people is and why we should do it, before leading the reader into how to undertake it. The book then provides practical examples of action and finishes with reflections about the whole process. Bringing together a variety of experienced researchers from a wide range of backgrounds in health and social care, including young people, the chapters provide insight for practical action, as well as critical and theoretical reflection. *Involving Children and Young People in Health and Social Care Research* includes discussion of:

- The reasons and motivations for involving children and young people in research
- Making sure that involvement is meaningful and not merely tokenistic
- Developing research methods that are commensurate with different ages and abilities
- Ensuring adequate training and preparation for children, young people and adults to make involvement meaningful
- Power and relationships between young researchers and adult researchers
- Sustaining young people's interest and motivation
- Addressing ethical issues that arise throughout the research journey.

Committed to partnership and participation throughout the entire process of the active involvement of children and young people in health and social care research, this text provides invaluable insights and is a resource for all those conducting research in and with children and young people.

Jennie Fleming is Reader in Participatory Research and Social Action and the Director of the Centre for Social Action at De Montfort University, Leicester, UK.

Thilo Boeck is Senior Research Fellow at the Centre for Social Action at De Montfort University, Leicester, UK.

Involving Children and Young People in Health and Social Care Research

Edited by
Jennie Fleming and Thilo Boeck

Routledge
Taylor & Francis Group
LONDON AND NEW YORK

First published 2012
by Routledge
2 Park Square, Milton Park, Abingdon, Oxon OX14 4RN

Simultaneously published in the USA and Canada
by Routledge
711 Third Avenue, New York, NY 10017

Routledge is an imprint of the Taylor & Francis Group, an informa business

British Library Cataloguing in Publication Data
A catalogue record for this book is available from the British Library

Library of Congress Cataloging in Publication Data
Involving children and young people in health and social care research / edited by Jennie Fleming and Thilo Boeck.
p. cm.
Child welfare--Research--Citizen participation. 2. Child health services--Research--Citizen participation. 3. Evaluation research (Social action programs)--Citizen participation. 4. Children's rights. I. Fleming, Jennie. II. Boeck, Thilo.
HV715.I58 2012
362.7072--dc23
2011049071

ISBN: 978-0-415-66349-6 (hbk)
ISBN: 978-0-415-52303-5 (pbk)
ISBN: 978-0-203-11631-9 (ebk)

Typeset in Goudy
by Taylor & Francis Books

Contents

Acknowledgements

Firstly we want to extend our gratitude to Lesley Lowes who conceived the idea for this volume and started the process of its creation. We were able to build on her firm foundations.

We would like to thank the contributors to this volume. They have all contributed honest descriptions and thought provoking accounts of their work. The volume is a testimony to their commitment to the involvement of children and young people in research.

We must acknowledge all the young people we have worked with on research projects – we thank them for their insight, knowledge, challenge, commitment and enthusiasm – and patience. They have taught us all that we know about working with young people on research projects.

We both want to thank Dave Ward and Bill Badham who have constantly been at our sides supporting and challenging us to always strive for more in our participatory research. Whilst offering encouragement they have never let us become complacent.

Notes on contributors

Thilo Boeck is a Senior Research Fellow at the Centre for Social Action at De Montfort University in Leicester, UK.

Vikki Butler is Senior Research and Policy Officer, Policy and Research Unit, Barnardo's Cymru, UK.

Liam Cairns is Director of Investing in Children, Durham, UK.

Claire Callens is the User Involvement Co-ordinator, NIHR Medicines for Children Research Network, UK.

Harrison Carter is an Associate Research Assistant at De Montfort University's Centre for Social Action, UK.

Dr Paul Chester is Visiting Academic at the Oxford Centre for Diabetes, Endocrinology and Metabolism and Honorary Associate Professor at Warwick Medical School and Honorary Lecturer at Barts and the London Medical School, Queen Mary College, London, UK.

Mayuri Chudasama is an Associate Research Assistant at De Montfort University's Centre for Social Action, UK.

Philippa Collin is a Research Fellow at the Institute for Culture and Society at the University of Western Sydney, Australia, and Programme Leader, Young and Well Cooperative Research Centre.

Iman Dalenius is an Associate Research Assistant at De Montfort University's Centre for Social Action, UK.

Susanna Dobson is an Associate Research Assistant at De Montfort University's Centre for Social Action, UK.

Dr Jane Ellis is Research Fellow in the Institute of Education, University of Warwick, UK.

Jennie Fleming is Reader in Participatory Research and Social Action and the Director of the Centre for Social Action at De Montfort University, UK.

Leah Fletcher is a Young Researcher with Investing in Children, Durham, UK.

Michael Gaffney is a PhD candidate at the University of Otago New Zealand where he worked for 15 years as a social science researcher.

Dr Alexandra Greene is currently Senior Research Fellow in Medical Anthropology and Director of the Nexus Programme in Child Health at the University of Dundee, in Scotland, and is about to take up the position of behavioural science lead in the Medical School.

Lyn Horrocks is Physiotherapy Lecturer at Cardiff University, Wales.

Dr Eleanor D. Kennedy now works with the Diabetes Research Network UK and as a freelance writer, producer, editor and consultant.

Mererid Lewis is Senior Development Officer at the Participation Unit, Save the Children, UK.

Dr Lesley Lowes is Reader/Practitioner at Cardiff University, and works as a paediatric diabetes specialist nurse at Cardiff and Vale University Health Board. She is co-editor of *Involving Service Users in Health and Social Care Research*, published by Routledge in 2005.

Dr Peter K. Mackie is Lecturer in Human Geography, Cardiff University, Wales.

Professor Nicola Madge is Associate Director for Consumer Involvement, Brunel University, UK.

Professor David R. Matthews is Emeritus Chairman of the Oxford Centre for Diabetes, Endocrinology and Metabolism and is Co-director of the Diabetes Research Network, UK.

Virginia Morrow is Senior Research Officer, Young Lives, Department of International Development, University of Oxford, UK.

Jenny Munro is a Senior Practitioner at the Otago Youth Wellness Centre, Dunedin, New Zealand.

Pritesh Nathubhai is an Associate Research Assistant at De Montfort University's Centre for Social Action, UK.

Jennifer Newman is the Consumer Liaison Manager, NIHR Medicines for Children Research Network, UK.

Dawn Pickering is Physiotherapy Lecturer, Cardiff University, Wales.

Dr Lorraine Radford is an independent research consultant; she was formerly Head of Research at the NSPCC (National Society for the Prevention of Cruelty to Children).

Kim Sabo Flores is the Associate Director, Thrive Foundation For Youth, California, USA.

Dr Darren Sharpe is Postdoctoral Research Fellow, Childhood and Youth Research Institute, Anglia Ruskin University, UK.

Anna Skeels was Manager of Save the Children's Participation Unit for Wales and is currently undertaking a PhD and freelance work on children's participation both in the UK and overseas.

Roger Smith is Professor of Social Work Research at De Montfort University, UK.

Melissa Stamp is a Young Researcher with Investing in Children, Durham, UK.

Ruth Taylor is an Associate Research Assistant at De Montfort University's Centre for Social Action, UK.

Nigel Thomas is Professor of Childhood and Youth Research at the University of Central Lancashire, UK, and Director of the Centre for Children and Young People's Participation.

Carly Tibbins is User Involvement Co-ordinator, NIHR Medicines for Children Research Network, UK.

Gabriela Todd is Senior Physiotherapist for Children and Young People Cardiff Pedal Power Project for All Abilities, Wales.

Shruti Uppal is currently training to become a Children and Families Social Worker at Goldsmiths, University of London, UK.

Karen Visser is a Physiotherapy Lecturer and Researcher, Cardiff University, Wales.

Introduction

Jennie Fleming and Thilo Boeck

As editors, we welcome you to this volume focusing on children and young people's involvement in health and social care research. We anticipate that this volume will be an essential resource and provide a follow-on to *Involving Service Users in Health and Social Care Research* edited by Lowes and Hulatt (2005), which, alongside others (for example, Percy-Smith and Thomas 2010) identified the need for a book dedicated to the involvement of children and young people in research. We have come a long way since research ignored children and young people, however their involvement is taking time to become widespread, and this volume makes a contribution to the debate about both the principles and practice of research with children and young people. It will, hopefully, encourage many more people to follow the example of the contributors and seek to find ways to actively involve children and young people in research.

Involving Children and Young People in Health and Social Care Research brings together contributors from a range of countries, as well as from a variety of backgrounds – including young researchers, academics and practitioner researchers. They are working in different sectors of statutory and voluntary health and social care services. The examples in the volume are centred on work in the English-speaking world – UK, USA, New Zealand and Australia; however, we anticipate it will be of relevance more widely. Alderson (in Christensen and James 2008: 276) points out that children and young people working as researchers is on the increase across the world. Research actively involving young people takes place in all corners of the globe – Hungary and Cyprus (Kellet 2010), Liberia, Sierra Leone and Northern Uganda (Wessells et al. 2010) and Bolivia (Punch 2002), to highlight a few, and they serve as a reminder of the importance of considering the examples in this volume in a wider context.

As the editors, our motivation to develop and produce this volume is shared by the authors of the chapters. It stems from our commitment to the value of working with young people on research projects and the increasing realisation that researchers – whether academics or practitioners – undertaking, or aspiring to undertake, research with children and young people, want and need practical guidance that arises from the real world. Whilst there is a growing body of literature on this area, there is still little where practice is explored in detail, the chapters in the volume do this.

There is an increasing emphasis on children and young people's participation in research by researchers, policy makers, youth organisations and funding bodies, with many now considering the active involvement of children and young people a requirement. The chapters provide insight for practice, as well as offering a more reflexive element. They create a combination of theoretical underpinnings, practical experiences and critical analysis. They focus on the specifics of the health and social care field, where there are often issues that are different from other settings.

All the contributors to the volume are experienced in undertaking research with and by young people and they have all chosen topics to write about that they consider important and relevant to a wider audience. We believe the variety of topics will ensure the volume will be of interest to a wide range of people from different professional groups and people with different levels of experience in research. Any contribution to such a broad area as involving children and young people in health and social care research cannot cover all the ground – it would be impossible to do so. The authors have written about issues that have arisen for them when doing research. It is not a comprehensive guide book or tool kit, rather a careful consideration and exploration of issues people felt were important. Each chapter can be read in isolation; however, the volume in its entirety provides a comprehensive, real life text offering the reader an exploration of some of the challenges of actively involving children and young people in research and some strategies to address these.

The authors provide honest accounts that are both critical and accessible concerning how to address and overcome the challenges arising in their research. Such challenges include:

- Understanding the reasons and motivations for involving children and young people, and young people's motivations for being involved
- Ensuring that involvement is meaningful and not merely tokenistic
- Ensuring adequate training and preparation for children, young people and adults to make involvement meaningful
- Developing research methods that are commensurate with different ages and abilities
- Relationships between young people and adult researchers
- Sustaining young people's interest and motivation
- Addressing ethical issues that arise throughout the research journey.

The age range of children and young people includes children from around four years old to young people up to 19. Though the majority of chapters are based on work with young people, some address the issues of working with younger children. The chapters are written by people with different perspectives and experience, this is reflected in the language they use. They have referred to themselves and young people in a variety of ways. Young people involved in research are referred to as children, youth, young people, peer researchers, young researchers, co-researchers, consumers and young adults. Adults are referred to variously as adult researchers, academic researchers, professional researchers, staff and practitioners. These reflect the variety of roles people have taken, the relationships between them, and the disciplines and countries they come from.

Structure of the volume

In order to provide a framework in which to present the diverse material in a coherent manner we have integrated them in the broader process orientation of the social action perspective (http://www.dmu.ac.uk/csa). We start by considering *what* research with young people is and then *why* we should do it, which leads the reader into Part 3 on planning and preparation and *how* to do it. The next phase is *action* giving a number of different practical examples of research with children and young people. The final Part 5 is the *reflection* phase of the process, and finishes with some reflections about the whole process.

The volume is divided into the following parts.

1 **What** – is research with young people? This chapter sets the scene and the parameters of the volume.
2 **Why** – should we involve children and young people in research? These three chapters consider the theoretical and practical motivations for working with children and young people on research projects.
3 **How** – to undertake research with young people. These four chapters explore planning and preparation, and consider things to think about before starting to work with children and young people on research projects.
4 **Action** – the six chapters in Part 4 are descriptions of research with young people. Many include strongly the voice of young people and one is created by young researchers themselves.
5 **Reflection** – the final Part 5 offers reflections on the experience of working with young people on research projects, and includes one chapter by young people.

Each part is initiated by a short introduction and the final chapter crucially reviews some of the themes from the volume and considers the further development of children and young people's involvement in health and social care research.

Part 1

What is research involving children and young people?

This first part (Part 1) contains just one chapter that considers the ways of involving young people in health and social care research – from enabling young people's perspectives on issues to be heard, to young people leading their own research projects, the essence of research involving children and young people.

It offers critical insight into the range of ways that young people are involved in research, and suggests there is no single 'right way' to involve young people but that consideration should be given to how to maximise their involvement and the impact they can have on all stages of the research process.

1 What is research with young people?

Jennie Fleming and Thilo Boeck

Introduction

The phrase 'involving children and young people in research' covers a wide range of meanings and understandings. However, researchers seeking to involve young people in research are all attempting to include children's voices into research. The primary purpose is to articulate young people's views, seeking to study children in their own right and from their own perspectives, and focusing directly on children and their life conditions, activities, relationships, knowledge and experiences (Alanen 2001:12).

Christensen and Prout (2002:480) further suggest there are four ways of considering research involving young people in which young people can be viewed as 'objects' to be studied; as 'subjects' in their own right; as social actors able to act, change and be changed by their actions; and as active participants in the research process, able to shape, change and challenge the research process and knowledge development. However, within each of these ways of considering research with young people, there is still room for considerable variety of practice. Authors in the 'Why?' chapters (Part 2) of this volume explore why people might take these various views of the potential for young people's involvement. In this chapter, the focus is on *what* various forms research involving children and young people can take.

Research involving young people is based on a recognition that 'our knowledge of the world around us will depend on the way that we look at it' (Agar 2005:34). Researchers involving young people consider that adult views of children and young people differ from children's and young people's views of themselves (Waksler 1991:viii); and they are acknowledging children and young people as reliable informants concerning their own experiences (Farrell et al. 2004). This interest in young people's perspectives is not completely new, Hine (2009:35) points to studies in the 1970s such as View from the Boys (Parker 1974) and Learning to Labour (Willis 1979), indeed Roberts (2008:261) cites research from 1875 that listened to and reported children's experiences of emigration to Canada. Such examples notwithstanding, in much main stream research young people have been primarily seen as sources of data and sources of information. However, there is a growing body of expertise that seeks to challenge this asymmetrical relationship between the researcher and the researched, and instead seeks the contribution of young people to the research itself. As Bennett with Roberts write:

> This means that researchers try not to use people taking part in research only as sources of information, but to establish relationships with them and also give them something back, with a view to achieving positive change. (Bennett with Roberts 2004:5)

In recent years, there has been a considerable increase in the interest of ensuring all aspects of research design enable young people's perspectives to be heard. This has been addressed both in careful consideration of how research can encourage the voice of young people to be heard and the increasing number of people seeking to enable young people to take a more active role in the research process itself. This is evidenced in a growing number of articles (for example, Wyness 2009; Franks 2011; Uprichard 2010) and books (for example, Christensen and James 2008, Heath et al. 2009) covering a wide range of aspects of what is sometimes called child-centred, or young-person-focused research.

Research seeking young people's perspectives and for their voice to be heard

Those undertaking research with children and young people view them as social actors with agency (Chapter 2) and seek to work with them on research in ways that have this at the core. Young people are seen as fundamental to the research and as active and reflective participants. They seek to undertake research with young people in a more contextualised way – 'looking up' and treating them as experts in their own lives, rather than from the standpoint of 'looking down' (Alanen and Mayall 2001). As Smith (2010:161–62) writes, children are not seen as 'merely objects of inquiry in relation to their unrealised potential, but as a source of knowledge and understanding about the forms and meanings of social interactions' and as having the capacity to make sense of and interpret social interactions. Hence, when young people's voices are being sought they have to be positioned as participating subjects, knowers and social actors, rather than objects of the researcher's gaze (Smith 2011).

Kellet (2010:86) suggests that 'in the stampede to privilege research *by* children, it would be foolhardy to overlook the very valuable research conducted by adults *about* children', and she emphasises the importance in this of being able to build rapport and trust between the young people and the researchers (see Chapters 10 and 17). The desire to ensure that young people's voices are heard and young people feel best able to take part in research projects requires careful consideration of research design and research process; for example, research methods or ethical considerations.

Christensen and James (2008:2–3) write that 'carrying out research with young people does not *necessarily* entail adopting different or particular methods', rather that methods should be chosen based on their appropriateness for the people involved, the context and the kind of question asked. However, Pain et al. (2002) suggest that when working with socially excluded young people good research should include a strong qualitative element. Many authors of this volume appear to agree, using research methods such as interviews, focus groups and social media. They write of how the design of research needs care to ensure that children and young people feel comfortable and able to participate (Chapter 17).

Understanding young people to be social actors has ethical as well as methodological implications, with new ethical dilemmas and responsibilities arising due to the greater complexity of the field (Christensen and Prout 2002:477). Health and social care research with young people may need different forms of ethical consideration because of the differing levels of risk and potential harm to those involved (Alderson and Morrow 2011). However, in all contexts, research ethics are concerned with respecting the people who are a part of the research project, and so inevitably, as relationships between people within research change, careful consideration needs to be given to how to ensure such respect is embedded in all aspects of the project. There are those who question whether research which is NOT participatory in any way can be considered to be ethical (Smith 2011:14). Those coming from an emancipatory perspective would challenge the legitimacy of research that does not seek to involve and empower those who are invisible or oppressed (young people) (Kellet 2005a).

A number of chapters in this volume are concerned with just this aspect of research – giving careful deliberation to how ethical considerations such as confidentiality (Chapter 11), consent (Chapters 5 and 17) and the role of adults as gatekeepers (Chapters 6, 10, 12 and 16) need to be approached to balance young people's rights for participation and protection (Chapter 5). In addition, Radford and Ellis (Chapter 11) write of how they consulted with young people and parents as to how best to approach ethical issues in research into domestic violence and abuse.

However, the developments in research with young people include not only bringing children's voices into adult research by using more participative methods, but also enabling children and young people to take an active part in research themselves (see, for example, Boeck and Sharpe 2009; Fleming et al. 2009; McLaughlin 2005).

Young people being active in the process of research

Some health and social care researchers and research institutions have responded to the challenge of young people's empowerment in and through research, and have made moves away from identifying and taking account of children's perspectives towards a greater emphasis on models of inclusion that ensure a more fundamental level of involvement: that is, through the active involvement of young people in all stages of research – the planning and preparation, undertaking information collection, analysing and disseminating of research projects. There are numerous different ways of involving young people in the process of research as is shown by the chapters in this volume. McLaughlin (2005) says we should not be dogmatic about how to involve young people in research. However, an area that needs consideration is the capacity for participatory research to demonstrate coherence with its own internal demands; that is, the extent to which it complies with what are by now recognised participation standards (see Chapters 3, 4 and 16). The initial question to be considered here is how participatory is it or could it be?

There are a considerable number of tools, practice guides and evaluative mechanisms available to support the implementation and assessment of participatory methods. UNICEF, for example, has developed a set of 'useful tools' to support young people's participation in evaluation exercises (Gawler 2005), as have Molina et al. (2009) and Horwath et al. (2011). Most have been written for the adults involved (Kellet 2005b; Kirby 2004). However, more recently, guides have been written directly for young people (for example, Sharpe et al. 2010). Some, though, appear to reflect a degree of confusion over a necessary distinction between 'participation' and engagement in research processes, and a more fundamental 'participatory' approach, which necessitates the application of rather different criteria of effectiveness. Pain et al. (2002) suggest a set of strategic principles that should underpin 'participatory action research' with young people:

- Use of a range of methods likely to 'engage young people' and reflect their 'priorities and concerns'
- Facilitation of 'whatever level of participation young people wish to have'
- Recognition that 'difficult issues' will arise, which may challenge established interests
- Creation of mechanisms by which findings will be disseminated and turned into action
- Inclusion of young people in change processes
- Establishment of sustainable mechanisms for replicating participatory inquiry.

(adapted from Pain et al. 2002)

In this framework, it might appear that the distinction between 'participation' (enabling young people's voice to be heard in ways that are meaningful to them) and 'participatory' approaches is blurred, and that 'inclusion' does not amount, of itself, to a guarantee that young people will be able to exert any degree of control about either the conduct or the outcomes of the research process. On the other hand, the determinant nature of young people's involvement is more clearly reflected in the reference to the choices they are entitled to make about their 'level of participation'.

Others have suggested an even smaller number of overarching principles that should be observable in participatory research practice. Boeck et al. suggest three key elements, for example:

> The project was, as far as is possible, defined by the young people
> All work carried out was based on equal partnership with the young people
> Everyone had a unique contribution to make. Everyone was able to learn from everybody else.
>
> (Boeck et al. 2009:10)

Even within these models, levels of engagement and involvement can vary. It may be that young people contributing to adult-led projects, or working together with adults on joint research or directing their own research, maybe with support from adults.

One of the most commonly referred to gauges of participation is Hart's ladder of participation (Hart in Badham and Wade 2005:7) which illustrates that involvement and importantly power and control can take different forms. Hanley (2004:9) developed a continuum with three points – consultation, collaboration and control. Fleming and Hudson (2009) have adapted this model with regard to research with young people and have included Hart's level of 'Tokenism'. It is important to see positions on a continuum such as this as flexible not fixed – it is possible for one research project to move from position to position at different stages of the research process, creating 'pockets of participation' (Franks 2011).

Tokenism is defined as 'the policy or practice of making only a symbolic effort' (Merriam-Webster's Online Dictionary). This means that there is no real attempt to involve young people and to give them some influence over the research or evaluation, but lip service might be paid to the notion of their involvement.

Consultation is the practice of asking for a specific population or groups' views and perceptions, perhaps of the substantive issue, as well as accessing their views about the design of the research. This level of involvement may come at the beginning of the research (and often does), but may also come at subsequent stages, depending on the design of the study.

Collaboration is more purposively a *partnership* between the researcher or practitioner and the young people. In this approach, the research often remains researcher led, but a two-way relationship is fostered in which the young people play an equal role and are often actively involved at all stages of the research process.

Young people controlled research – the young people themselves are fully engaged in and in control of the research, which only involves professionals or adult researchers if they are invited by the young people (adapted from Hanley et al. 2004 in Fleming and Hudson 2009:118)

Fleming and Hudson suggest tokenism unfortunately is 'all too common in research with young people' (2009:117). A similar point is made by McLaughlin (2005:1396) when he writes of illusionary participation where young people's participation 'is mere sham'. The writers suggest such tokenism would manifest itself when, for example, arrangements are not suitable for young people's participation, their opinions are not valued, they have no influence over any decisions and they have nothing to gain from the process. Another aspect of tokenism to be aware of and avoid is manipulation, which Hart defines as 'adult-led activities, in which youth do as directed without understanding of the purpose for the activities' (Badham and Wade 2005:7).

As young people's participation in research has become more widespread, there are inevitably those who involve young people in research for pragmatic rather than ideological or epistemological reasons. They involve young people because everyone else is, funders require it, or they see it as a way of getting things done. As the body of experience, knowledge and skill of both young people and adults involved in research has grown, it is to be hoped that these types of 'involvement' have diminished, and it is less likely that 'good intentions slide into colonial smothering' (Roberts 2008:282), and that young people and adults are better able to recognise these actions for what they are.

However, participation is more often driven by values and the commitment to young people's human rights (Chapters 2 and 4). It is also a methodological position – that participatory research makes for better research. For all the authors in this book participation is a genuine feature of practice, rather than just a rhetorical commitment.

Consultation

Consultation largely involves asking people for their views to inform your decision making, however they may, or may not, be acted upon (Hanley 2004). Consultation can be tokenistic when people have no intention of acting on the findings and so consultation can have a bad name. However, serious consultation, with a commitment to act on what young people say and feedback to them as to what has happened as a result of what they have said can be a way of them having influence over aspects of the research. Badham (2009) suggests that consultations can be targeted and focused, time limited and of immediate relevance, however it is important to guard against them being unrepresentative, with no ownership or momentum.

Some authors in this volume have incorporated consultation into their work to ensure that elements such as ethical issues (Chapter 11) or awareness raising about diabetes research (Chapter 12) are addressed in ways that take into account the views and opinions of young people.

Collaboration

There are many examples of research collaborations between young people and adults. Kirby defines collaboration as involving 'the active, on-going partnership with young people in research' (Kirby 2004:10). The contributions which young people can make to projects may include identifying meaningful research questions, planning and design, data collection, data analysis and final presentation, collaborating with researchers, and disseminating findings and recommendations, or combinations of these. Data analysis has been seen by some as a particularly challenging element of research for young people, although there are increasing accounts of addressing this (Coad and Evans 2007; Chapters 7, 14, 15, 16, 18 and 19). Certainly from our own work we have learnt that young people readily understand the principles of thematic analysis – looking for patterns in data, contrast and paradoxes, and exploring the significance of these (Coffey and Atkinson 1996), and can use these techniques extremely well to make sense of the data they have collected (Chapter 13). Alderson (2008) has found that young people often concentrate on the stages of dissemination and acting on findings, as they want to see their research leading to change. McLaughlin (2006) outlines the benefits of young people playing a key role in dissemination to other young people. There is always a danger, however, that it is assumed that young people (for example) will know what other young people will respond to – this suggests a homogenised view of a highly diverse group.

A number of the authors in this volume identify their research as being a collaboration between young people and adults – the young people employed by a university research centre talk of shared decision making (Chapters 6 and 19). This notwithstanding, it is important to remind ourselves that 'whilst good conversations are achievable within participatory dialogue' (as chapters in this volume testify), it is important for researchers to remember and be aware of the power differentials that remain (Smith 2011:14).

An interesting point to note is that in collaborative projects the influence and roles taken on by young people often increase throughout the project. For example, Thomas (Chapter 14) writes of how young people became increasingly committed to their project and ultimately had a more 'hands on' role than had been anticipated. We also found this to be the case when working on a research project with young people as volunteers: they chose to have a much greater involvement in aspects such as analysis than we had anticipated at the outset (Chapter 18). Within such projects, young people can, of course, *lead* certain aspects of the project – this is true in our experience; for example when young people might be responsible for the information collection using tools and processes developed out of discussions with adults.

Young people lead research

Another form of young people's involvement in research is when young people have been encouraged to identify themselves as potential researchers and choose topics based on their own interests, for example through the work of the Young Researchers Network or the Children's Research Centre (Chapter 8, Kellet 2010).

Such projects are initiated and lead by young people with the young people having the power and control over decision making. This could be a group of young people undertaking research themselves. This does not mean there is no role for adults; however, adults are involved on the invitation of young people and are there to share knowledge and skills with them on their terms, with the project being lead by young people. Whilst it is still relatively uncommon, young people do lead research projects. Many but not all of these examples are connected with schools and colleges. There are, for example, young researchers in American classrooms where young people undertook small research projects on issues of concern to themselves. As the teachers involved write, 'students choose their own cause, research it, create a plan of action to positively affect the cause, act upon it, reflect on their progress, and present their entire project to the class' (Berdan et al. 2006:51). Such projects include young people investigating local landfills in their impact on the health of the community, book choices from the library and scoping the need for a youth centre in their neighbourhood.

Within this volume there are examples of young people-led research, though these still often start with the suggestion of research coming from adults, and then the young people leading from there (for example, Chapters 8, 9 and 18).

Participation for change

Research itself is a political activity (Mayall 1999:5). It is not a neutral exercise in knowledge and evidence creation. Its methods are socially constructed; it can meet the ends of the powerful, but can also be a means of exposing unacceptable and shifting policy and practice (Becker and Bryman 2004:29). There is a long-standing emancipatory dialogue associated most particularly with feminist (Oakley 1981) and disability (Oliver 1992) research that can contribute to consideration of issues of power and power inequalities in all research.

As research involving young people has developed, participatory research is carried out with groups who are potentially vulnerable, almost by definition. In other words, it is often this very aspect of their lives that is the focal point of the investigation. Research is carried out with young disabled people (Chapters 7 and 10), young people in care (Smith et al. 2002), young refugees (Franks 2011) and orphans and vulnerable children in Uganda (Cheney 2011). However, there is a danger in focusing on children and young people as solely 'in need', victims or problems, rather than as competent agents (Checkoway and Richards-Schuster 2003:298). Many authors in this volume recognise that children and young people are often seen as vulnerable, and challenge discourses of young people as passive and powerless agents (Chapters 2, 11, 18 and 20). The reasons they may be seen as vulnerable are linked to 'their physical immaturity, lack of knowledge, experience and other material resources' (Smith 2010:197). Importantly Smith goes on to stress that this does not mean that children and young people should '*only* be viewed through the lens of vulnerability, or that this should imply a lack of competence'. Perceptions of powerlessness and vulnerability can be used to impose top-down interventions upon young people, viewing them as in need of adult guidance and protection (Johnny 2006), without the ability to make decisions for themselves.

Much research with young people is based on an explicit awareness of power differentials, seeking to challenge injustices in society and working towards a model of empowerment. Young people obtaining knowledge about their situations 'from their insider perspective has the potential for change and transformation. By leading their own research and actively interrogating their own evidence, they are able to offer informed views about social practices that affect their lives' Kellet (2010:22).

This connects with what young people that we work with tell us, that one of the most important things about being involved in research is that it should lead to change – that things improve in some way for young people. Alderson too has this experience, saying: 'young researchers are usually keen to produce findings that will achieve changes in, for example, provision of services, and respect for their rights' (Alderson in Christensen and James 2008:279). This leads Heath et al. (2009:75) to question if participatory research should be judged by the same criteria as mainstream research, they use the term 'catalytic validity' and suggest that this capacity to 'allow marginalised voices to be heard and to challenge dominant discourses' should be considered an indicator of research quality. There are a number of chapters in this book that reflect this link between research and action and change (Chapters 5, 9, 13, 14, 16, 18, 19 and 20) reflecting its broad significance in the field.

Conclusion

This chapter has offered a critical reflection on the range of ways and models of undertaking research with children and young people – describing and defining the 'what' of young people's involvement in research. In so doing, with the exception of tokenism, we have tried to avoid a judgement 'that this way is better than that'. We suggest that different models can have different places and roles. There is no one single way of working with young people on research projects. What research with young people looks like will vary, depending on the young people, the topic, the funding, the adults involved and many other factors. Such an understanding will perhaps reduce the unintended consequence of the greater participation of young people in research becoming 'tyrannous' (Gallacher and Gallagher 2008:501).

Framing existing knowledge and setting out these paradigms is of itself a contribution to the debate – taking the discourse further. It is no longer acceptable to have loose definitions masking the true nature of what is happening within some research projects that talk of children and young people being actors but in fact being treated as objects. Now is the time to build on and connect the 'pockets of participation' (Franks 2011) to strive to find appropriate ways to maximise the involvement and impact of young people in research and ensure it is indeed as participatory as possible.

Acknowledgement

With thanks to Roger Smith for some of the material included in this chapter.

Part 2

Why?

The following three chapters consider *why* we should involve children and young people in health and social care research. The chapters consider the theoretical and practical motivations for involving children and young people on research projects. All three chapters recognise that the cornerstone of the *why* question is the recognition of children's rights based on the United Nations Convention on the Rights of the Child. This has been a major driver to promoting children's participation; and hence children's rights which have also begun to occupy a more central place on policy and practice. Within this, there has been an increasing emphasis on children and young people's voices, in both policy and academic debate.

A second argument for *why* we should undertake participatory research with children and young people is explored by Morrow. She introduces sociological theories of childhood, through the lens of the new sociology of childhood, and explores why theories matter, and why children and young people can and should be included in research about their lives. This is echoed by Smith, and Skeels and Lewis, who all highlight the importance of acknowledging children's and young people's agency, focusing on them as social actors and recognising that childhood is socially constructed. This is why children and young people are often best placed to comment on their specific situations thus become co-constructors of knowledge. Smith also picks up on this and suggests that there has been considerable progress in terms of involving children and young people in research in recent years, in parallel with the wider social movement towards increased recognition of children's rights.

Smith and Morrow both highlight that, despite this positive recognition of sociological approaches in the study of children, they are still not mainstream and social policies in the UK persist in viewing children as 'outcomes' – as future beings. It is only relatively recently that participatory approaches have begun to gain any prominence or been accorded legitimacy.

The third argument in this part (Part 2) is developed by Smith, who argues that participation is not only a matter of principle, but also a key element of improved research quality. As such it has the potential to enhance the quality of the findings: through effective and ethically sound engagement with participants, it may lead to deeper and more comprehensive understanding of the subject matter. He highlights that the distinction between 'participation' and participatory approaches is blurred; and he explores how inclusion does not guarantee that young people will be able to exert any degree of control about either the conduct or the outcomes of the research process.

In Wales, the Participation Unit – working with the Children and Young People's Consortium – has developed a set of national standards for children and young people's participation to help address the gap between rhetoric and reality. Coming from a health perspective, Skeels and Lewis argue that the standards for practice in health can also provide a rationale for young people's participation in research.

Participatory research involving children and young people has faced and continues to face a number of challenges in establishing its scope and legitimacy, both in methodological terms and in relation to those subjects or areas of inquiry which it is entitled to consider (Smith). There are also many questions that remain about the impact and benefits of young people's participation in social and health care research: is participation simply a 'conduit to understanding young people's lives' or does participation change health and social outcomes for children and young people more broadly? Though Skeels and Lewis suggest that the practice of children's participation in research is still patchy and far from inclusive or mainstreamed, they also point towards an explosion of interest in children's participation across disciplines, especially within medical and social science. Smith is optimistic about the fact that children's perspectives and voices have become more prominent in a range of settings.

2 Sociological theories of childhood

Reasons for involving children and young people in research

Virginia Morrow

Introduction

This chapter introduces sociological theories of childhood, through the lens of the 'new' sociology of childhood, and explores why theories matter, and why children and young people can and should be included in research about their lives. The chapter is structured as follows. The first section briefly explores how ideas about children within sociology have changed. The second describes the 'new' sociology of childhood, including a discussion of children's agency. The final section illustrates this theoretical perspective with two examples of studies where children and young people have undertaken research in collaboration with professional researchers.

Childhood

The past two decades have seen an increasing recognition of the importance of childhood as a separate stage in the life course, as the subject of social and political interventions. The near universal ratification of the UN Convention on the Rights of the Child (1989) has raised awareness of the situation of children globally. There have also been waves of concern about the effects of rapid social change on children's lives in Western societies. On the one hand, childhood might be viewed as lasting longer and longer as children are expected to stay on in education for increasing periods – into their 20s. On the other hand, some commentators talk of childhood 'disappearing' (Postman 1982). Discussions about children and childhood are often emotive and raise difficult questions and challenges. We all think we know about childhood, whether we are parents of children or whether we remember our own childhood experiences; in this sense, we all have our own theories and constructions of children and childhood. How do we make sense of these differing approaches and claims about childhood, particularly when these change over time? This chapter will introduce some of these ideas, explore why they matter and how they are relevant to personal and professional interactions with children and young people. How we think about and understand children and childhood matters enormously because theories and ideas affect how societies, governments, policy makers, practitioners and parents, deal with and engage with children and young people in everyday life and practice.

Various social science disciplines such as psychology, anthropology and sociology have influenced understandings of 'childhood' throughout history and into the present. Understanding that these disciplines provide differing perspectives on childhood is key. Sometimes theoretical assumptions or perspectives are explicit, but at other times they have to be deduced or inferred.

Changing ideas about children and childhood

How were children understood in the past? How has childhood changed? The French social historian Phillipe Ariès (1979:128) made the controversial claim that 'In medieval society the idea of childhood did not exist: this is not to suggest that children were neglected, forsaken or despised'. In emphasising the idea of childhood, Ariès indicated that childhood is socially constructed, in that children have differing roles and undertake differing activities, according to historical period and culture. Ariès argued that children existed alongside adults, and once they were past infancy, they participated in the life of the communities around them, working and playing with adults, with no distinctive practices (or clothes) focused on them *as children*. Gradually, bourgeois boys were singled out for special treatment in the form of education, and this was eventually, over the course of two or three centuries, extended to middle-class girls, then to working class children. So, for example, during certain periods of history, children were expected to work, firstly with their families, and then as wage labourers, in order that they and their families could survive. This is still, of course, the case across the majority of the world.

From children in sociology, towards sociology of childhood

Up until the mid-1980s, sociologists rarely considered childhood as anything other than a phase of the life course that involved 'socialisation'; that is, the process whereby children became civilised, functioning adults. The study of children was dominated by developmental psychologists. Sociologists focused instead on families, and that usually involved studies of parents, not children. From its earliest roots, sociology had relied upon a particular view of children and childhood. Emile Durkheim, the French thinker and one of the founders of sociology, suggested that childhood is a period:

> in which the individual, in both the physical and moral sense, does not yet exist, the period in which he [sic] is made, developed and is formed … the educationist is presented with a becoming, an incipient being, a person in the process of formation.
>
> (Durkheim 1911/1979:150)

It was this idea, that children are 'blank slates' (tabula rasa) upon which culture could be 'written', that dominated sociological and social thought during most of the 20th century. To argue that children could be viewed as fully social beings capable of acting in the social world was quite radical (Waksler 1991). However, during the late 1980s and early 1990s, sociologists increasingly acknowledged that research specifically related to children and childhood was underdeveloped (Qvortrup 1987; Prout and James 1990). Similar points were made by feminists about 'malestream' sociology, which had focused on men's lives and formal institutions, and had ignored the everyday lives of women, until the second wave of feminism in the 1970s brought attention to the structural position of women (for example, Oakley 1974).

The Danish sociologist, Jens Qvortrup, was the first to break from the emphasis on the sociology of the family in the mid-1980s (Qvortrup 1985). He noted that family sociology tended to be about parents, or at best parent–child (usually mother–child) relationships, and not about children as a separate social group. There were plenty of 'sociologically relevant discussions of children's problems and problem children', but few studies that were grounded in children's experiences of their daily lives (Qvortrup 1987:3). James and Prout's edited book, *Constructing and Reconstructing Childhood: Contemporary Issues in the Sociological Study of Childhood* (first published in 1990) proposed a framework for understanding childhood thus:

- childhood is understood as a social construction; ...
- childhood is a variable of social analysis; ...
- children's social relationships and cultures are worthy of study in their own right, independent of the perspective and concerns of adults; ...
- that children are and must be seen as active in the construction and determination of their own social lives, the lives of those around them, and of the societies in which they live.

(Prout and James 1990:8)

Social constructionism is 'a theoretical perspective that explores the ways in which "reality" is negotiated in everyday life through people's interactions and through sets of discourses' (James and James 2008:122). In other words, it relates to the idea that different realities arise from the interactions people have with each other and their environments (James and James 2008). In this sense, sociological theory argues that 'reality' is socially constructed. The idea that individuals are involved in ongoing 'making' of everyday life and meanings through their actions is the core idea underpinning a school of thought referred to as symbolic interactionism. A range of other taken-for-granted ideas can also be seen as social constructions – ideas such as adolescence, youth, teenager or generation. This interest in childhood as a social phenomenon was also growing in other European countries throughout the

1980s and 1990s. From a macro-sociological perspective, Qvortrup argued that the 'professionalization' of childhood (the ways in which children have become the focus of specific professions, and how an expertise has been generated about childhood through, for example, psychological, psychiatric and pedagogic institutions) ought itself to be the subject of sociological enquiry:

> The postulate that childhood (as a structural element and a status position) changes in time and space in accordance with the dominant adult society's needs and interests seems so evident, indeed almost trivial, that we may be surprised that it is almost impossible to find this perspective represented among sociologists.
>
> (Qvortrup 1987:6)

Qvortrup led an important comparative study of childhood as a social phenomenon across 16 different countries (between 1987–1992), under the auspices of the European Centre for Social Welfare (Qvortrup et al. 1994). In the USA, Barrie Thorne (1987) was also pointing to the neglect of children within sociology, and observed that research 'has either ignored children, seen them as objects of adults (primarily women's) labour, or confined them to questions of socialisation and development' (Thorne 1990:101). Thorne's book *Gender Play* (1993) demonstrates how young children's interactions with their peers regulate behaviour in gender-specific ways.

Over the past two decades, there has been a flourishing of sociological research on childhood. In the UK, the Economic and Social Research Council supported a programme of research focusing specifically on children and young people during the 1990s. The trend towards increased focus on children and young people as social actors has continued globally (see, for example, Corsaro 2005, in the USA; van Krieken 2010, for Australia). The growth in interest in children and childhood from researchers, theorists and practitioners from a variety of disciplines and locations was reflected in the establishment in 1993 of the journal *Childhood: A Journal of Global Child Research*, which provides a forum for a broad range of discussions relating to children and childhood.

Mayall (1994) argued that this new field of sociology emphasises:

> how far we adults fall short of implementing children's rights, what children's own experiences and discourses tell us about their understandings of the rights and wrongs of their daily lives and what resistances children make to the childhoods proposed for them.
>
> (Mayall 1994:2)

The 'sociology of childhood' involves moving beyond understandings of childhood as a period of socialisation (the study of what children are becoming) to a sociology that is interested in how children experience their lives in the here-and-now. The key point claimed for this new field is an understanding of children as follows.

> [T]he child is conceived of as a person, a status, a course of action, a set of needs, rights or differences – in sum as a social actor … this new phenomenon, the 'being' child, can be understood in its own right. It does not have to be approached from an assumed shortfall of competence, reason or significance.
>
> (James, Jenks and Prout 1998:207)

Building on these ideas, Alanen and Mayall (2001) identify three key approaches within the broad category of 'sociology of childhood' that help us to think about children and childhood. The first is sociology of children, and understands children as agents and as active participants in constructing knowledge. From such a perspective, childhood studies is focused on:

> studying children in their own right and from their own perspectives, … taking children as the units of research and focusing the study directly on children and their life conditions, activities, relationships, knowledge and experiences.
>
> (Alanen 2001:12)

The second approach is what Alanen refers to as the deconstructive sociology of childhood. This emphasises how *childhood is socially constructed* and that ideas about childhood change through time and space (and reflects Prout and James' argument that childhood is a social construction). The analytic process of deconstruction is used to question taken-for-granted or commonplace assumptions about childhood.

The third approach is the structural sociology of childhood, in which childhood is understood to be a permanent social category in society.

> Its members change, but childhood, in its relations with the other major social group – adulthood – continues as an essential component of a social order where the general understanding is that childhood is a first and separate lifespan whose characteristics are different from the later ones.
>
> (Mayall 2002:23)

The structural sociology of childhood is perhaps the least well developed of the three approaches, not least because it can be difficult to trace the political and economic constraints and forces that operate to shape children's everyday lives, if we focus entirely on what children have to say about their circumstances.

Children's agency

The idea that children are social actors in their own right recognises and values children's agency. Agency is a concept that is understood differently by different disciplines, and indeed by different theorists within the same discipline. The relationship between 'structure' (institutions and practices that organise and constrain social life) and 'agency' is arguably not one that is resolvable in any straightforward way (regardless of the age of the actors). Within sociology, agency tends to be taken to mean 'the capacity to act'. Giddens, one of the leading social theorists of the late 20th century, for example, suggests that 'agency refers not to the intentions people have in doing things, but to their capability of doing those things in the first place' (Giddens 1984:9). He attempts to locate the 'logical connection between action and power' by suggesting that

> to be an agent is to be able to deploy ... a range of causal powers, including that of influencing those deployed by others. Action depends upon the capability of the individual to 'make a difference' to a pre-existing state of affairs or course of events.
>
> (Giddens 1984:14)

While Giddens, in common with most mainstream social theorists of this time, would (presumably) not have considered children to have agency (see Ennew 2000), we can use Gidden's notion to impute agency to children. It is not difficult to see that at the (micro) level, particularly within family relationships, neighbourhoods, or schools, children and young people have agency, or the 'capability' to make a difference. This begins from the moment of conception, and at birth a baby's cries influence parents' behaviour. Market researchers claim that children have the power to influence parents' shopping habits – they call this 'pester power' (see, for example, McDermott et al. 2006). As noted, mainstream sociology had not, until recently, paid children's agency much attention. Furthermore, from a sociological perspective, children lack the power of authority, the power that is derived from adult status, and thus it can be said that they occupy a powerless position in society. Many childhood sociologists are interested in the interaction between structure and agency, and how this plays out in the context of relationships between adults and children. They focus on how these relationships are constrained, or affected, by broader social factors, such as those embodied by institutions, or affected by social policies, political processes, or economic and environmental considerations. The sociology of childhood thus accounts for children as both constrained by structures and as agents acting in and upon structures (Prout and James 1990). It acknowledges that children do not exist in a vacuum, or merely within families, but in social worlds that are affected by broader social processes (see James, Jenks and Prout 1998).

There are a number of key questions that sociology of childhood asks:

- How can we better respect children and their rights in our thinking, communication, research and practice?

- How can we understand the complexities of children's everyday lives while respecting their different circumstances?
- How can we undertake research with children and young people to advance their interests?

Why is it important to include children and young people in research?

There are a number of reasons why the active involvement of children and young people in research is not only justified but necessary in specific circumstances. First, children and young people are often best placed to comment on their specific situations. As Boyden and Ennew suggested in 1997, 'research about children's lives is ... essential if policies and programmes are to become more responsive and relevant to their concerns and needs' (Boyden and Ennew 1997:10). Children and young people themselves are and can be co-constructors of knowledge, especially when it comes to understanding their daily lives and experiences. They may have differing views and will almost certainly have different experiences to those of adults. So, for example, children and teachers will experience school differently; children in hospital settings or within the social care system will experience these settings in specific ways that adults may not fully appreciate or understand. However, it is only recently that research has begun to explore how such services are experienced by children and young people, and their views add valuable insights into how services can be improved. Let us look at two very brief examples.

1. The involvement of young people who use mental health services in a consultation that has in part led to a change in regulations about young people as inpatients in adult psychiatric wards (Office of the Children's Commissioner for England/Young Minds 2007 and 2008 for responses). This involved a consultation with a small number of young people about their experiences of mental health care as they made the transition from child and adolescent mental health services to adult mental health services. Their accounts of their experiences were a central element of the report *Pushed into the Shadows: Young People's Experiences of Adult Mental Health Facilities*.
2. An evaluation of a teenage pregnancy prevention service that involved peer researchers (Fleming et al. 2009). Young people undertook the consultation themselves, developed the questions for parents and practitioners, and contributed to the final report and dissemination of findings. Several of the peer evaluators were young parents themselves, and they wanted to use their experiences to contribute to the improvement of sexual health services for young people. The research team concluded that the involvement of young people as researchers was beneficial in a number of ways. Firstly 'it strengthened the research in terms of the

development of information collection tools' (Fleming et al. 2009:289); secondly, peer researchers developed excellent rapport with young people; and, thirdly, their insights were invaluable for data analysis. The final report has led to a commitment to improve teenage sexual health services in the city.

McLaughlin (2005), in a paper exploring some of the practical possibilities and limitations of involving young service users as co-researchers, describes some of the key benefits. Young co-researchers are more likely to 'speak the same language as other young people and be able to create rapport and a right of entry to shared meanings that are usually inaccessible' (p.225); they provide an 'insider view which should be considered alongside other explanations and views of the same phenomena' (p.225) (see also Chapter 19). Thus, theoretically, young people are understood as social actors, 'able to change and be changed by their experiences' (p.226). However, McLaughlin cautions against dogmatic approaches to involving children and young people as co-researchers – it may not be justified or appropriate for all social research. He also highlights some of the ethics questions that need to be carefully considered. These relate to valuing and using the work of young researchers, involving them in dissemination activities, as well as to child protection, confidentiality, and dealing with unanticipated risks, and thinking carefully about managing relationships at the end of a research study involving young people (see Chapter 6).

Discussion

Children and young people are increasingly involved in research, as the examples in this volume show, and research has begun to explore their experiences of, and views about, matters that have previously been approached only from adult perspectives. Increasingly researchers are moving away from ideas about research *on* children and young people to research *with* children and young people. However, eliciting children's views does require some theoretical reorientation, because professionals working with children and young people tend to be trained in simplified versions of developmental psychology which may inadvertently disempower children and young people because adults know best what children need (see Woodhead 1990/1997).

Sociological approaches to the study of children are helpful in critical analysis of childhood, but they still are by no means mainstream and are still marginal. Social policies in the UK persist in viewing children as 'outcomes' – as future beings – and the emphasis remains on individual children's well-being, rather than exploring collective responsibilities towards children and young people. There is thus a need, in research and practice, to shift the focus from 'the child' (since this implies a universal category), towards 'children' (plural). Not only does this avoid the awkwardness of writing he/she, but it also emphasises the idea of children as a social group.

At the same time, differing childhoods are structured (like adulthood) by social class, gender, ethnicity, dis/ability, age within the broad category of childhood, and rural/urban location. A structural analysis would explore processes of social exclusion, social justice, and the politics and economics of why certain groups of children and young people fare better or worse or have access to more or less favourable resources.

Accompanying these developments is a growing interest and need to pay much greater attention to the ethics of research and practice with children (Alderson and Morrow 2011). This emphasises respect for children and young people's dignity and competencies, acknowledging what they can do, not what they can't do or need support to do. More work needs to be done in the area of research methods and professional practice in terms of finding ways for children to express themselves, drawing on their competencies. In research, for example, there is a recognised shift from adult-oriented methods such as one-to-one interviews, which may be intimidating for children not used to communicating in this way. A range of creative and innovative research methods are being documented, ranging from photo-elicitation interviewing to children's forums. However, the power dynamics between researchers (adults) and participants (children) remain an obstacle to be overcome, particularly in analysing data and interpreting findings (see Chapters 7, 14, 16, 18 and 19). Future social research could aim to illuminate the interconnectedness of the 'micro-social' with the broader socio-political contexts in which the everyday lives of children are played out.

Acknowledgement

The author would like to thank Professor Anne Graham and Dr Renata Phelps for permission to reproduce in this chapter some material from Morrow, V. (2011) *Understanding Children and Childhood*. Background Briefing Series No 1 (2nd edn). Lismore: Centre for Children and Young People, Southern Cross University.

3 Why participatory research?

Exploring principles and practice

Roger Smith

Introduction

There are many ways of carrying out investigations into the lives of children and young people, but until relatively recently participatory approaches have not gained much prominence or been accorded legitimacy. However, the picture does appear to be changing, and as children's perspectives and voices have become more prominent in a range of settings (Smith 2010), so it has also been acknowledged that they can and should have a place in the process of exploring and accounting for key aspects of their lives. This is reflected in a growing body of work that seeks to translate these aspirations into sound and valuable research inquiries.

Aspirations and challenges to involving young people in research

There is no doubt that there has been considerable progress in terms of involving children and young people in research in recent years, in parallel with the wider social movement towards increased recognition of children's rights. As this body of work has developed, there has also been considerable evidence of a critically self-aware ethos that has ensured that 'good practice' has been a continuing aspiration of such research activity (Woodhead and Faulkner 2008; Uprichard 2010). Despite these welcome developments, it is important to retain the critical edge, already mentioned, and be ready to acknowledge where things may go wrong. We should be sensitised to the possibility that a preoccupation with achieving the preconditions for good inclusive or participatory research may tend to override the requirement to ensure that the work undertaken is sound and meaningful. If participatory research becomes routinised or rule bound, this may in the end be detrimental to the quality of its outputs, mightn't it?

If, for example, young people decide that they do not wish to be centrally involved in the design and conduct of a research study, but merely want to be respondents (see Smith et al. 2002), does this fall within or outside our working definitions of participation in research? This kind of question highlights the continuing challenges of incorporating flexibility in our approach without compromising the underlying principle of seeking and supporting active engagement of children and young people at all stages of the process. Participatory research is believed to be an effective means of representing children's and young people's perspectives directly in our means and processes of inquiry; but this, in turn, necessitates the adoption of a principled approach to its realisation. In other words, we must practise what we preach.

These observations prompt further consideration of how such principles can be embedded in inclusive research practice in ways that enable them to be adapted to the needs of the specific inquiry in hand. What are the benchmarks against which we can judge whether or not and to what extent particular research investigations meet the necessary criteria of participation and inclusiveness; and how do we ensure that such considerations are balanced against more formal and standardised expectations that we should demonstrate adherence to recognised criteria of quality and legitimacy in research?

Why involve young people? Emerging trends

A series of parallel developments has prompted a greater sense of openness and 'possibility' around the choice and implementation of social research, especially in applied settings in the recent past. In the world of policy, for example, the United Nations Convention on the Rights of the Child (UNCRC) pushed children's rights to the fore, with the result that this has become an area of significant progress since 1989. At the same time, and from a very different starting point, it is apparent that the recognition of the value and validity of a much greater variety of research practices has followed a similar trajectory. Thus, acceptance of the worth of qualitative research strategies has been paralleled by an increasing emphasis on children and young people's 'voices', in both policy and academic debate. In the public sphere, for instance, developments have included the government-sponsored Children and Young Persons Unit, and the creation of Children's Commissioners for each of the constituent countries of the United Kingdom. At the same time, it is well documented that the academic world has taken an increasing interest in 'listening to children: and hearing them', as Roberts (2008) puts it. As these strands have converged, a change in the manner in which research is conceptualised and carried out has also been a predictable consequence. As a degree of legitimacy has been achieved for the idea, the challenge has shifted to become a matter of effective implementation, firstly through the conduct and acknowledgement of pioneering research studies, and then through subsequent attempts to rationalise the emergent messages in the quest for consistent and high quality practice.

Following the acknowledgement of children's agency (Corsaro 1997; Chapter 2), and as Alderson (2001) has demonstrated, early steps involved recognising the normality of children and young people's own research activities, as a day-to-day feature of their schooling, for example; or as a way of articulating concerns about health and safety in developing countries. Historic limitations to their investigative roles have resided not in their own lack of competence, but in 'Western adults' limiting attitudes, in constraints and concerns for protection over participation rights' (p.150). Not only are these paternalistic attitudes problematic in that they limit children's access to and contribution to processes of inquiry, but it also appears that the investigative field has in the past been implicitly restricted to those areas in which children and young people are expected to have an interest (Chapter 19). Thus, their views have only been sought in relation to matters that are recognised as affecting them directly, such as play or family life. Their 'issues' are therefore seen and addressed as specific to them; the wider social world is not their concern, apparently (Uprichard 2010:7). So, participatory research involving children and young people has faced and continues to face a number of concrete challenges in establishing its scope and legitimacy, both in methodological terms and in relation to those subjects or areas of inquiry which it is entitled to consider.

As we might expect, in facing these challenges there are demonstrable stages through which the project of developing participatory research with children and young people has progressed. Thus, for example, the emerging recognition of children's distinctive interests and needs, perhaps associated with the UNCRC and the Children Act 1989, led to a greater emphasis on finding out about their experiences directly. This point was underlined by Hill (1997:180), who contrasted such approaches with earlier studies drawing on recorded data and adult assessments of children's needs. At this point, the concern was mainly to elaborate a range of methods that would do justice to children's perspectives, whilst respecting ethical safeguards concerning informed consent and confidentiality (p.179), and addressing practical concerns such as the 'desirability' of matching researchers with children and young people according to their characteristics, such as gender or ethnicity. It was only as a concluding observation that the idea of involving children in 'the planning and dissemination phases of research' (p.180) emerged. And yet, within a relatively short period of time, the centrality of children and young people to the entire research process has been established much more strongly.

As children's rights have begun to occupy a more noticeable place on policy and practice agendas, so has there been evidence of a greater willingness amongst organisations and practitioners to seek to give substance to good intentions, driven to a considerable extent by the voluntary sector. At the same time, and in parallel, legitimacy has been accorded increasingly to research 'from below' across many aspects of social life, especially in areas in which 'minority' interests have been identified (Alderson 2008:276). Children's capacity to act as researchers is now recognised accordingly. Indeed, the argument is now advanced that children and young people may be better placed than others to carry out certain types of research activity, especially concerning their own lives (Alderson 2008:278).

Increasingly, too, there has been an emphasis on the importance of including children as researchers irrespective of age, circumstances or characteristics (see, for example, Davis et al. 2008). The experience of carrying out research with young children, for instance, has itself contributed to the recognition that they have the capacity to engage in complex and difficult subject areas on equal terms. As Alderson demonstrates (2008:283), children have a very wide range of skills, techniques and insights to bring to the research process, and this has been consistently under-acknowledged. This leads us to observe that participation is not only a matter of principle, but also a key feature of improved research quality. In some cases, she suggests, the involvement of children is probably crucial to the achievement of the desired results (p.284).

Inevitably, though, as research with and involving children and young people has developed in scale and scope, new questions have also emerged quite rightly as to the ethics and principles that should inform this area of activity (Alderson and Morrow 2011; Powell 2011). At the same time it has also become increasingly important to try to establish quality criteria, and to understand better how to make judgements about the quality of the research undertaken. As Spyrou (2011) suggests, it is no longer enough to seek justification in the simple fact of obtaining 'children's voices'. Inclusive and participatory research approaches need to be able to establish appropriate and distinctive mechanisms for evaluating and assessing methods of inquiry that may bear very little relation to conventional approaches, in order to support their claims to legitimacy or moral superiority.

Standards and expectations in participatory research

It is certainly the case that as children and young people have become much more fully recognised as research participants, so has there been considerable effort expended on developing principles and guidance to ensure that their involvement is based in sound ethical and methodological foundations. Some of these principles are understandably grounded in established concerns about safeguarding and the avoidance of risks of harm and exploitation; and some are similarly concerned with demonstrating the quality and value of the research undertaken; but others have come to prominence more recently, and concern the extent to which participation is central, how far young researchers control both the process and its products, and what the fundamental aims and intentions of the research exercise are (see Smith et al. 2002).

An inclusive orientation to research practice has the potential to enhance the quality of the findings generated, precisely because it offers stronger guarantees of effective and ethically sound engagement with participants, and is likely therefore to lead to deeper and more comprehensive understanding of the subject matter. Accordingly, demonstrating the value of participatory research as claimed depends critically on 'getting it right' in practice, and ensuring that those principles on which it is based are developed and applied throughout its implementation and dissemination.

To illustrate this point, even a relatively obvious consideration such as the need to avoid risks of harm or exploitation becomes increasingly complex when we try to unravel its implications (Chapters 6, 10, 11, 13 and 17). It is, in the words of Alderson and Morrow (2011:23), a problem that 'is often invisible and elusive', made more challenging because of the tension between different perspectives and alternative judgements of the nature and extent of any risk identified. These issues are further complicated by virtue of the fact that much participatory or inclusive research is carried out with groups who are potentially vulnerable (see Chapter 1). Attempting to promote research led by children and young people who have been victimised in some way might be problematic if it raises the possibility of duplicating previous 'risky situations' or evoking uncomfortable memories. As Alderson and Morrow illustrate (2011:25), this problem relates in part to the question of who is involved in judging the level of risk; that is to say, it could be the participants, it could be their parents or carers, it could be research partners, it could be an external body such as a research ethics committee, or it could in some cases be a statutory or other agency which retains a level of responsibility towards the young people concerned.

Participatory models of research could adopt the view that it is proper to leave the determination of risk and the judgement about what safeguards are needed to those at the heart of the inquiry process. They are likely to be more aware of the kinds of issue that might affect participants, and which may not be so obvious to professional researchers, to whom 'some risks might not occur' (Alderson and Morrow 2011:27) and who may similarly take a rather monolithic and 'top down' view of other risks (p.29). In Alderson and Morrow's view, this suggests that there may have been a prior tendency to 'skew' decisions about the dangers (or otherwise) of some forms of participatory research, where an implicit conflict has been assumed between the 'protection' rights of children and young people and their 'participation rights' (Powell 2011:2). Nonetheless, formal decision-making bodies, such as project funders and ethics committees, may have difficulty in accepting that participatory research can also incorporate its own mechanisms for identifying and safeguarding those involved who may be at risk of harm: 'To contrast welfare with participation could imply that participation can only be risky and non-beneficial to the child (Alderson and Morrow 2011:29).

This argument is helpfully elaborated by Skelton (2008) in her account of an inclusive (rather than participatory) study carried out with young lesbians and gay men. In this case, choices over the engagement and recruitment of research participants necessitated an approach that did not draw attention to young people's sexuality, and so it became necessary to adopt a snowballing approach to the task of obtaining a sample, using voluntary and public-sector organisations as the conduit for this task. In this case, the ethical framework for the study was clearly informed by the experiences and interests of the young people concerned, and, in fact, applying participatory principles enhanced the safeguards available, ensuring privacy and a sense of confidence in the research process. Skelton contrasts this outcome with what the formal rules of an institutional ethics committee might have demanded, in terms of securing 'written consent from parents or guardians' (Skelton 2008:32; Chapter 6).

Despite this, we must also acknowledge that it is not axiomatic that a participatory research exercise will necessarily promote or guarantee the safety and security of those involved, whether as researchers or participants. Indeed, the ethical standards to be applied are likely to be very similar to those that operate in conventional research practice; differences of implementation do not diminish the underlying importance of these principles (Chapters 6, 11, 16 and 17).

As with the case of protection from harm, participatory research is also inevitably concerned with the question of quality. The preceding example from Skelton seems to offer pointers in this respect too. She argues that the ethical recruitment process adopted had significant implications for the conduct of the subsequent fieldwork as well.

> The method of snowballing became important as we tried to reach young people who still remained outside of the voluntary and public 'support' structures. For many young people these interviews were the longest period of time they had had the chance to talk with an interested listener about themselves, their identity and their socio-spatial experiences.
> (Skelton 2008:32)

This point is further supported by another example from the same article, where Skelton describes the processes whereby a study of the experiences of young women in South Wales *became* participatory as it evolved. This developmental trajectory 'was an unforeseen benefit....The project evolved in situ and the methodology was driven by the young women themselves' (Skelton 2008:31). Here, it seems, the argument in favour of this kind of approach rests on claims of enhanced relevance, sensitivity and 'fit' between the initial research question and the investigatory methods ultimately employed. In this way, participatory studies are, in principle, able to claim that they incorporate inherent advantages in terms of the direct representation of the realities of children and young people's experiences. Clearly, though, there is work to be done in translating these inbuilt potentialities into practice, and in demonstrating that the research process does not simply take assumed advantages for granted (see Chapter 1).

Taking control?

From the young people's point of view, it appears that crucial aspects of involvement are the level of agency and power they are able to achieve in the research process and the quality of communication and resources available to them to support their involvement. We can expect that any investigation is likely to be subject to external constraints, such as funding limits and commissioners' demands; and, at the same time, the initial impetus for research will rarely originate unprompted with children or young people themselves (Franks 2011). Thus, in a project with which this author was involved, the concern to investigate the health needs of socially excluded young people (Smith et al. 2002), could only indirectly be attributed to pressure from that source, and was certainly not the original idea of the specific groups who became involved as participant researchers. However, they were able to take part in shaping the next stage of the process, and influence the emerging focus on the question of 'stress' and emotional well-being.

It has been acknowledged previously that a participatory approach has been easier to support and embed in some aspects of the research project than others. Thus, it may be possible to demonstrate compliance with participatory principles when involving children in the fieldwork phase of an inquiry, without necessarily either ensuring that from the outset of the study or sustaining it in the subsequent phases of analysis and dissemination, say. Franks (2011:20) suggests that it is quite common in research involving children and young people for them *not* to be involved at the design stage. But, she argues, '*total* ownership' would depend on them taking charge at every stage, from initial idea all the way through to dissemination and subsequent use.

Furthermore, as Alderson points out, there may well be conflicts of interest as to which stage of the research is most important.

> Research in schools and universities, which mainly aims to add to knowledge, tends to concentrate on the middle stages of projects: collecting and analysing data and writing reports. In contrast, young researchers are usually keen to produce findings that will achieve changes in, for example, provision of services and respect for their rights.
>
> (Alderson 2008:279)

So, another important test of the level of participation achieved is, quite simply, whether or not children and young people got what they wanted out of the exercise. In one instance I can recall, involving young people who were 'looked after', this was simply to present the video recording based on their consultation exercise to a group of elected representatives. To attempt to use the material generated for any other purpose would have undermined the 'control' they had over the process. Despite the fact that what we saw showed young people who had been in care in a very positive light, the recording was destroyed, as they had stipulated.

Ceding overall control has implications at the level of detailed implementation, too, as children and young people would then be expected to make (informed) choices about methods, sampling, data collection and analysis (Alderson 2008:283). They may, of course, need support to develop the necessary skills, as would any researcher (see Chapters 7 and 8), but this is rather different than conceding control of the research activity itself to an expert 'from outside' (Kellett 2009). This relationship between young researchers and the inquiry itself has ironic consequences, too. In the case of the investigation of young people's health needs referred to earlier (Smith et al. 2002), one group of young women involved exerted their control by deciding that they did not want to play a full part in constructing and carrying out their component of the study; they opted instead for the adult project researcher to interview them according to a standard schedule in a very conventional manner. This finds echoes, too, in Franks' (2011:21) similar observation that young people engaged in research might in fact 'be more empowered by being given the option to have an experienced interviewer ask their questions on their behalf'.

This paradox helps to highlight some of the challenges we face when we come to evaluate the questions raised earlier both of the extent to which research activities can be judged to be participatory, and of how far they should be expected to comply with a pure model of participatory research. Further complexity is added by the additional considerations of ethical compliance and quality, as we have already observed. Franks (2011:22) also points out that we cannot necessarily assume that a participatory approach will lead to 'better' data, such as when young people might be reluctant to share their experience of being bullied with their peers (Chapter 19). Clearly, unequal power relations are not just restricted to the inter-generational dimension. As she observes, it may be helpful to think 'in terms of pockets of participation, which may not necessarily be evenly dispersed throughout the [research] project'.

Achieving participatory goals inevitably involves a process of negotiating the tensions between competing principles and between ideals and reality. Franks (2011:23) argues that 'total participation is in all probability a false goal', and suggests that one way to address this is to 'develop participative ownership of specific parts of the research process'. This approach to finding an accommodation with real-world factors may improve outcomes, seemingly. Both 'quality' and 'ethical' motivations can be addressed, by ensuring that participation principles are mediated by other important considerations, such as the need to include different interests 'where research is cross-cultural'; and to avoid imposing excessive expectations and thereby 'putting [young researchers] into difficult situations' (Franks 2011:23).

The benefits of participation: The value of a principled approach

Perhaps we can conclude by noting that the rationale for participatory research is strengthened when we can demonstrate it has contributed to the quality of the experience and the knowledge generated. Whilst we can stipulate a number of important conditions to be met in initiating and delivering inclusive and participatory investigations (Chapter 1), these are not enough in themselves to guarantee either that the products of these activities will be of good quality or that they will safeguard and promote the interests of those concerned (either direct participants or children and young people from the wider community). There are perhaps two distinct, but necessarily overlapping sets of questions to be considered to be able to undertake an evaluation of participatory research.

First, we will need to apply tests of the extent and integrity of 'participation' by young researchers, such as:

- Were young researchers involved from the start, and throughout the process?
- Did they lead/take responsibility for key decisions, such as specifying research questions, methods, sampling, analytical approach and use of outputs?
- Were they responsible for making choices about task allocation and the division of labour?
- Were they able/enabled to make informed choices and exercise relevant research skills?
- Were they fully representative of the group/interest that was the subject of the inquiry?
- Did the research achieve what they wanted?
- How far they were they able to retain control of its dissemination and subsequent use?

But, alongside these run other significant questions too. As we have already observed, a participatory approach has the capacity to enhance quality and introduce greater ethical sensitivity into the research process. However, there are no guarantees in this respect, so we must also consider a number of further key questions, including:

- In what ways was the quality of the research enhanced through participation?
- How might it have been compromised, for example, because of limitations in the kind of methods available?
- How did a participatory approach support good ethical practice?
- How were ethical challenges dealt with, such as the sharing of personal details or the generation of unrealistic expectations?

Sinclair (2004:114) has suggested that 'the growth in children's participation activity' has not been reflected in a substantial body of evaluation, and that despite the view that participation is an unqualified good, there is still a need to monitor and evaluate such activities to improve, rather than to challenge, their achievements. This is equally true of young people's participation in research. In the same way, the inherent features of equality and justice built into the good intentions of participation do not, of themselves, guarantee fair and non-exploitative outcomes in a world where inequalities and oppressive treatment are deeply embedded in human relationships.

We can conclude, then, that it is not contrary to the spirit of inclusion and participation to remain concerned about conventional research questions to do with validity, rigour, quality and ethical integrity. The important task is to ensure that these questions, themselves, are framed in the same spirit; and that we raise them in order to enhance rather than derail participatory research activities involving children and young people.

Participatory research is a positive and desirable project because it offers direct and undistorted access to children's and young people's perspectives and experiences, and allows them to take the lead in shaping and articulating the research process and its messages. In order to demonstrate the validity of this claim, we must therefore also recognise and act on the practical obligations following from our assertions of principle. In other words, the validity of the initial claim is revealed (and, indeed, has been revealed on many occasions) by the quality of the work undertaken with and by children in many and diverse settings.

4 Using national standards for children and young people's participation to inform health research

Anna Skeels and Mererid Lewis

Introduction

An online search on any medical or social science academic database will result in a plethora of papers on children's participation in health research settings. This is symptomatic of an explosion of interest in children's participation across disciplines and sectors, due to, among other things, the almost worldwide ratification of the United Nations Convention on the Rights of the Child (UNCRC); the subsequent changing conceptualisation of the child as 'social actor' and competent decision-maker and the rise of 'childhood studies' as a discipline, and an increasingly consumer-focused society (Chapter 2; Kirby et al., 2003; O'Kane, 2008; Wyness, 2009). The popularity of children's participation is such that some have described it as a participation mantra. They have also, however, contrasted the rhetoric with the practice of children's participation, pointing out that this is patchy, experimental and far from inclusive, embedded or mainstreamed (Lansdown, 2001; Sinclair, 2004; James, 2007).

By way of contrast, much of the literature attempts to highlight what is felt to be 'genuine' participation and what is thought to constitute a good quality participatory process. Discussion includes, for example, the importance of choice and informed consent (Chapters 6 and 11), feedback and respect, and various models of participation point out the difference between tokenism and meaningful participation (Chapters 1 and 3; Hart, 1992; Shier, 2001).

In Wales, the Participation Unit – working with the Children and Young People's Participation Consortium for Wales, 2007 – has developed a set of national standards for children and young people's participation to help address the gap between rhetoric and reality. These standards attempt to both define and enable children and organisations to measure the quality of the process of children and young people's participation. Linking the Participation Standards to a national kite mark, awarded through a self-assessment process and external inspection by local teams of young inspectors, the Participation Unit presents a system that attempts to drive up the quality of participatory practice across Wales.

In this chapter, we explore the 'fit' of these Participation Standards to children and young people's participation in a health research setting in

Wales. We look at the raft of policies and legislation that support children's participation – broadly and also specifically in the field of health – and, using a case study, apply the Participation Standards to research practice in health, and suggest that participation standards can also provide a rationale for young people's involvement in research.

We argue that consistent and high-quality participatory practice, defined and measured by children and young people themselves, is a key step towards ensuring a good quality participatory experience, a more effective and needs-led service delivery and better outcomes for health care research.

Children and young people's participation in Wales

At the beginning of the 20th century, the notion of the child's need to be protected and cared for was a central principle of the Declaration of Children's Rights, endorsed by the League of Nations in 1924. The 1959 Declaration on the Rights of the Child continued this paternalistic theme, and it was not until the 1970s that there was a formal recognition of the political and civil rights of children, including their right to have a voice and to be heard (Boylan and Dalrymple, 2009).

The United Nations Convention on the Rights of the Child (UNCRC), adopted in 1989 by the UN General Assembly (Child Rights Alliance, 2009), became the cornerstone of children's rights worldwide and has been a major driver to promoting children's participation. Article 12 of the UNCRC requires that state parties shall:

> assure to the child who is capable of forming his or her own views the right to express those views freely in all matters affecting the child, the views of the child being given due weight in accordance with the age and maturity of the child.
>
> (OHCHR, 1989: 4)

The National Assembly for Wales has not only adopted the UNCRC but has also used it as the basis for all policy making on children and young people (National Assembly for Wales, 2004). Within this approach, there has been strong Welsh Assembly and cross-party support for the strategic development of children and young people's participation. In 2010, the new legislative framework of the Children and Families Measure[1] (Wales) incorporated, as one of its broad aims, a goal to help young people participate effectively and responsibly in the life of their community. Furthermore, a proposed Rights of Children and Young Persons (Wales) Measure will place a duty on Welsh Ministers to:

> have due regard to the United Nations Convention on the Rights of the Child (UNCRC), when making decisions about the formulation, review or change of policies, or about proposed legislation.
>
> (Welsh Assembly Government, 21 January 2011)

From 2014, the duty will be applied when Welsh ministers exercise any of their functions. This will result in Wales having a statutory commitment to the UNCRC and to protecting the rights of children and young people in law.

In addition to policies and legislation, structures and mechanisms to support and enable children and young people's participation in policy and service development in line with Article 12, have been developed in Wales. Funky Dragon, the Children and Young People's Assembly for Wales, has enabled children and young people's elected representatives from across Wales to meet and question ministers and officials to lobby for change at a national level. Furthermore, young people from Funky Dragon were instrumental in driving forward the Participation Standards discussed in further detail below.

Children and young people's participation in health

The generic rise in the children and young people's participation agenda in Wales has manifested itself across the different sectors – education, social services, youth justice, youth service – and health. As children's participation has its roots in Article 12 and the UNCRC, so does the child's right to health. In Article 6 'the child has the inherent right to life, and the State has an obligation to ensure the child's survival and development' and in Article 24 'the child has a right to the highest standard of health and medical care available'.

A raft of legislation, statutory guidance and policies support both children and young people's right to health and to participation in Wales. For example, the standards set out in the National Service Framework (NSF) for Children, Young People and Maternity Services (2006), the Health Care Standards for Wales (2005) and the All Wales Universal Standards for Children and Young People Specialised Health Services (2008) all specifically reference children and young people's participation. The Welsh Assembly Government document *Our Healthy Future: A Public Health Strategic Framework for Wales* (Welsh Assembly Government, 2009) includes a chapter specifically on 'enhancing participation', and other key documents, such as the *General Medical Guidance* document for all doctors working with 0–18 years olds and the Child and Adolescent Mental Health Service (CAMHS) strategy document, *Everybody's Business*, instruct practitioners to take the views and opinions of children and young people into account in their service delivery.

More recently the proposed Rights of Children and Young Persons (Wales) Measure (Welsh Assembly Government, 2011) and the Children and Families (Wales) Measure (2010) also have great potential for children and young people's participation in matters that affect them, including their health. Similarly, the recent reorganisation of the National Health Service (NHS) has emphasised the effective engagement of citizens, including children and young people, and the need for services to meet local and individual need. At a local statutory level,

Children and Young People's Single Plans and Local Participation Strategies in local authorities across Wales make reference, in varying degrees, to children and young people's participation in health, and initiatives such as Healthy Schools bring together children's participation, education and health. Within the voluntary sector, Save the Children has worked to raise awareness of children's rights, including their right to participate, in various health settings in Wales. The Save the Children leaflet for children and young people, entitled *Your Health, Your Rights* (2009), elaborates on the 'right to have your say' and what this involves in a health setting.

> You have the right to ask for support and have someone else to help your views be heard if you want them to. This could be a family, friend, health worker or someone independent called an advocate. You have the right to make a complaint if you are not happy about any health service you use – talk to your doctor, nurse or the health service manager first. If this does not sort things out you can make a formal complaint. Staff in any health service should give you information on how to do this. You also have a right to give your views and ideas on health services that you have used or might need in the future.
>
> (Save the Children, 2009).

Finally, and most importantly, young researchers from Funky Dragon, the Children and Young People's Assembly for Wales, undertook extensive consultation with thousands of other young people mapping the realisation of their specific rights under the UNCRC, including Participation and Health. The results were written up into a report called *Our Rights: Our Story* (Funky Dragon, 2007), which fed into the 2008 UK state party reporting process to the UN Committee on the Rights of the Child.

Standards for participation

Alongside the rhetoric of children's participation in health research settings, it is important to be able to establish how this is being translated into practice. It is also crucial to make sure that the quality of the process of participation is acceptable and consistent across Wales. In order to do this, it is important to set standards and to be able to measure effectively against them (Chapter 3). In England, the National Youth Agency have developed Hear by Right (Badham and Wade, 2005), a model of organisational change putting children and young people at the centre of what organisations do. At the UK level, CAMHS have worked with the Health and Social Care Advisory Service (HASCAS, 2008) and drawn on the Hear by Right framework to develop quality standards for children and young people's participation in CAMHS, which aims to feed what children and young people say into what services do. There are seven quality standards, in keeping with the 7S model of organisational change used by Hear by Right:

- Shared values
- Strategies
- Structures
- Systems
- Staff
- Skills and knowledge
- Style of leadership.

The process of meeting the CAMHS standards is through self-assessment and is colour and number coded across four levels from red/0 (not achieved), through amber to green/3 (achieved fully). For each level, you are provided with 'guidance notes/what to look for' to gauge which level you have reached.

The Participation Unit based in Save the Children in Wales has worked in partnership and consulted with a range of groups of children and young people across the country to develop national standards for children and young people's participation across all settings. The standards are:

- Information
- It's your choice
- No discrimination
- Respect
- You get something out of it
- Feedback
- Improving how we work.

The Participation Standards are accompanied by a set of key performance indicators, each of which specifies the evidence required (as part of the self-assessment process but also for external inspection by young inspectors) to demonstrate that each standard has been met.

The Children and Young People's Participation Consortium for Wales (2007) are complementary to, but different from, the Hear by Right framework, drawn upon by CAMHS. Both sets of standards are useful to drive forward improvement in children's participation, but in different ways. The CAMHS standards are more specific to a health setting and are, as with the Hear by Right model, exploring the cultural change involved in participation; that is, what an organisation needs to do in terms of its value systems, training its staff and identifying resources that will support children's participation. The National Standards focus more on the key elements of the process of participation; such as, there must always be appropriate information available and feedback to participants about the impact of their views, opinions and participation. In terms of measurement, the Participation Standards provide clearer guidance for measurement and foster a more consistent approach, since specific criteria must be met and evidence produced. We go on to look in more detail at the Participation Standards in a health research setting and their applicability in improving research practice in this context in Wales.

Participation Standards – Case study in health research

It is highlighted in The Research Governance Framework for Health and Social Care (Department of Health, 2005) that health and social care research is wide ranging and therefore it is difficult to apportion one set of standards or good practice guidelines to this body of work (Department of Health, 2005). The Framework does, however, identify five key domains common to all areas of health and social care research. The Participation Standards may be seen to correlate and be complimentary to many aspects of these five domains. For example, *The Health and Social Care Research Standards* state that:

> 2.4.3 All those conducting health and social care research must open their work to critical review through the accepted scientific and professional channels. Once established, findings must be made accessible to those participating and to all those who could benefit from them. This may be through publication and/or other means appropriate to the type of research. Data relevant to findings should also be accessible.
>
> (Department of Health, 2005:14).

Similarly, the Participation Standards also set out a commitment from practitioners to the service user with regards to feedback. The Participation Standards, however, require a commitment from adults to *give* feedback to children and young people – not just to make it available as they are required to do in the Health and Social Care Research Standards – and are also required to feed back in a more defined way with an agreed timescale.

In addition to corresponding to certain guidelines that researchers already have to adhere to, the Participation Standards can be seen as a useful checklist for health researchers to follow to ensure that when involving children and young people in the research process, their involvement is meaningful and that a quality participatory process is followed that will ultimately enrich the process and lead to better outcomes.

Examples of the use of these standards in such contexts can be seen in the following case study.

Case study: ALPHA Young People's Advisory Group

A Young People's Advisory Group was set up to inform the work of health and social care researchers and the Centre for the Development and Evaluation of Complex Interventions for Public Health Improvement (DECIPHer). In order to give the young people ownership of the group, they were given the freedom to name their group and design their own logo. The young people decided to name their group, ALPHA (Advice Leading to

Public Health Advancement). Aged between 14 and 19 years old, 25 young people have registered as members of the group, with regular attendance of approximately 12 young people at the monthly meetings. The young people travel from south-east Wales and south-west England to attend the Advisory Group, and through their involvement have influenced the design and delivery of research projects and the development of guidelines for researchers on producing young person friendly materials, as well as resources on focus groups and logic models (Daniels, 2011). Since establishing the Advisory Group, the practitioners and researchers have increasingly worked using a participatory approach and process, following the Participation Standards. In addition to following the Participation Standards themselves, the Advisory Group developed guidance called *Advice for Involving Young People* (ALPHA, 2011) to support researchers to work better with young people and meet the Participation Standards in their own research practice. The following sections both show how the standards have been demonstrated in the research and also sets out the ALPHA group's advice for putting each standard into practice.

Standard 1: Information

The practitioner supporting the ALPHA group used a wide range of methods to contact children and young people, including phone texting, letters, email and Facebook. The young people were consulted regularly on the ongoing issue as to the best way(s) to remain in contact, concluding that different approaches suit different young people and contexts. The practitioner then maintained contact with the young people as they had identified best suited their needs, which was via email and letter.

The ALPHA group's advice for research practitioners is to:

- Explain the research information provided (written and verbal)
- Make sure opportunities for participation in research are advertised
- Provide the time and resources to create appropriate information
- Provide feedback on every aspect of the research process
- Highlight the risks involved in participating in the research.

Standard 2: It's your choice

In line with Standard 1, where there needs to be varied means of circulating information to children and young people, the practitioner working with the ALPHA group used a number of different methods to recruit the young people. Fundamental throughout, however, was the emphasis on young people exercising their choice regarding their participation. The methods for recruitment included using informal networks (typically teachers and youth workers) and young people bringing their friends to the session, with numbers increasing via this snowball method. A young person involved in ALPHA commented that this was a real strength of being part of the group. He said, 'They were really flexible with us if we couldn't attend some meetings, which meant it was easier to stay involved over a longer time'.

The ALPHA group's advice for research practitioners is to:

- Provide information on participating in the research – what, how, why, impact and outcomes
- Explain what happens if they change their mind
- Make it possible for young people to opt in/out of the research process
- Use appropriate methods (ask participants what they want!)
- Allow input into the research design
- Change how researchers recruit young people – are there invisible barriers?
- Beware of excluding 'naughty' children.

Standard 3: No discrimination

Contact was made with groups supporting specific sub-populations of young people, including young gypsy travellers, black and minority ethnic (BME) communities, young offenders, disabled young people and lesbian, gay, bisexual and transgender (LGBT) young people to ensure that a wide range of young people could access the Advisory Group. As a result, the young people attending the meetings were from a range of socioeconomic backgrounds, although it was recognised that the group would benefit from having greater representation from more diverse backgrounds. As noted in the previous standard, due to the flexibility of the group, young people were given the freedom to invite new people all the time, which meant a greater number of young people would have the opportunity to be part of the group.

The ALPHA group's advice for research practitioners is to:

- Translate information into a shared/common medium
- Support access for differently abled groups of children and young people
- Challenge the established hierarchy.

Standard 4: Respect

A number of researchers from the University of East London, Cardiff, Bristol and also Swansea universities came to talk to the young people and to listen to their ideas, views and experiences of health-related issues. Topics covered included the take up of free school meals, methods for teaching young people personal and sexual education (PSE), youth homelessness, young people's well-being and interventions to support self-esteem. When a researcher asked the ALPHA group about the best way of feeding back research findings to young participants, he found that the response was informative and 'provided key information about the various spheres of influence that may impact on an individual's social and emotional well-being'. He also said that the young people's views aided their literature review and encouraged them to explore areas that they had previously overlooked. Furthermore, the researcher said that the feedback the young people gave on participant responsiveness was useful in allowing him to expand his focus during participant observation but also in enabling him to develop areas which he could use as themes during his interviewing phase with young people (Daniels, 2011).

The ALPHA group's advice for research practitioners is to:

- Get feedback from young people as to how they have been listened to, taken seriously and treated fairly
- Choose methods that help everyone to contribute, not one method. Some people prefer to write rather that speak
- Make sure everyone has a chance to give their views
- Give feedback on how views have been taken into account
- Be honest about how much say young people have and how it will be taken into account
- Have an action plan to take forward things that young people say and involve young people in that action plan. Ensure attentive listening.

Standard 5: You get something out of it

Whilst the content of the sessions with the young people became more research focused as the sessions progressed, the importance of ensuring that the young people enjoyed the experience and bonded as a group was not neglected. Residential courses were run; two experienced youth workers were employed to support the group and a variety of opportunities were offered to the young people. Some of these opportunities included the young people representing the DECIPHer centre at a national conference in London and being supported to produce films on public health issues such as homelessness and eating disorders. A young person involved in ALPHA commented that he had gained a lot from being part of the group, such as 'teamwork; research skills; learning about public health issues and learning to accept others' views'. The young people were all given hoodies with the name and the logo that they designed for ALPHA on it, which they valued as it gave them ownership of the group. They also had the opportunity to visit a similar young people's group in Bristol. One of the aspects that a young person from the group said that he enjoyed most, however, was simply 'seeing our opinions being valued by the researchers'.

The ALPHA group's advice for research practitioners is to:

- Ask young people what they want and why they are there
- Provide opportunities for new skills/qualifications

- Consider providing compensation for expenses
- Provide opportunity for making new friends
- Give feedback.

Standard 6: Feedback

The researchers consulting with the ALPHA group gave feedback via email, where appropriate, to the group about their input. The young people were also involved first-hand in the development of guidelines for researchers on producing young person friendly materials therefore could see the evidence of their input clearly in the production of these materials.

The ALPHA group's advice for research practitioners is to:

- Ask if, how and when children and young people want feedback
- Discuss if feedback is possible
- Make feedback age appropriate
- Make feedback appropriate for the group
- Make it on-going
- Ensure two-way involvement in research and feedback process
- Inform people beforehand
- Involve young people in feedback development
- Make feedback engaging
- Make feedback constructive.

Standard 7: Improving how we work

The young people contributed to the production of materials to promote public involvement in research for DECIPHer. Young people reviewed guidance for researchers looking to produce public friendly materials and, using this as a basis, produced a guide that was forwarded within Cardiff Institute of Society, Health and Ethics (Daniels, 2011).

The ALPHA group's advice for research practitioners is to:

- Go to schools
- Ask questions and listen to answers
- Provide training for young people and adults who want to work with young people
- Enable two-way feedback in a fun (non-threatening) way
- Give positive feedback as well as how to improve.

This case study shows that, in addition to existing specific health care policies and frameworks, the National Children and Young People's Participation Standards for Wales can be used as both a rationale and an effective guide for encouraging and supporting the process of children and young people's participation in health research, with positive results.

Despite discussion of a positive participatory process, there are, however, many questions that remain over the impact and benefits of young people's participation in health research. Does their participation improve retention in trials? Is participation simply a vehicle for understanding young people's lives? Does participation change health outcomes for children and young people more broadly?

Much participation activity in general has been at a tokenistic level because there has so far been little call to evidence the outcomes of children's participation in research, only that it has occurred (Kellet, 2009a). It is clear that a more systematic approach is required to evidence the outcomes and impact of children's participation in order to answer these questions. However, by following a rigorous and high-quality process, such as informed by the National Children and Young People's Participation Standards for Wales, research is more likely to produce better and more meaningful outcomes for all.

Conclusion

It can be said that many health researchers do not have a culture of involving children and young people in their work, either in the production of research or in the dissemination of its outputs. Despite this, there is the beginning of a cultural shift in many areas towards recognising the value of children and young people's voices and the importance of making their participation in research meaningful, with the caveat however of needing sufficient time, money and mapping of the outcomes. According to a researcher who met with the young people from the ALPHA group, he felt that the researchers had had their beliefs challenged as they 'had previously underestimated the insight and meaningful contributions that young people can make to the research process' (Daniels, 2011).

As the principles underpinning public involvement in DECIPHer state:

> We are committed to ensure that as researchers we [are] willing to change the way we undertake our work to ensure that public participation is meaningful and provide adequate support and opportunities for the public's involvement.
>
> (DECIPHer, 2009:2)

Indeed, a young person involved in the ALPHA group commented that:

> People shouldn't assume that young people are not interested in research. We are. The key thing is making the research interesting and relatable to young people. You could do this by building in ice-breakers and games. That way we can get involved and enjoy it.

Feedback from a practitioner in the field of social work suggests that one way to ensure a meaningful process for the participation of children and young people is to follow the National Children and Young People's Participation Standards for Wales:

> The Participation Standards embody children's rights principles such as being listened to, non-discrimination, and best interests in a really practical way. They help promote a child rights based approach for individuals, teams and services. They can also be applied in a range of settings – as a checklist for undertaking research with children, in planning pieces of work or in evaluating our practice – this flexibility is a real strength and should help engage all sectors and all levels.

It is recognised that the National Children and Young People's Participation Standards for Wales are one of an abundance of guidance mechanisms informing children and young people's involvement in health research, however it is maintained that they provide a useful, clear and simple reminder or checklist of best practice for providing a good quality participatory process for children and young people. The examples used show that this holds true in a health research setting.

Acknowledgements

With many thanks to Philip Daniels, Iwan Matheson, Anne Crowley, Trudy Aspinwall, Rhian Croke and Lee Hind for their input and advice.

Note

1 A 'measure' is the specific term used by the Welsh Assembly under the 2006 Government of Wales Act for what is called a 'law' at Westminster.

Part 3

How?

The following four chapters consider the *how* phase of involving young people in research. They consider aspects of planning and preparation needed before working with young people on research projects, such as recruitment, ethics, training, support and developing more equal relationships. The chapters build on the previous part (Part 2), demonstrating some of the practical implications of recognising young people as active social agents in research.

All four chapters in Part 3 consider aspects of giving up our adult role of 'knower'; to really partner with young people to create something new. Sabo Flores writes that this means following the young people's lead and feeling comfortable with the fact that we might not know where they are leading. She says moving both young people and adult performances from 'knower' to 'questioner' is a radical yet necessary step in youth–adult partnerships.

5 Moving to the inside

Employing young people as researchers

Jennie Fleming

Introduction

The commitment to work with young people on research projects takes many forms – as the chapters in this volume testify. The terms on which young people are involved and remunerated also vary considerably. In some projects young people are unpaid volunteers, in others they receive vouchers, in yet others they are paid and in some projects their involvement is long term, while in others it is for a shorter time. The rewards and remuneration for young people are affected by a range of factors including the views of the young people themselves, the budget, the organisation's ability to remunerate and how it will affect the payment of benefits, to name a few (Pryse 2009; see also Chapters 14 and 16). This chapter explores the benefits and challenges for a university research centre which decided to employ young people aged 18 and under as Centre for Social Action staff. It also outlines in some detail the processes for recruitment of the young people as research staff, and how young people were involved as decision makers in this process and how young people view their role. It concludes with reflections from other university staff and also from people who have commissioned the team to work on research and evaluation projects.

Rationale for employing young people

The Centre for Social Action has a long history of working in partnership with people on issues and concerns in their lives both in practice (Arches and Fleming 2007) and research (Fleming and Ward 2004). We have worked to avoid extractive research, which mines young people for information (Petrie et al. 2006:35). Rather, we have worked with young people to ensure their perspectives are included throughout all stages of the research process. We have found that involving young people questions the principles behind the research, asking in whose interests it is being done and encouraging consideration of the power dynamics that inevitably arise within research. Working with young people on research projects has encouraged us to think more deeply about how research can promote change for children and young people. It also questions the rigour of the research process by identifying from the outset the need to understand the context of the enquiry and recognises that young people, as experts by experience (Fleming and Ward 2004; Chapter 3), are likely to be central to that. This approach values their first-hand experience as a basis for knowledge (Beresford and Evans 1999:673; Chapters 1, 7 and 8).

We had worked with young people both as paid and unpaid co-researchers on a number of research projects. For those who were paid, none were employed by the university but usually by partners in the research, for example youth organisations. Much of our work is commissioned and task focused. As a result, our relationship with the young people involved was quite transitory as our contact with them ended when the specific project ended – a not uncommon feature in working with young researchers (Blackburn et al. 2010:24).

We were keen to work with young people over a longer period of time for a number of reasons. We felt it was important to look to maximise their involvement and impact in our work and we thought that having an on-going, long-term and developmental relationship with a group of young researchers would enable us to do this. We wanted to practise what we preach in terms of young people's participation; Hear by Right considers the engagement of young people as staff and is one of the indicators to develop the active involvement of young people in decision making (Badham and Wade 2005:15). Checkoway and Richards-Schuster (2003:27) write that 'If both parties share interpersonal and institutional power, they take a step toward quality participation. If the power remains largely in adult hands, however, they do not.' We hoped that including young people more systematically in the organisation as insiders, as part of the university, would go some way to creating such 'quality participation'.

The journey to recruiting Associate Research Assistants

The journey from making the decision that this was what we wanted to do to the appointment of the young people was quite a long one. Many parts of the university were involved in the discussions, including Human Resources (HR), Finance, Health and Safety and senior management, to name a few!

The support of the faculty's HR partner was crucial, and a face-to- face meeting with them early on gained their commitment and detailed information as to what needed to be done. At the time the university did not have any employees under 18 years old and there were issues of safeguarding to be addressed. Otherwise, most of the issues were those that related to the appointment of any staff, for example that those interviewing had undertaken the recruitment and equal opportunities training. We agreed the appropriate job title would be Associate Research Assistant (ARA) and the posts were created formally through the university's HR processes. The posts are exempt from the age discrimination legislation initially under paragraphs 8 and 29 of the Employment Equality (Age) Regulations (2006), as we stated the case that the age was a genuine occupational requirement (HMSO 2006; these regulations have now been incorporated into the Equality Act 2010). The best option was agreed to be for the young people to be appointed as staff on bank contracts and paid an hourly rate for the time they work, with no fixed hours of work. As members of staff they would have staff ID and access to the wider university facilities, such as the library (the local ARAs have made good use of the staff access to the library and borrowing books in their college work). The posts not being full-time, enabled those appointed to combine working for the university with school, college and other paid work and commitments. The process involved a number of different parts of the university working together to approve the posts, whilst recognising that these are research posts, and that they are different because they are age exempt for younger people.

Part of the approval process was agreeing the job description and person specification. These were important both to be able to evaluate the post and ensure the correct pay grade, but also so that young people interested in applying and their parents or guardians could fully understand what the post entailed (for example, independent travel to and from meetings).

For the first round of recruitment we were able to work very closely with a group of young people to develop the job description, person specification and application form, and devise the selection process. These young people were key members of the team for the whole first recruitment and selection process. We agreed with the young people and HR that the role description was 'To advise, plan, undertake, record and reflect on research and evaluation projects, working with children and young people, workers and managers on various projects both short and long term.'

The first time around we appointed five young people all aged 16. At the end of their first year, three were in a position to have their contracts renewed and these three worked with us on the recruitment of three more ARAs. They were able to reflect on their own experience, and ensure that their opinions and ideas were integrated into the latest selection process.

Much has been written about the involvement of young people in the recruitment of adult staff and it is common practice in many youth organisations (e.g. Spicer and Evans 2005; Burke 2008; also Chapters 13 and 14). There is also literature about young people's involvement in recruitment of other young people; however, this tends to relate to their involvement in recruitment of fellow members of clubs, boards or groups (Big Lottery Fund 2010). Less appears to be written about the involvement of young people in the recruitment of other young people to paid posts. It is suggested that involving young people in staff recruitment can have benefits for the young people involved in terms of building their confidence and gaining a better understanding of interviews and selection processes, as well as being able to add it to their CVs (IDeA 2010). Importantly some people have also found it leads to the 'right people being selected for the role' (IDeA 2010) and makes use of the young people's experience (Howard 2011). These benefits were all noticed in the recruitment process outlined here.

Whilst we were committed to involving young people in the selection process, these posts are university posts and so had to also satisfy all the policies and procedures set out by the HR department. Certain elements – such as the use of scoring sheets and guidance, record keeping and confidentiality of the equal opportunities forms – had to be in line with routine recruitment and selection procedure. These were explained to the young people, and their role and ability to make decisions clearly was explained to them.

Recruitment process

The first stage of the process for the second recruitment was to meet with the ARAs to learn from their experience from the first recruitment process. They did recognise that their views might be influenced by the fact that they were successful and chosen to be ARAs, and that the process might have been perceived differently by those who were not! We discussed the application form and how the selection day had felt, plus what elements we should keep and what we should change. The ARAs said they felt that the application form had provided them with an 'opportunity to talk more about our ability to learn and work in a team than an ability to research; it took into account our lack of research experience', the interview questions had been 'challenging, but it was possible to find an answer to them', and they had appreciated the variety of exercises at the selection day and said that they had been helped to feel as comfortable as was possible at such an event.

With the ARAs we discussed at length exactly what we were looking for in a candidate. Was it research skills and knowledge? Critical reflection? Commitment to children and young people's rights and particularly participation? Ultimately we agreed that we could not necessarily expect research skills and we were well placed to teach them. So the interest in supporting young people to create change, commitment to improving the lives of young people through research, group experiences and communication skills were the focus of the questions on the application form.

We agreed a very wide-ranging strategy for letting young people know about the opportunity. We advertised in local schools, colleges, clubs and youth organisations; we contacted specialist groups and workers (e.g. the Participation Worker in the city, Leaving Care groups, the youth group at the LGBT centre) with an advertisment. All young people who expressed an interest were sent an information pack about the post, job description, person specification and application form. The pack included information from the existing ARAs about their experience of the work for the Centre:

> It is unlike anything I've done before. When I first started working I was unsure what to expect and felt extremely unequipped to do my job. However, everyone you work with is really friendly and willing to help out in just about any way. The training weekend lets you know more about what you can expect to be doing, who you will be working with and what is expected from you. Working alongside people of different ages who had much more experience than me was at first daunting, but I soon came to realise that I have just as much to offer and learn as everyone else and that if we all help each other along we can make a great team.
>
> It is a very challenging job, putting you in situations that may be out of your comfort zone, but doing it with all the support you could expect and need. I've learnt more on this job than I ever would have imagined and have gained knowledge and experience that will last me my life. It's been especially interesting to see how research takes place from start to finish and how many different ideas and important points people can come up with when you throw young people into the mix.
>
> One of the rights of children is to be heard. Going to the organisations that work with young people, there needs to be a researcher there who is a young person. Young people bring a different light to research. There is a certain stigma of what a researcher looks like and for us to go to the organisations not looking like that stereotypical researcher for young people is important.

In agreement with our HR department, all young people under the age of 18 years old had to have parental or guardian consent to apply, and a form for this was included in the application pack. Whilst this was a very important part of the process from the university perspective, it seems it was less significant for the young people and their parents or guardians, as one of the ARA said, his parents 'didn't have much input into me becoming an ARA. They simply signed the consent form trusting I had everything sorted'. A parent said, 'We did not think twice about giving our consent, though on reflection I am glad we were asked as she was only 16 at the time'. She went on to say:

> The application process seemed very good. We thought the whole process of filling in the form and, even more, going to the selection day was excellent experience. It didn't occur to us that we should be involved in any way, although I think I did give her some advice about what to wear. I think it was obvious that you were treating her like an adult and we felt it was right to do the same.

On both occasions we received more than 20 quality applications from young people offering a range of experiences. The interview team (two young people and two adults) read all the applications and scored them on a scoring sheet we had previously agreed together that related to the person specification. We then met for a shortlisting session. We went through the applications one by one, and to make sure one person's opinion did not have undue influence, we took it in turns to be the first to review each application. There was considerable consistency of opinion about the candidates between the four of us, and no discernible difference between young people's assessments and the adults.

Those invited to interview were sent information about the day, which told them about the activities they would take part in. They were also sent a travel risk assessment, and once more parental/guardian consent to attend the interview and to take up the post if successful was sought for under 18 year olds (all of them). We offered parents or guardians the opportunity to speak with us about the work and what it might entail, just one guardian did so, asking about practical arrangements. We also contacted the referees candidates had suggested – many of these were teachers from school or college, but also included workers of youth groups, places young people volunteered, social workers and friend's parents.

Information and selection day

We arranged what we called an Information and Selection Day as the purpose was just that: to enable the young people to gain more information about the posts and for us to be able to make a judgement as to who were most suitable. We tried to set up the day to enable the young people to feel as relaxed and as comfortable as possible, and to be able to find out all they wanted and also best show what they had to offer (Fleming et al. 2009). In planning for the day we considered carefully what it was we were seeking to assess and what the best method to do this would be. We started off with introductions and being very clear to the candidates what was assessed and what was not. Three of the ARAs attended the day, but only two were involved in the assessment process. One, who had not been available to be part of the shortlisting process, was able to meet and greet the candidates, answer questions outside the selection process and be a point of contact throughout the day.

Involving young people in the recruitment process appeared to enable the candidates to open up and ask some insightful questions of the ARAs about the role and work. The ARAs' responses gave the candidates an indication of what the experience might entail. They were asked what they had gained from being ARAs, to which they had a range of responses:

> I am so much more self aware – how I am with people. I am much more observant. I see so many things differently from what I have learnt from this job.

> I was quiet and not at all confident when I started, but I have learnt so much. I was able to go and stand up in front of big group of adults and tell them what we had found out.

Those already employed were also asked what had surprised them about working as ARAs. Their responses included what they had learnt, how they are treated within the team and also what they had learnt from the young people they had met during the research projects.

> That we have learnt so much about research and evaluation.
>
> I thought Jennie and Thilo would be in charge and we would do what they told us, but it is not like that – it is team work.
>
> I didn't know what to expect, didn't really know what we would be doing when I applied. I guess I thought it was almost like a volunteering role, but it is employment – and the trust and responsibility that go with that.
>
> For me one of the surprising things has been to see other young people's passion about changing things for young people and how that is happening.

And what they had found the most challenging aspects of the job:

> Actually going into the organisations for the first time and trying to engage with people – staff and young people. We were on their ground but we were asking questions about it – it felt a bit cheeky to be honest.
>
> Trying to take authority of a group as a researcher – that was a challenge.

The rest of the morning was spent on observed group exercises and presentations. Finally they individually wrote a reflection on what they had thought of the morning session.

After lunch each young person had an individual interview. We allowed 20 minutes for these but most did not take this long. The panel consisted of two ARAs and two older academic staff, and we had an agreed scoring sheet that we each completed for each candidate. The interview covered a number of areas: their experience, skills and qualities, and what they thought was needed to be a member of the team. We also asked about making change, and how they might have been part of this plus children and young people's rights. The first question was about their interest in the post and they told us they were interested in the posts as they thought it was an 'interesting and unique experience', and they wanted to expand their 'skills and use skills and experience I already have'. They also highlighted their desire to be part of improving the lives of other young people.

On both occasions we have had really difficult decisions to make when it came to whom to offer the posts to. If we had had the finances we could have appointed more. Recruitment policies allow for the manager to notify candidates of the outcome informally, so the Centre Director rang all the candidates on the day after we had made our decisions. Obviously the appointment calls were a pleasure. However, the calls to the unsuccessful candidates were tough calls to make, that needed to be handled with care. They were all sent formal letters by HR as well.

After the young people had been appointed, we asked them what they had thought of the selection process. These comments, of course, are from the successful candidates.

> All the candidates were friendly towards one-another with no tension in the air even though we were in competition with one another. Also the current staff, who were judging us, were calm and approachable and made us all feel welcome. The activities we had to do were quite unusual but in a good way as it was mainly teamwork exercises so we got to know one-another even more. I think the fact that some of the current staff were my own age helped me feel more relaxed and even the adult staff were friendly towards us and didn't act superior.

> Having two young people on the panel – it showed the ethos of the Centre from the beginning.

Reflections on the employment of young people as researchers

The HR department have been supportive of the appointments from the beginning – ensuring that all the correct practices were being followed. The HR partner had the following reflections about the employment of the young people.

> I was concerned to ensure that the DMU [De Montfort University] employees who would be working with the ARAs had CRB [criminal records bureau] clearance and appropriate training, so the HR could confidently say that those involved had the appropriate credentials. I needed to know that parental /guardian consent allowing a successful ARA to be employed had been obtained. The age exemption was not problematic in any way. This was a genuine occupational requirement and I am not aware of HR receiving any query regarding the age exemption.

As mentioned earlier, employing young people under 18, who can be considered a vulnerable group (Chapter 1), does create safeguarding issues for HR and there is a greater of duty of care towards them compared with over 18s. HR took care to make sure all necessary steps to ensure the safety and well-being of under 18s, for example CRB checks and risk assessments were carried out.

Importantly she finished by saying:

> I briefed my colleagues to let them know that HR would support the recruitment of the ARAs and that they would be treated like any other

employee. HR is keen to continue supporting the recruitment of ARAs because the project is developmental for young people and the benefits to them would be invaluable. Also, it helps to support DMU's equal opportunity policy.

A senior manager within the School considered that the employment of young people as researchers fitted with the university's commitment to lifelong learning and professional development, saying:

> We believe strongly in providing opportunities to develop a culture to encourage life-long learning. The employment of young people as members of staff who work alongside academic staff on all aspects of research provides us with the opportunity to engage with young people, to actively participate in their development and to benefit enormously from the valuable contribution that they bring to the work of the School. We believe the employment of these young people in this way is exceptional and demonstrates commitment to engagement with young people but also the uniqueness this brings to our work.

Some of the projects the ARAs have worked on have been commissioned by organisations working with young people. These organisations find the fact that the Centre has recruited, employed, trained and supported young people as researchers demonstrates our commitment to both children and young people's participation and rights and the desire for quality research.

> Young researchers being a part of our evaluation team is vital. Young researchers make a significant contribution – not only do they add a fresh perspective, unique experience, passion and enthusiasm – it is also important to us on another level. As an organisation that promotes children and young people's right to participate, we believe that research and evaluation should be undertaken in partnerships with young people, not about them.

Another person said:

> The already embedded young researchers added another dimension to the evaluation. The young researchers had the potential to regard the issues of the young people we work with very differently from the 'standard' academic team – they definitely added value with the potential to tap into the needs, explanations and issues that our clients face and how they regard their engagement with us. The employment of the young researchers, rather than working with young people as volunteers, showed a real commitment to young people's involvement and that they were valued members of the team. It also meant that the evaluation team would have already directly dealt with many of the

issues that we would have to grapple with. They had direct, hands on experience to draw upon and not just a theoretical understanding of youth participation.

Conclusion

The case for involving young people more fully in research has been made convincingly throughout this volume and, like others, we have found working in collaboration (Chapter 1) with young people on research projects has changed the way we both undertake and understand research. By collaboration we mean the purposeful partnership between the younger and older researchers, a two-way relationship in which the ARAs play a more equal role and are actively involved at all stages of the research process. Being employed goes some way to balancing the asymmetrical power relations between adults and young people in research (Hodge 2005). It means the ARAs can be involved in deciding what opportunities to pursue and how to approach them, and have an input into early design discussions. They can be more involved in dissemination work, presenting at conferences and writing chapters for books (Chapter 19). They have also developed their own research ideas and subsequent proposals, though so far they have not been successful in attracting funding. However, they plan to continue to do this and so begin to move outside the current predominantly adult-set institutional boundaries of their participation and use their knowledge, skills and experience to undertake their own research on issues they identify of concern to them – youth-lead research (Chapter 1).

However, there is still more to be done in negotiating the tensions between the principles of participation and the requirements of research and practice; we need to continue to be critically self-aware and strive to develop and improve practice. This model of bringing young people inside a research centre as colleagues is not perfect, nor is it without its challenges, however it is a model we are keen to both sustain and develop further.

See Chapter 19 for reflections from the ARAs themselves about their research work and on the role of young people in research.

6 An exploration of how ethics inform the design of social research with children under 11 years of age

Vikki Butler

Introduction

Research institutions, commissioners and organisations can outline their principles and values, but researchers have the responsibility to implement ethical practice, proving that they have weighed up the sometimes conflicting interests of those involved, and resolved any ethical dilemmas through their day-to-day management and design of the research process. Taking an interdisciplinary approach to ethical practice can draw on health research guidelines (for example, Royal College of Nursing 2007), university ethical procedures, social care principles, and national policy such as the National Children and Young People's Participation Standards for Wales (Welsh Assembly Government 2007; Chapter 4), but also requires individual researcher reflection. This chapter will draw upon the author's experiences gained from five research studies in order to explain ethical dilemmas and solutions faced in the course of implementing social research with younger children.

I will briefly outline key elements of these studies as they are referred to throughout the chapter.

- Generation 2020 (Butler 2005) involved 67 children under the age of 10, examining their perceptions of their own participation in services within the city and county of Swansea.
- The Homezone Feasibility Study (Bevan et al. 2006) was a community planning study in an area of social regeneration involving 187 children and young people aged between 3 and 17 years.
- 'Young People's Experiences of, and Solutions to Identity Related Bullying' (Butler 2007) explored 10–17 year olds' experiences of bullying in the docks areas of Cardiff.
- 'Understanding Children's Communication of their Emotional and Psychological Well-being' (Newman 2007) was a partnership project between Swansea University Psychology Department, Barnardo's Cymru Research and Policy Unit and Cardiff's Children and Young People's Partnership, researching communication of emotional well-being with 46 children aged between four and 10 years old.

- An Evaluation of the Impact of the City and County of Newport's 2008–11 Single Plan is a current study. It explores the impact of strategic planning from the perspectives of children and young people and has involved over 230 children and young people, including 46 nursery aged children.

I will discuss establishing informed consent with children and issues surrounding parental consent before examining ethical research design.

The process of gaining consent

Informed consent is routinely sought in social research, and this is no different when undertaking research with younger children. At its simplest, informed consent is agreeing to take part in research and understanding what it entails. Consent, assent and competence are three concepts used to gauge the level of understanding participants have of the research they are agreeing to participate within. Whilst gaining informed consent is crucial to ethical research practice, gauging levels of understanding may not be the most useful way of establishing informed consent, particularly in relation to younger children. Assent has been defined in varying ways, but is generally agreed to be ensuring a child has an understanding to agree to participate in research. It is often used in medical and health research to distinguish between agreed participation in a study and legally mandated consent (Twycross 2009). Some researchers use it interchangeably with 'consent', whilst others suggest that it is understanding the project generally, but not the details. To ensure clarity of terms, I use the term 'informed consent'. Competence to consent is sometimes judged through the Gillick Principle, which does not rely on age but on having a level of intelligence to understand what is being suggested and the issues at hand (Alderson and Morrow 2004). The problem with defining competence is that it risks excluding those who are deemed incompetent. To exclude a group of people on the basis of researcher-judged competence is problematic and would result in social research extending a partial world view.

The National Children's Bureau research guidelines (Shaw et al. 2011) suggest that informed consent should be a process. This moves away from deliberations regarding competence to focus upon the practicalities of implementing a process that will enable participants to give their full consent. Informed consent then becomes about giving explanations of consent, anonymity and confidentiality and how to implement planning and reflection mechanisms throughout the fieldwork process.

Children and informed consent

When considering children's involvement in research the consent of children themselves must be sought. Children do not always remember verbal explanations of research, may not fully understand the purpose of research when it is first explained and are entitled to a clear documented process. So all the studies have used a paper-based consent form. To ensure that children have information they can refer to after an initial meeting, half of the consent form is in the style of a pocket-sized leaflet containing pictures, researcher contact details and colour coded sentences. I have never had a child contact me about the research, but presenting contact details demonstrates researcher availability and reciprocity. This is a small way of overcoming existing adult–child hierarchies. Colour coded sentences enable a researcher to read the leaflet with reference to colours and pictures, ensuring that a child with low literacy levels can understand the content. Researchers are masters of words, often using a wide and complex vocabulary. However, we need to study the word and speech patterns of children in order to be able to explain complex ideas such as anonymity, confidentiality and child protection procedures in language a child will understand. The other half of the consent form contains the child's details and a box where they can sign their name, draw a self-portrait or leave a thumb print. The two halves of the form are separated by a tear off; the child keeps the leaflet and the researcher takes the form. The wording and detail on the form will vary according to age and context.

For informed consent to be a process it must be referred to during the fieldwork, preferably in subsequent research sessions, but this will depend upon a study's design. If only one research meeting is being undertaken, consent, confidentiality and anonymity can be explained again at the end of the fieldwork meeting and, where possible, throughout the interview, focus group or activity. For example, in Generation 2020 (Butler 2005) children did not like the fact the research was anonymous and asked if they could be named. During the fieldwork a child said something about both their parents' parenting skills and the school's approach to learning. Anonymity could then be explained concretely through researcher comment: 'That's interesting. And it's important this is anonymous so that I can report your true feelings without giving your name.' This approach enables children to understand the research processes as well as reduce expected adult–child hierarchies. If the fieldwork does enable a series of meetings or sessions, each session can include a short summary of consent, asking the children what they remember was on the form and what it meant. In this way the researcher undertakes capacity building through engaging with the children's current understanding of the research process. Similarly, children may not understand the term 'research'. If the fieldwork is undertaken in a series of meetings, the researcher can remind the child or group of children what they have found out from the previous meeting and give a synopsis of what other children have commented upon. This builds capacity for the children, enabling them to understand how activities or interviews create data and how different data sets can be complied. Generation 2020 (Butler 2005) and the Evaluation of Newport's Single Plan included taster research sessions to enable the children to experience the types of method we would use and how we would gather data. This enabled them to know what they would be consenting to as they had no previous experience of research. Gaining full informed consent also enables the research participants to have informed choice. Firstly, this is that they are informed about research, so they can know whether they want to participate, and, secondly, they are informed of the issues that will be discussed and feel confident to express their opinions.

Engaging with adults – Is their consent needed?

People under 16 are in the position of having an adult responsible for them. There are no rules governing what consent this adult may need to give, it is a matter of balancing children's rights, family relationships, and the laws regarding guardianship and child protection. Barnardo's Cymru research guidelines state that:

> The consent of parents or guardians should be routinely sought except:
>
> - Where it is clear that participation in the research involves minimal risk (i.e. risks no greater than those in everyday life) and will not infringe the rights or impact upon the welfare of participants
> - Where parental or carer permission is impossible or would not protect the child or young person (i.e. where relations have broken down)
> - Where the young people concerned are resistant to parent/ carer consent being sought in the grounds of their rights to privacy and confidentiality AND where the emotional and social maturity and particular vulnerabilities of the young people have been evaluated and the risks of participation are considered to be low.
>
> (Barnardo's statement on ethical research practice, Barnardo's 2008: 3–4)

Each of these points will be examined with reference to specific projects undertaken with children under 11.

It is not hard to gauge what is 'minimal risk' if the emotional well-being of the child is going to be affected by the subject area of inquiry. For example, when designing the research for examining children's communication of their emotional well-being (Newman 2007), the topic area could be sensitive and so we sought parental consent. Similarly, we sought parental consent for the evaluation of Newport's Single Plan when undertaking interviews and participant observation in a nursery with three and four year olds on the grounds of their age. However, for Generation 2020 (Butler 2005) parental consent was not sought because the subject matter was about everyday life and of minimal risk. In all the studies where parental consent has not been sought, ethically parents still need to be informed about the research their child is involved in. This can be done either through a parental information leaflet, sometimes with an accompanying opt-out form. This enables parents to have researcher contact details should they have any queries and to withdraw a child from the research.

The need for parental consent needs to be carefully considered when a child does not want to talk to their parents about participation in research because of family conflict. When undertaking the evaluation of Newport's Single Plan, this issue arose with two young carers, causing an assessment of the merits of the children taking part with the risk to emotional well-being and fragile parental relationships, given the subject matter. As the subject area was not sensitive, we provided parental leaflets, but did not seek parental consent. In a different context, it may have been necessary to avoid fieldwork with these individuals. Occasionally there are situations where it is not possible to seek parental consent, such as when a young person is in care and not in contact with their parents, or when a study is street based. Street-based studies are common in community development projects that utilise participatory appraisal (Chambers 1994; Govan et al. 1998). When undertaking the Homezone Feasibility Study (Bevan et al. 2006), the fieldwork I undertook was street based using participatory appraisal and unstructured interviews with children and young people. It was impossible to get parental consent, but we sought written informed consent from the children and young people and provided information leaflets for the parents. Ethically this study combined community development research practice with social care guidelines for outreach youth work.

Lastly, with regards to consent, adults who have a responsibility to children but who are not their parents, require some consideration. They do not need to give their consent, but may have some legal and moral obligations to the children they work with, which will require them to weigh up whether a particular research project should occur within their work sphere. Commonly referred to as 'gatekeepers' these adults are in a position of responsibility because of the vulnerability of children, but will hold various perceptions of research. For example, schools are in loco parentis and may want to choose which pupils a researcher works with or require them to work with a whole-class group, thus denying children a choice to participate. Some schools and play clubs perceive research as a part of the normal activities and so do not feel there is a need to gain any consent. This occurred in Generation 2020 (Butler 2005), but was addressed through giving information about ethical research to gatekeepers and the use of parent information leaflets. Some gatekeepers will want all the children to participate because they feel the subject inquiry is important. This occurred in the identity-related bullying research (Butler 2007), requiring careful facilitation and dialogue between a youth worker and those children who did not want to participate. Occasionally, gatekeepers will have a perspective regarding children's ability to undertake research. For example, when disseminating Generation 2020 (Butler 2005) a council official suggested that children do not know their own minds, and, similarly, when submitting the research design of the study regarding children's communication of emotional well-being (Newman 2007) to scrutiny, a strategic educational official suggested that children aged between five and eight cannot comment upon emotional well-being and therefore the research was pointless. Having a clear ethical stance, a comprehensive research design, and appropriate methods and information for gatekeepers can aid discussions with adults who hold a perspective that does not see children as active agents (Chapter 2), and also safeguard existing important relationships that a child may have with adults who work with them.

In conclusion, informed consent can be fully established from younger children when incorporated into the research design and fieldwork. Parent information leaflets and parent opt-out forms are useful pragmatic mechanisms for taking account of parent or guardianship responsibilities and realising children's rights. Where parents do opt out or consent is not given, fieldwork cannot go ahead with the child. For this reason it is important to assess whether parental consent is needed, and whether there are existing conflict situations for the child that may affect parental consent. Our experience shows it aids the research process if gatekeepers are involved in discussions and given information.

Ethical practice and the design of fieldwork

Researcher affect upon participants is commonly documented in terms of gender, age, cultural background and other variables, including political beliefs. However, an additional researcher affect to consider when working with younger children is the differences in psychology and constructions of social meanings between an adult and a child (Alanen and Mayall 2001). This is not to suggest that adults know better, just that they know differently (Kellett 2010) and bridging these differences needs to be started within the research design. The topic of research inquiry needs to be explained to children in a way that is relevant to their lived lives (Shenton 1999). For example, when undertaking the evaluation of Newport's Single Plan the research had to be explained in terms of their experiences and opinions of school, play clubs and doctors, rather than the quality of service delivery. To ensure that adult–child differences are reduced through the design of the fieldwork, consideration should be given to the choice of fieldwork sites, creating a timetable that offers time to develop rapport and the accessibility of methods.

Choice of fieldwork sites

Fieldwork requires a setting appropriate for the task that ensures all ethical issues can be accommodated. Unless contacting individual children and their parents for a research inquiry, the research participants are likely to be sought from schools, play clubs or support services. Schools can be difficult locations to undertake research in because in a school setting children are used to doing what they are told by adults and seeking to give the right answer, which can make open dialogue with an adult difficult (David et al. 2001). For example, only after our third meeting in both Generation 2020 (Butler 2005) and the evaluation of Newport's Single Plan did primary school children realise that the researchers were not teachers, began to call us by our first names rather than 'Miss' and would express opinions, checking that we would not be telling a teacher or their parents. However, a nursery school was an excellent location for undertaking the evaluation of Newport's Single Plan with three and four year olds because it was a structured play environment that lends itself to participant observation and short unstructured interviews. Leisure environments such as play schemes or youth clubs can provide good fieldwork locations, but tend to be quite hectic and on a drop-in basis, making consistent fieldwork difficult to achieve – but the identity-related bullying study (Butler 2007) found them to be a rich environment for participant observation. Support services, such as a young carer's group, enable focused and consistent fieldwork, but these are only available for certain specific groups within the child population. Regardless of exact location, the purpose of the research needs to be communicated clearly so that the research activities are distinguishable from school lessons or play sessions. There also needs to be space for the research to occur so that it is outside a classroom setting. Generation 2020 (Butler 2005) and the evaluation of Newport's Single Plan used a school library, enabling individual or small group research methods and for children to choose to participate. When children have not wanted to participate in the research, gatekeepers may be able to provide an activity for the child in a different location, or the child can be included in research activities but not have data recorded or be interviewed. If no extra space is available or the gatekeepers are keen for all the children to participate, the researcher may need to consider revising their fieldwork location choice.

Time to build rapport

Children may need some time to think and consider new ideas, to be able to give informed consent and to establish rapport with the researchers. When researching children's understanding of emotional well-being (Newman 2007) and Generation 2020 (Butler 2005), we found that younger children aged five and six needed a series of sessions in order to get to know the researchers and feel confident to give their opinion. This is in contrast to nine and 10 year olds who gained confidence more quickly. With regards to capacity building, children will give their ideas and opinions once they are sure about what they are being asked. Capacity building assists children's confidence, but requires careful consideration in order to avoid researcher bias. For example, during Generation 2020 (Butler 2005) we asked about aspirations for play services. A few children said they had not been to a playground. The next research session involved pictures of different kinds of toy and playground so children could pick which ones they would like to try, and this enabled interviews regarding play development and the barriers to accessing play services. Children are not always used to being asked their opinions or experiences and so may need time to get used to interacting with an adult in this way. Children also need to know what you have done with what they have said, requiring the planning of a feedback session.

Choosing a method – Deciding between group work and individual work

The length of a research session or meeting will depend upon the choice of methods and whether it is individual or group work being undertaken. Children under 11 tend to have experience of the world through learning and playing with each other. Their social worlds are orchestrated through peer groups, with them rarely being alone or with an adult on a one-to-one basis outside the home. If choosing to work on a one-to-one basis, the design needs to be flexible in terms of the length of research meetings, and to allow time to build rapport and reduce adult–child differences. Small-group work can yield the best qualitative data. When exploring children's understanding of emotional well-being (Newman 2007), we designed the research to be a series of activities for groups of 6–8 children. This ensured that no child was intimidated by a large group or by the intensity of one-to-one work. Methods can be chosen so that children work individually with the researcher in a group setting, or as a group working together. A research design of small groups will work only if the children already have a shared group identity. When the location is loosely structured, such as a play scheme or nursery school, children like to know how long you will be in their club or school so that they can undertake usual activities but also choose to join in the research for a short or long amount of time when they are ready.

Occasionally a session will not work because of an incident external to the research, such as an argument. Sometimes children who have experienced an incident will choose not to participate for that particular session or will be disinterested. While opting out of a research session may be inconvenient in terms of consistency of data, it does show that a child has understood one of the principles of informed consent – that they can choose not to participate without having to give any reason why. The advantage of having a series of research meetings is that if there is disinterest you can come back next time, with a backup plan of different methods, or when the child or children are in a position to be able to participate. If informed consent is undertaken as a process, there will not be continuous disinterest, because children will choose to opt out.

Ensuring accessibility and choice of methods

Adults tend to communicate in their social world through talking, whilst children communicate whilst doing other things, such as activities, playing or learning. Therefore, the methods used to ask research questions must be accessible to the children themselves (Chapter 10). Additionally, different groups of children will be used to playing and doing activities in different ways. For example, many boys over eight in all the studies did not like drawing and some girls did not like physical games, but both genders enjoyed Play-Doh and sculpture. Both genders under eight enjoyed interviews facilitated with the use of puppets, and when facilitating mapping techniques boys of all ages and across different areas of Wales would not write on pink Post-It notes.

When working with three and four year olds in a nursery, we examined family relationships using a doll's house and wooden figures that included representations of different ages, ethnic groups and disabled people. We could then play with the children, and ask them to show their family and housing situations and start interview questions. Planning a series of research sessions ensures that gender and other social variables can be taken into account in the choice of methods, and enables triangulation so that data can be cross-referenced from different sessions to ensure validity and reliability.

Vocabulary has to be meaningful to the participants, and for children this may mean having to design differently worded research questions for an older age group to those used for a younger age group. When exploring children's communication of emotional well-being (Newman 2007), we had to frame research questions differently for five year olds compared to eight–nine year olds. For example, when exploring expressions of happiness, we asked the five year olds 'What makes you happy?', but with the nine year olds explored emotional well-being with questions such as 'What does it feel like to be happy?'. The older children understood concepts of emotional well-being and feelings, whereas the young children needed less abstract discussions that related to their experience. Although it may compromise reliability and generalisability, ensuring accessibility may result in different methods and phrasing of questions for different ages.

Utilising creative methods enables accessibility for children. There are plenty of toolkits available regarding research methods for working with children (EYSIP 2001; Funky Dragon 2011) and for the social care sector regarding participative practice which can be adapted for research settings (Dynamix 2002, 2009; National Evaluation of the Children's Fund 2010). The research designs for all the projects discussed in this chapter included physical games, participatory appraisal and mapping, visual methods such as photography and film, and talking tools such as puppet- or art-based interviews. All the studies combined activities, participant observation and interviews, to enable children to express experiences and opinions. However, if using creative methods as an interview technique, there is a need for the researcher to devise robust recording mechanisms. For example, any activities involving drawing had unstructured or semi-structured interview questions to accompany them. The drawing would act as a tool for interview, with the researcher making notes and attaching them to the artwork to ensure robust recording, including documenting age, gender and other social variables relating to each child. Children may ask 'Why are you writing?', prompting an explanation that it is impossible to remember everything they have said and that their words are important. They may also ask to hear some of the researcher notes. Giving explanations and reading fieldwork notes aloud to a participant aids rapport and helps to break down child–adult hierarchies.

By applying traditional sociological and social anthropological observation techniques and principles as used in classic ethnographic studies (Foote Whyte 1943; Becker 1963; Goffman 1961), gaps in data created by the need to be flexible and accessible can be filled with rich observations allowing for theoretical contextual analysis. Observation yields data regarding social norms of a group, interactions between children and memorable events, and includes researcher reflexivity (Okely 1992; Ellis and Flaherty 1992). Reflexivity is an important tool in ensuring adult–child differences, that power relations between the researcher and the participants are being fully addressed and for assessing how well informed consent is being achieved.

To conclude this section, for social research to ethically engage with younger children, practical factors such as time and location need more emphasis than studies with adults may require. The ethical stance of realising children's rights, undertaking protection and engaging with children as active social agents has a practical application to the fieldwork process and research design (Morrow 2009).

Conclusions

The aim of this chapter was to outline pragmatic steps that can be taken when considering the ethics of undertaking social research with children under 11. It has avoided deeper philosophical discussion to focus upon mechanisms in research design for implementing ethical practice. At their simplest, ethics are a set of philosophical considerations to aid good responsible research. However, the interpretations of 'good research' and 'responsible research' will vary both between different research communities and according to the theory of childhood held (Chapter 2). We need to embrace how to undertake meaningful and ethical research with younger children rather than thinking vulnerabilities and the need for protection mean that younger children cannot be involved in social research (Chapters 1 and 3). This is both impractical and denies children their rights. Children are a part of the social world and without their perceptions and experiences being documented, we gain a partial view and an inaccurate perspective, whether that be for informing social theory, explaining social meanings and experiences, or supporting social policy development.

7 How to make involvement a positive experience

Ensuring adequate training, preparation and support

Darren Sharpe

> Bespoke and high-quality training can enable young people to lead a high-quality research project. The young people in the three case study projects [at the Office of Public Management] took part in training sessions provided by the National Youth Agency. The sessions covered developing a research question, and methods of dissemination and achieving impact. The training gave the group the knowledge base they needed to decide their research question, choose data collection methods and analyse and present findings in a robust and engaging way.
>
> Anne Hedges (Researcher Associate at Office of Public Management)

Introduction

Once children and young people have been identified and recruited to be researchers, they will need to be effectively trained and prepared. This chapter outlines an innovative research skills training programme pursued at the Young Researcher Network (YRN). Our experience at the YRN provides a tested approach in how to help train, prepare and support groups of children and young people thinking of or about to embark on health and social care research. The chapter looks at different aspects of the programme and associated techniques to build skills, confidence, and resilience among children and young people. In my observation good research skills training has the potential to unlock in children and young people the desire for life-long learning and to enhance their skills and knowledge alongside addressing issues that matter to them. A common concern among youth participation groups I have worked with is that of not feeling fully involved in decisions about their own health and social care, nor in the wider development of health and social care services. So, now, as we stand against a time of public expenditure cuts, how do young people effectively get their voices heard? One way to ensure that young people have a say is through high quality research for, with and by young people.

The Young Researcher Network

The Young Researcher Network (YRN) is a project of the National Youth Agency (NYA). The NYA is a national, expert, developmental organisation that support those who work with young people in England. It is a registered charity and aims to advance youth work in order to promote young people's personal and social development, and their voice, influence and place in society. The YRN involves a network of organisations that support and encourage young people's active involvement in research in order to influence and shape youth policy and practice. The YRN supported to completion over 25 research projects led by young people by providing a grants programme, research skills training, seminars, conferences and capacity building. During this period I worked as a Development Officer for the NYA, working directly to set up and coordinate the YRN. The idea of the network arose from the new requirement for local authorities to go beyond merely 'consulting' young people. The Local Government and Public Involvement in Health Act (2007) refers to the 'duty to involve', requiring that councils inform, consult and involve people in decisions on the design and delivery of local services. Impetus also came from the United Nations Convention on the Rights of the Child (UNCRC) in the form of guidelines for the proper conduct of research involving children and young people (Beazley et al., 2009), as well as a plethora of other government acts (see the 'Why' chapters in Part 2).

Thus, the main purpose of the YRN was to provide young people[1] with the necessary tools by which they could empower themselves to have an informed voice to help influence and shape youth policy and practice that would in turn help to secure positive outcomes for young people in England. Most of the young people involved in research through the YRN were not academics. They were volunteers, pupils, looked-after disabled young people, members of the youth parliament, service users, learners and more. Training in basic research skills supported them to carry out quality research where they set their own questions. Without exception they saw research as a tool for change, in the tradition of action research – research that leads to action. It is for that reason that it has already had a real impact on their lives and communities.

Principles of the YRN training programme

Our goal was to make research skills training accessible, relevant and fun for young people in order to gain and sustain their cooperation and full attention. I am a totally committed service-learning teacher/researcher[2] and therefore made it my focus to work with a diverse range of young people to support them to become the authors of their own research projects. In practice, this meant approaching training (and support) with two integral factors in mind: the nature of the phenomenon under investigation and the biographies and/or life-circumstances of the young people involved. The latter will often inform how the former is approached. In the light of young people's diversity and individuality the training was rarely experienced as a one-off-event but sequenced according to where the group were at in the research process (detailed later) and paid due recognition to their position in order to develop critical distance. They in turn researched some of the challenges that young people face as they seek to build livable lives in the UK. These included, poverty, drug and alcohol abuse, HIV/AIDS, gang and gun culture, homelessness, bullying, health, sex and sexuality, lack of family life, cultural, recreational and sports facilities, access to good education, training and productive employment.

Although young people were often researching sensitive and politicised issues, fun was at the centre of the research enterprise. By fun I mean that young people were encouraged to think creatively, innovatively, enjoy and take pride in what they were doing. My own experience suggests that training needs to feel alive and not be an abstraction from the daily lives of the learner. This often entails fostering activities and technologies, for example sports, gaming, arts and crafts, food, and youthful spaces that form the architecture and fabric to young people's daily lives. It is this liveliness and connectedness that, in part, gave research skills training the power to transform how young people saw and experienced their projects. For instance, each time that we met we took practical steps like structuring in leisure activities in combination with outdoor and flexible learning opportunities (Barnes and Sharp, 2004) including traditional classroom teaching. These small steps honoured the limited free time young people have nowadays and their different learning styles. Each time we met with groups of young people it was a unique opportunity to hear not only what they know but more so on what they did not yet know and wanted to try and find out. They realised that they did not always have to be right, they developed the confidence to ask questions and learn through discussion. To paraphrase Socrates, learning is best achieved through dialogue, and debate is the best source of knowledge.

It is vital these opportunities, normally positioned at the front of a research project, are not squandered but used to the full throughout the research project. Research training can be experiential; that is, learning underpinned by dialogue through experience and testing out new ways of doing research. With this in mind, the planning stages always took into account slippage time in the research process owing to absences and/or haphazard decision making. In equal measure I also planned in time for things that can take longer than normally expected – for example, CRB checks for young people, gaining ethical approval when involving young people in research; or things that have a greater chance of going wrong – for example gaining informed consent from parent/care giver and also child/young person (Chapter 6). Frustratingly, going up dead ends is part and parcel of the research process and does not equate to failure or give you reason to stop. Below are the key lessons that I have learnt when helping groups of young people set up research projects:

- not trying to claim too much from research
- not raising expectations too high
- being sensitive around time and commitment
- acknowledging the trade-off from other aspects of their lives
- making research literature accessible and available
- help with travel arrangements and expenses.

Preparation for young people to be researchers

In this section, we look at the different types of training offered at the YRN. Our initial call for youth-led participation groups brought together young people from across England. They came from emerging, established and advanced research groups with a diverse range of needs and experience in doing research. We held conferences where we ran taster workshops to introduce young people to the ideas of networking, qualitative and quantitative research approaches and scientific standards before deciding a central research question. Then followed the YRN basic research skills training programme which was designed to provide in-depth training in a plethora of different research methods and techniques aimed primarily at young people, but was also of benefit to support workers. Support workers used the sessions as a chance to refresh themselves on research methods and techniques.

> Young Researcher Network helped us get training, interview skills training, analysis training, training for proposal writing so we've got loads of new skills. We also did training on ethics and public speaking.
>
> Jason Crawford (a young researcher)

How did we do this? First, we commissioned professional researchers to help design and deliver sessions in the generic programme, along with ourselves, in order to maximise on the accumulated experience and knowledge in the field. The challenge here was to pitch the training at the right level to ensure cooperation and sustained engagement from learners. In other words, we wanted to give young people who are not considered 'academic' a voice and a chance to flourish, and to give the 'academic' young person a chance to think outside the box and to see that the non-academic have inspiring ideas. This way it gave all young people value. So we bought the groups together in a range of different ways in order to network and learn from each other. They were pulled together by region, research themes and at key stages of the research process. This loosely followed the eight conventional stages (Sharpe, 2009, 2010) in a research project, from unpacking the topic to the dissemination of the key findings.

In addition to the generic training each youth participation group also had individual support to help them decide on what they wanted to find out in their research project. We went out to each of the projects and ran group-centred brainstorming sessions, bought in selected materials, encouraged them to go online to find out as much as they could about their topic area and to share this information with the network. Once they had interrogated the information and decided upon what they wanted to know and/or change, the next step was to work out who they wanted to listen to them. Only at this stage did the groups spend time writing down their central research question. Once they settled on a central research question, they could plan how they would carry out the research – the *methods* they will use. In the preparation of the research plan we also encouraged them to think about how they would be sure their research can aim to do no harm, and to help and be useful to other people. This is what we call the ethical framework. In the preparation stage the groups also thought about how they will tell people what they have found out in their research. These different activities can be made into fun workshop sessions (see the YRN toolkit) that will also help to form the group, stimulate discussion and give rise to new ideas and shared understanding.

Alongside working with the young people to help them develop the skills and knowledge to undertake research projects, there is also planning and preparation to be done by the adult workers involved. We also found it important to plan early how to remunerate young people's involvement; this can be by cash payment or high street vouchers. Accreditation should also be considered and can be done in a number of different ways; for example, Award Scheme Development and Accreditation Nework (ASDAN), City and Guilds, National Open College Network (NOCN) or a certificate of attendance. Accreditation requires a time commitment to oversee the completion of portfolios and external assessment. All these efforts are worthwhile if the young people decide that this is what they want. Bear in mind that accrediting training will require additional time and effort on the part of the young researchers and the internal assessor.

Below are the lessons that I have learnt from coordinating and delivering a research skills training programme. They are:

- Try to establish dialogue with the human resource department before you embark on recruiting young people (see Chapter 5)
- Investigate and decide upon the appropriate accreditation route and find a local registration centre
- Try to demystify research terms and concept – this is the first barrier to overcome
- Complete a project plan – this will help to plan the project and identify all the significant stages in the process and then

- Match young people appropriately to research activities (i.e. skills audit) – this will mean research activities are discussed thoroughly and roles are properly negotiated.

Creative research methods

In this next section, we now turn to look briefly at the multisensory and multimedia techniques used at the YRN. We trained a number of youth participation groups in using a range of methods including photo-elicitation techniques, video diaries, collages; participation methods for example timelines, walkabout interviews. As well as traditional techniques such as, on and offline surveys (see Office for Public Management, 2010), questionnaires, interviews and focus groups. Some traditional methods posed a significant problem where the young researcher was semi-literate or lacking in confidence. For example, Mencap's Pengwern College was an emerging young researcher group made up of five young people with learning difficulties with moderate communication problems and two support workers. The group's mission was to set up an evening club for residents at the college. They worked together with the principal and college governors to establish the social group, but before they could get the go-ahead they needed to research: (a) what students wanted; and (b) how the club would be made sustainable. Most, if not all, the students at Pengwern College experienced moderate to severe communication problems, therefore collecting their views and opinions needed careful consideration. To overcome barriers in communication, the research group organised a field trip for a group of students to a local theme park to help stimulate ideas on activities that they would like to see ran at the proposed recreational club (see also Chapter 10). The young researchers creatively planned for the walkabout interviews to serve as a device to stimulate ideas, which they would, in turn, develop into a questionnaire tailored to fit with each student's communication plan.

Projects like this illustrate the potential benefits in the training of creative methods that increase inclusion and flexibility and have the enjoyment factor. This gave the young researchers greater freedom to capture ideas and fresh insight and fun ways to help answer their central research question. In fact, many of the methods and methodologies used at the YRN have had to be innovative to include young people who have limited speech, who may have varying learning needs, have challenging behaviour, and come from marginalised and vulnerable groups, to reveal aspects of their lives and experiences of services. Other methods commonly used include mapping, a weekly timetable, charts, drawing scenarios, card games, vox pop and 'big-brother' style diary rooms. There are a range of techniques for listening to young people and for widening participation which shift the balance away from the written or spoken word, to approaches that focused on visual or multisensory methods (Barker and Renold, 2000; Devine, 2002; Lightfoot and Sloper, 2002; Shemmings, 2000; Sloper and Lightfoot, 2003; Clark et al., 2003,

Curtis et al., 2004). Our experience at the YRN demonstrates how young researchers are keen to use and mix multimedia and multisensory methods to generate and present data. The lessons I have learnt from training young people in creative and innovative research methods have been:

- To encourage young researchers to stretch themselves and not let them rest within their comfort zone
- To develop young people into competent researchers – not postgraduate researchers
- Not to rely upon past methods and techniques to answer new lines of inquiry
- To support young people to build new skills that are transferable to other areas of their own lives (e.g. problem solving skills, critical thinking, IT skills, interview and observation skills, report writing and presentation skills all enhance their school and college performance).

Analysis and reporting on research findings

This section looks at training in data analysis and interpretation. This is an important stage in the research process and should be handled with much care and consideration. The analytical framework should be identified at the early stages of the research process before starting the fieldwork and data collection. It is possible to mix your analytical frameworks, but they must conceptually fit with the data collection methods and be able to answer the research question. There are lots of textbooks that will help select the appropriate type of analysis for the methods the group have used. However, do not leave the analysis to the end. Support workers should encourage the group to start making sense of the information as they collect it. Data analysis is a time consuming activity, but one that can be shared across the team as well as inviting other youth participation groups to share in this task. Get the Life U Want (GLUW) worked together with members from the local Youth Council to help make sense of the data they had collected.

Prior to this stage, GLUW needed training and guidance to develop an analytical framework to fit with the mixed methods. They used a statistical analysis programme to run cross tabulations and frequencies, using the numeric data collected in the survey, and a thematic analysis for the oral accounts generated in the interviews (see Sharpe, 2012).This is in contrast to much of the analytical frameworks used in the YRN which have been qualitative in orientation – thematic, specifically. This is due in part to its accessibility to young people who were unfamiliar with the relevant theory. Where quantitative methods have been used, the difficulty has been with sample populations not large enough to allow any higher-level statistical testing or generalisations to be made that would be valid beyond the locality of the studies. This does not mean, however, that quantitative approaches should be avoided. On the contrary, like GLUW, young researchers should be trained in, or at the very least receive tasters of, both qualitative and quantitative approaches in order properly to make up their minds on the best approach to follow in any given research project.

Next, training in the write-up of research should stress how to capture and express the key messages. The training should aim to clarify and justify all the steps and strategies that have been employed, from the justification of why the group selected the topic, sampling strategy, methods, analysis/interpretation, findings, and to the discussion, recommendations and, most importantly, what next (see the YRN toolkit). They might choose to produce different outputs for multiple audiences. It is important that they recognise the different audiences and try and communicate research findings back to young people involved in the research.

The audience includes the community they are doing the research on, senior managers and directors who can influence and/or champion your recommendations, and other interested parties. For example, GLUW comprised four young researchers with care experience and two support workers They carried out research into the experiences of education, support and counselling for young people in care. Using evidence collected through surveys and qualitative interviews, GLUW presented their findings (e.g. the end to inappropriate separation of siblings when entering care) to the Children Services directors, elected members, senior managers and youth work practitioners at a special event organised at a local museum. Delegates on the day praised their work and were able to identify where policy already existed to deal with specific recommendations, but also acknowledged where policy was not being turned into practice. GLUW continued to use their research to advocate for change to positively improve the educational experience and support services for young people looked after in Bradford.

The lessons I have learnt in doing training in the analysis, write-up and the dissemination with young people include:

- Provide taster training in both qualitative and quantitative analysis from the outset
- Ensure that the analytical framework and methods correctly match to effectively address the research question
- Start the analysis early
- Feed back to key stakeholders
- Negotiate quite early on with all key stakeholders upon the format(s) of the report and plan/budget for the launch event.

Managing research ethics whilst working with young researchers

In this next section, I will look at training in research standards and ethical practice (see also Chapters 6, 11 and 17). All research carries an element of uncertainty, and the professional researcher will plan for and try to overcome these risks. Professional researchers will question their ethical approach according to the methods used, the measures they use to reach conclusions and what happens next. Young researchers may see only one aspect of the research process – influence change – and not have an eye on all aspects of the research process. Young researchers should be encouraged to gain a full understanding of the research process and not be expected to passively move from one activity to the next without first knowing why. They should be supported to take on responsibilities appropriate to their skills and abilities, and the amount of time that they can commit to undertaking the piece of work.

Providing good research ethics training in YRN not only taught young people how to stay safe, but also accountability in their decision making and actions. Good research skills training makes great effort to help young researchers express themselves naturally, honestly, and empirically. How young researchers then translate the learning into an ethical code of conduct is dependent upon how they are supported and steered. For instance, the National Children's Bureau (NCB) group wanted to explore how young people are portrayed in the media and what impact this has upon them. Although a lot of research has been conducted on the media representation of young people, there has not been much focus on the views of young people themselves, or the opinions of journalists. To explore what young people and journalists felt about the media portrayal of young people, they conducted media-story analyses and consultations, focus groups, interviews and an online survey.

The group met during their school holidays to discuss all the ethical considerations of their research project. Each young person was given a project folder and part of this was a section on ethics. They looked at the YRN ethical framework (Sharpe et al., 2010) as well as NCB's ethical framework (National Children's Bureau, 2003), and one member of the group attended the YRN ethics training.

They discussed the points of informed consent, anonymity and confidentiality (see Chapter 6), as well as exploring the limits to confidentiality if a child protection issue arose. In relation to informed consent, they decided to create an information leaflet. This explained who the team were, what the research was about, why the research was happening and what would be involved if they decided to take part. It also made people aware of their rights if they took part in the research, as well as explaining that child protection concerns would be classed as more important than keeping information disclosed confidential or anonymous, in relation to reducing harm.

As well as all participants receiving an information leaflet, the research ethics that the group were abiding by were reiterated at the start of the focus groups and interviews. To help with possible disclosures or other unforeseen incidents, a project worker attended the focus group as a silent observer.

It is important to ensure that any research work young people undertake is done in an ethical fashion. Ethical considerations should thread throughout the research process and should help guide the group's thinking and practice. Points to consider include:

- Build in training on ethics covering informed consent, anonymity, confidentiality and data storage
- Plan to complete a pilot study to test your methods, and make necessary changes
- Remember to ensure that young researchers are familiar with your organisation's child protection and safeguarding procedures
- Discuss and establish a protocol for reporting of disclosures
- Make young researchers clear about their role
- Debriefs are essential and regular group-centred support sessions desirable
- Develop a person-centred entry and exit strategy to enable young researchers to leave the group (and return) without it negatively impacting on the project or equating to personal failure.

Conclusion

To summarise, there are no hard and fast rules to how you go about training and preparing young people to be active researchers. The first stages of training aimed to form the team, develop collective understanding around the research topic (see Chapter 8), start identifying gaps (not deficits) in skills and competencies and develop the central research question. These steps still count if you are intending to work with an emerging, established or advanced group of young researchers. Each research project warrants a fresh look, with the young people being sufficiently trained to tackle the new problem. A poorly planned and implemented research skills training programme can result in an ill-equipped and unprepared team unable to effectively make key decisions, collect valid or reliable data, stay committed. This could result in an uncompleted project.

The training and support outlined in this chapter should in practice help young people to develop critical thinking skills to arrive at a good research question leading to the production of trustworthy and credible findings. This is a tightrope that, increasingly, young researchers and professional researchers must walk together. Regardless of the quality of training the young people receive, they will always require on-going support to cope with the pressures of doing user-led research. Whether working with young people who want to be researchers or you target unrepresented or marginalised groups to get involved in research, the gain is vast for both groupings. The skills obtained in good research skills training are transferable to other areas of young people's lives (i.e. training, education, and employment) and will be useful since we live in a knowledge economy and networked society.

Young people as knowledge agents and networkers should be something we should all champion and attempt to mainstream in all organisations that seek to work for, with or are run by young people.

> People take us more seriously. That's what empowerment is. Empowerment: you know you can do it.
>
> Daniel Crawford (a young researcher)

Helpful online resources

The Young Researcher Network Research Toolkit can be located at http://nya.org.uk/dynamic_files/yrn/YRN Toolkit Dec 2010.pdf. This document provides an overview of the advice and guidance offered to groups of youth researchers involved in the Young Researcher Network.

Other YRN training materials can be found at http://www.nya.org.uk/integrated-youth-support-services/young-researcher-network.

Examples of related youth research

Reports relating to some of the projects referred to in this chapter, as well as other examples, can be downloaded from http://www.nya.org.uk/integrated-youth-support-services/young-researcher-network/yrn-research-reports.

How to involve children and young people in research:

http://www.nya.org.uk/integrated-youth-support-services/young-researcher-network/yrn-research-reports

http://www.participationworks.org.uk/resources/how-to-involve-children-and-young-people-in-research

Qualifications:

ASDAN: http://www.asdan.org.uk/Qualifications

National Open College Network (NOCN): http://www.nocn.org.uk/qualifications

City and Guilds: http://www.cityandguilds.com/uk-qualifications.html

Notes

1 In the chapter, children and young people are abbreviated to 'young people' for simplicity and owing to the fact that the core age group was 15 to 19 at the YRN. The term 'young researcher' has been used interchangeably to denote the different roles and responsibilities young people take on in research projects (also called active researchers, peer researchers, user-controlled researchers, applied researchers, youth researcher and co-researchers). Young people's involvement in research can be on issues about children and young people or about other people's issues, as peer researchers or co-researchers, and be research projects led by children and young people or led by adults involving children and young people, or even as

commissioners. It is important not to get bogged down with labels, but to focus on practice, as young people can often take on different roles (see Sharpe, 2009).

2 According to Delgado (2000), service learning is a method of teaching, learning and reflection used in youth and community services. As a teaching method, it falls under the philosophy of experiential education. More specifically, it integrates meaningful community service with instruction and reflection to enrich the learning experience, teach civic responsibility, encourage lifelong civic engagement and strengthen communities for the common good.

8 Transforming relationships between adults and youth through improvisation and performance

Kim Sabo Flores

Over the years I have had the great privilege of speaking and writing about my partnerships with young people. Each time, I am conscious of the fact that I am speaking for youth rather than with them, and I grapple with how I will adequately tell our stories. Each time, I feel deep absence of the youth voice in my writing and in the other youth development literatures. I wonder why these literatures are rarely written for and by them. As I begin this chapter, I am wrought with similar tensions and discomforts. Questions about my authority bubble up: Who am I to write about effective youth–adult partnerships? What do youth really think about my capacity to act as a true partner? Am I any good at it? How do adults become experts in youth–adult partnership – and where are all the youth experts?

As these questions swirl in my head, my writing comes to a screeching halt, and I desperately search for support and encouragement from the dozens of young people with whom I have worked. I fill my office with youth journal excerpts, interview data and written reflections, and look for something that will make me feel more authentic in my voice. Just when I am about to give up, I re-read the introduction to my book *Youth Participatory Evaluation: Strategies for Engaging Youth* (Sabo Flores, 2008). A young colleague, with whom I had worked many years prior, wrote this reflection on an evaluation project that we developed together for her youth-led organization. She states:

> What if we were *treated as experts* of our own environments and experiences? What if we were *offered tools and guidance* to look at the *big picture*, to collect information that would *directly affect our lives*? Would our experience of adults be different? I believe we would be deeply affected. We would be less fearful of the systems put in place to govern our lives. We would feel empowered to make changes based on information we gathered from ourselves and our peers.
>
> (Ortiz, 2008: xv)

Upon first glance, the quote seems to suggest that all participative youth research and evaluation projects transform youth–adult partnerships or at least youth's views of adults. As I ponder this thought, I reflect on the tools and curricula that both my colleagues and I have developed. All are useful in supporting adults working with young people on research and evaluation projects. However, the question remains: Would the use of these tools, in and of themselves, radically transform youth–adult relationships in the ways that Naomi Ortiz describes? The answer of course is a resounding "no." In fact, I have observed adults using these activities while remaining very much in power, relating to youth as "students" or "little banks" to be filled with expert research and evaluation knowledge. Indeed, I have seen participative youth research and evaluation projects that are set up by adults with pre-determined subject matter and end products that may or may not be related to or directly affect a young person's life and that are not at all connected to a serious analysis of the big picture.

So why, after more than two decades of framing youth as assets (King et al., 2005; Pittman et al., 2000), do adult researchers have such a difficult time creating partnerships with young people? Because it requires a radical shift in our cultural performance as both youth and adults. It requires new relationships, new values and even new language. Richard Learner questions:

> Do we even have words to depict all the important, valuable, admirable, and positive things that a young person can do? Have we forgotten how to affirm their positive characteristics? This collective amnesia is more serious than you may at first realize. Our lack of vocabulary isn't innocuous – it's a symptom of a much larger public and scientific problem that has serious implications, both for individual teenagers and for our society at large. ... When we view teenagers as deficient – as if something's wrong with or missing from them – it affects them.
>
> (Learner, 2007:6–7)

Indeed, our collective amnesia has made us forget that notions of childhood, adolescence, and even adulthood, are social constructs that continue to shape our performances and limit our capacity for true partnership with young people (see Chapter 1). In this chapter, I will illustrate how improvisational techniques and strategies can help us to literally perform our way out of these predetermined roles so that we can create together.

In order to illustrate the nuances of improvisational activity in everyday life, I have created a one act theatrical dialogue between Naomi Ortiz and myself, using her exact words. The dialogue includes scene notes (tips) and improvisational activities that can be used to help youth and adults develop new roles and ways of working together. While some of the activities are specific to participative youth research and evaluation, most can be used when working with youth on any project. This creative adaptation was done with the full consent of Naomi Ortiz, who said "I'm glad that my words can have another life and be useful."

Evaluation and research as performance: A one-act play

Scene I: Accepting offers

[Kim] I was asked to work with Kids as Self Advocates (KASA), a US national, grassroots project created by youth with disabilities for youth with disabilities. KASA was founded on the knowledge that youth can make choices and advocate for themselves if they have the information and support they need. When I met KASA, they were under pressure to find an adult who could help them garner the information needed to create an evaluation plan. Their previous partnerships with adults had failed and they had fired several adult consultants prior to calling me.

When the KASA staff reached out for my support, I was terrified to work with them, fearing that I too would let them down. I knew almost nothing about the lives of young people living with disabilities, and I certainly did not think I was any more skilled than the consultants who had just been fired. From the start, I was aware that I would need to develop my skills as a partner to these youth.

[Naomi] When I met Kim, we were in the middle of an "organizational development" process, which meant figuring out what the project does, how it works, and why it works. When we were told that we were expected to come up with an evaluation plan, it seemed overwhelming. By the time Kim came on board, she had heard of our issues in working with other evaluators to develop a plan for our project. Other evaluators had not grasped what we meant when we said we wanted "an accessible process." They did not understand why having everyone involved, no matter what their disability, was essential. (Ortiz, 2008:xiv)

[Kim] During our first conference calls, the youth board members told me that the previous consultants had not really taken their specific needs into consideration when delivering assistance and trainings. These adults, I was told, just "didn't understand them" and weren't taking time to learn about their unique set of needs. At the end of our first conversation, the young people were not convinced that I could do better and asked me, "So what do you need from us?" I was immediately relieved because I understood that the youth were making me an "offer." They wanted me to do better than the other consultants and were willing to help me.

(Scene note: In improvisation, accepting offers is key to making the relationships work. The key to accepting offers is to take all offers seriously and build with them. In this case, the youth were offering to help me create a new performance as an adult partner – and frankly I needed the help.)

Accepting offers sounds easy, however it can be very difficult, especially for adults who aren't accustomed to following young people's lead.

Accepting offers means having to recognize the offers and being open to new possibilities. It means following the youth's lead and feeling comfortable with the fact that you will not know where they are leading. It requires giving up our adult role of knower; it means we have to really partner to create something new – something that has never before existed. In order to practice accepting offers and giving up your "knowing performance," try the following activity.

Activity: Accepting circle (modified from the Improve Encyclopedia)

Ask the group to sit in a circle. Invite one youth to turn to the right and begin the game by making eye contact with her neighbor. Then make a small gesture, perhaps with a little sound. The neighbor then tries to do exactly the same. Pass the gesture and sound around the room, asking each player to accept the offer and send it to the next player.

Although we expect the gesture/sound not to change, it will. Once this happens, the next player should accept the changes. After the group has gone around the circle one or two times, discuss the activity. Make sure that both youth and adults participate in the activity and discussion. To ignite a conversation, you might want to ask some of the following questions:

- What was it like to accept an offer from your peer or from an adult? How did it feel?
- Did you want to accept the offer or did you want to change it? Why?
- What happened when offers where changed? How did this feel? How did it change the dynamics?
- What does it feel like to accept offers when you don't think they are "right"?
- Did you have to give up your pre-conceived thoughts about what is "right" and "wrong"?
- Do you think we could do better if we tried it again? If so, let the group try the activity again.

Scene 2: Advancing offers

[Kim] I responded as openly and candidly as I could so that the youth could learn more about me and my fears and anxieties. "I want you not to fire me," I said. We all laughed and then I added, "No really, I'm serious. I want to do whatever it takes for you not to fire me and I think I'm going to need your help." In an effort to build trust and commitment to the work together, I accepted their offer, and I advanced it by placing a demand on the young people.

(Scene note: In order to keep improvisations moving, you need to both accept offers and advance them without denying what came before. In improvisation this is often referred to as "yes and." For example, in the above scene, I listened to what the youth were offering me (i.e., help), I accepted their help by saying "yes," then I advanced the conversation by adding "and I want you not to fire me.")

Advancing requires that you stay in the moment, listen carefully, and build with the last thing that was given. A good tip to keep in mind is that when you advance an offer your objective is to make your partner look good. The "Yes And Game" will help you and your group practice accepting and advancing offers, while making your partner look good.

Activity: The Yes And Game

During this activity you will be creating a collective story. Each participant will use only one sentence at a time. The group will build the story by listening closely to what the person before said, accepting the offer, and then advancing the story by adding something that is connected. After each person says her sentence, the following person must say "yes and" – and then add a sentence. The "yes" marks an acceptance and the "and" marks an offer to the next person. Tell the group that we always want to set the next person up for success – so remember to try to make your partner look good.

Begin the story by asking the group to create a title. You may want to select a title that has something to do with the focus of your group (i.e., research, evaluation, participation, etc.). Once the group has selected a title, choose one person to start the story. Once again, make sure that both youth and adults participate in the activity and discussion. Go around the room with each person adding one sentence at a time. Continue until there is a logical end to the story. At that point, say "the end," and applaud the performance.

Stop the story any time you hear someone saying "no but" either literally or figuratively. This will be obvious because the storyline will be broken. After the first go around you may decide to assign a director to listen for breaks in the story. See if the group begins to identify these breaks on their own.

(Variation: Once the group has perfected the "one sentence story" try to have them build a story using one word at a time.)

After each story is completed, ask the group to talk about their experiences. The following questions can be helpful conversation starters:

- Were you able to accept offers?
- Did you listen to one another differently than usual?
- Were you able to advance offers and make the next person look good?
- Were you more conscious of creating with one another than in normal conversation?
- Were you surprised by what you said or what you created? Why? Why not?

- How was this conversation similar or different from everyday conversations?
- What did you learn that could be used in our work together?

Scene 3: Build with everything

[Naomi] When we were told that we were expected to come up with an evaluation plan, it seemed overwhelming. I was particularly resistant. To me, as a disabled young person, evaluation meant that an adult (usually non-disabled) made a judgment about what kind of classroom I could be in, what kind of say I could have in the care of my body, and even the extent of my participation in the community. Evaluation represented power over every element of my life, as I believe it does for most young people. (Ortiz, 2008:xiv)

[Kim] Early in the process of working with KASA, the youth board members told me that they were constantly barraged with teachers and doctors who were evaluating their competency, and making judgments about their abilities. In fact, many of them would never be granted full license to make decisions for themselves. Evaluation was power, held and wielded by others. For these reasons, the KASA board members knew that their members simply weren't going to be interested in participating in an evaluation – no matter how youth driven. So how was I, an untrusted adult, going to create an evaluation with a group of youth who found the idea repugnant? My insecurity once again crept in, but quickly I realized that I needed to build with everything I had available to me, even those things I wanted to avoid – their anger, their negative past experiences with consultants, and my fear and anxiety.

(Scene note: Build with everything you have. This is one of the most difficult tips because most of us aren't good at building with what we dislike. Instead, we annihilate, erase, and try to modify them; we create rules about them, work around them, and ignore them. Who really wants to build with anger, fear, and incompetence? However, in improvisation, denying these realities (or these offers) can bring the performance to a screeching halt. This is the same when working with youth. Young people are accustomed to being denied their stories, being told to restrain their anger, to settle down, and to behave. When their feelings, their stories, and their realities, are used as creative tools, something unusual happens. These "ugly" things become valuable materials. As youth and adults remove their moral judgments, more creative space is available to play with and recreate these stories and feelings.)

When beginning any youth–adult partnership, particularly those focused on research and/or evaluation, the youth's and adult's values, perspectives, and feelings about evaluation and research must be well understood so that they can be used as valuable tools. Below is an activity that will help your group perform and play with these "uglies."

Activity: Reflection on a word

Begin this exercise by asking the participants (both youth and adults) to shout out the first thing they think of when you say evaluation or research – depending on which you are doing. Tell them not to think about their answers too much because there are no wrong answers. As they shout out answers, write them down on flip-chart paper. Try to encourage them to shout them out as fast as possible, without interrupting one another.

Once they have exhausted their responses, review and try to summarize what they have said (have the group help you). For example, "It seems a lot of you think research is done by scientists" or "we all think evaluation is about judging people." Create a discussion by asking some of the following questions:

- According to these responses is research/evaluation positive or negative? Why?
- How did you come to this understanding of research or evaluation?
- Have you ever participated in research or evaluation? What was this like?
- Who typically does research and/or evaluation?
- Can youth do research or evaluation? Why? Why not?

After you have discussed the word evaluation or research, ask the group to tell you the first thing they think of when you say participation. Once they have exhausted their responses, ask them how participation is like/unlike research or evaluation. Keep the group moving and shouting out their answers. There are no wrong answers so don't let the group begin to debate. At the end, try to summarize what the group knows about participation. Create a conversation and ask some of the following questions:

- When have you participated in something?
- Are there different types/levels of participation? If so, what are they?
- How are research/evaluation and participation different? How are they the same?
- What do research/evaluation and participation have in common?
- How are they different?

After you have discussed the participation, ask the group to tell you the first thing they think of when you say "adult". Once they have exhausted their responses, ask them how adults are like or unlike either evaluation or research and participation. Once again, keep the group moving quickly, there are no right or wrong answers. At the end, try to summarize what the group has said – try to remain as neutral as possible. Create a conversation and ask some of the following questions:

- Are all adults the same or different? How?
- What do adults and research/evaluation, and participation have in common? How are they different?

- Have you ever had an exceptional experience with an adult? What was that like?
- What qualities does the group need in an adult partner?
- What would an adult partner be like? What would his/her qualities be?

Scene 4: Performing questions

[Naomi] Ultimately, it is not the answers to our questions that hold power but the questions themselves. Asking the individuals who are most affected by their own experiences what their questions are regarding their life, their world, or the project they are involved in gives them a chance to present a framework that is authentic, real, and useful as a benchmark against which to measure change. We all crave validation and have hopes for our future. By creating the space for young people to participate in their own evaluation, we can build a vision that will give us all hope.

(Scene note: Asking questions is foundational in research and evaluation. However, many youth and adults have been taught that asking questions may illustrate their ignorance. We have been socialized to speak and share our opinions only when we know the correct answer. Shifting both youth and adult performances from "knower" to "questioner" is a radical yet necessary step in youth–adult partnerships. Practice your question-asking performances by using the following activity.)

Activity: Performing questions

Let the group know that in order to create a research and/or evaluation project they will need to learn how to perform as question askers. Have the players (both youth and adults) imagine that they are all anthropologists who that have just landed on Mars. You have just come into contact with an intelligent life form. Imagine what types of question you would want to ask this creature. Invite the group to shout out their questions as quickly as possible. Try to list them quickly on flip-chart paper.

Invite one member of the group to perform as the "anthropologist" and another to perform as the "alien." Then set a scene in which the anthropologist is interviewing the alien (perhaps this is on Mars public television – have the group decide the exact scene). Ask the anthropologist to use any or all of the questions that the group brainstormed. If the anthropologist gets stumped, they turn to the audience and ask them for questions. Allow players to switch roles and do this a number of times. After the performances are completed, have a conversation with the youth, asking the following questions:

- What was it like to ask that many questions?
- Did you remember to listen and accept offers from your partners?
- Did you need to listen differently so that you could ask the next question?
- Did you learn anything that we could use in our group?

Scene 5: Relate to youth a head taller

[Kim] On a freezing cold day in Chicago, I met with several KASA youth board members to plan a larger evaluation training session that I was to conduct with the full team. I was eager to learn everything about the young people so that I could better conduct the training. About three hours into the meeting it became painfully clear to me that all of the techniques I typically used with youth just wouldn't work with this group. Due to a variety of physical disabilities, it was necessary to choose activities that did not require movements around the room. I was told, for many, the materials I had brought would be too complex. I finally realized that it would be much easier for this small group of bright youth to learn everything I knew about evaluation than for me to learn everything about their board members. These youth were experts at negotiating all the physical and intellectual needs of the group and they were certainly capable of learning evaluation strategies. So I asked them if they would be willing to lead the evaluation training with their peers. I told them that I would teach them what they needed to know about evaluation, then they could translate the material into useful activities for their youth board members. I promised to stay in the room during the training, as a resource.

At first I was worried that the young people would see this as a failure on my part or, worse, a cop out. Instead, they were pleased with my redirection, and took on full leadership of the process. The workshop was one of the best I have ever attended. I won't say that the young people surprised me, because I really knew they could do it. But I will say that they went far beyond my expectations and were able to develop a training that highlighted an advanced understanding of evaluation.

[Naomi] Kim listened to our frustration and then surprised us all by agreeing that she did not have the expertise needed to complete the plan. Instead, she told us that we did! It took hours for Kim to explain the process to a few of us. Then *we translated* the language, *processes, and activities* to make them accessible for our community. As disabled youth, we are often viewed as the most vulnerable, the most "unable" to know what we need. To have a nondisabled adult tell us that we could be the experts to decide what would work for us was profound. This philosophy shifted my view of adult–youth partnership and, most of all, challenged my ideas of what my role as a co-chair of an all-youth board should be. Through this experience, youth board members became more than "leaders." We became responsible for our own community. (Ortiz, 2008:xiv)

(Scene note: Much of the research and practice related to play and performance has grown out of social cultural theory that "stresses the interaction between developing people and the culture in which they live." This theoretical framework grew out of the seminal work of Lev Vygotsky (1978), who argues that development is both a product and process of "mind in society." From a Vygotskian perspective, development is not something that occurs within an individual child, but is the relationship between what a child can do independently and what a child can do in collaboration with others. Development is a participatory and relational activity that occurs when children and youth creatively imitate others who are more advanced, and when they are seen as who they are becoming, or a head taller (Vygotsky 1978:102). Young people and adults need others to see and relate to them in advance, so that they have the space and courage to explore new roles and ways of being in the world. The following activity will help you practice relating to one another as a head taller.)

Activity – Talk show: The evaluation/research expert

Invite several youth to perform as evaluation/research experts. These experts will be on a panel and interviewed by a television talk show host. Ask someone from the group to volunteer to play the talk show host. The host may ask any questions that he/she wants and then invite the audience to ask questions. Remind the "experts" that they do not need to know the right answers to the questions and that they should feel free to invent answers, as long as they are playing their expert roles. After the performance has ended, use the following questions to guide the discussion.

Questions for experts:

- What was it like to be on a panel of experts?
- How did the experts relate to one another?
- Did you say or do anything that surprised you?

Questions for the group:

- How did the experts relate to the talk show host? To the audience?
- What was it like to be in the audience?

Questions for the host:

- What was it like to be the talk show host?
- Did you listen to what the experts were saying carefully? Why or why not?
- How did you decide which questions you would ask the experts? What did you want to know from them?
- How did you feel the experts related to you?
- How did you feel the audience related to you?

Creative encouragements

My goal in writing this chapter was to offer you a new mindset, posture and approach to use when undertaking research and evaluation with young people. The dialogue between Naomi Ortiz and myself, scene notes, and activities have provided a framework for how to build performance environments in which everyone can develop. Remember to accept all offers, advance offers, listen carefully, build with everything you have (the good, the bad, and the ugly), relate to youth as a head taller, and give up the adult performance as "knower." I promise that these shifts will radically change your relationship with youth (Chapters 1 and 3).

There are several specific toolkits and books on participative youth research and evaluation that I would highly recommend that contain specific research and evaluation activities, including a wide variety of data collection and analysis methods. However, as you use all of these tools, including the ones in this chapter, I encourage you to keep creating and improvising so that the activities and tools become unique to your context, and so that they continue to develop and evolve. Invite youth to help, they'll know what to do!

Epilogue

In 2007, SCILIFE Archive (issue 4, no.3, 2007) named Naomi Ortiz one of the "most dynamic and articulate young disability rights activist[s] today." (This archive is on spinal cord injuries (SCIs).) She became the project director of KASA, a US national organization, and continues to promote participative youth research and evaluation in her work, assuring that all youth have the right to ask their own questions and create their own knowledge.

Part 4

Action

The following six chapters form the action phase of the research process and all are descriptions of working with young people on health and social care research projects. The chapters describe a number of aspects of involving children and young people in research; together they cover all aspects of the research process – though the emphasis in each chapter is on different aspects. Researchers and evaluators are making constant judgements when working with young people – addressing tensions and challenges such as reducing paternalism, the benefits versus costs of participation, ensuring children's right to autonomy and choice, and how to keep to the principle of justice.

The importance of considering power relationships has already been highlighted by authors in previous chapters (Smith, Fleming, Morrow and Sabo Flores) and is also given prominence in these action chapters. Gaffney and Munro pay close attention to these issues as they arose in the process of a service evaluation. In an attempt to address the power differentials between adults and young people they set up a young people's advisory group, whose primary role was to consider young people's interests in the evaluation. They found this promoted reflection and was helpful in keeping young people's interests to the fore.

Fletcher and Stamp explore the importance for young people to have ownership of the project and feeling that what they said mattered. This is also reflected in Chester et al., who work with young people with diabetes to consider the importance of research and their participation in it. They developed a project with young people to let young people know more about research and how they might be involved.

A number of the chapters discuss how to sustain interest and enthusiasm over a period of time. Sense of ownership is one of the factors, and, in addition, as highlighted by Sharpe, Chester et al. and Thomas found that fun through play, relaxation and engaging activities helped sustain the interest of young people over a period of time. However, Gaffney and Munro recognise that sometimes participation can stem out of a sense of obligation or young people wanting to give something back for the support they received from the organisation they were evaluating.

A crucial factor for long-term engagement and perseverance is identified by Fletcher and Stamp – young people's interest in the topic and their determination to see change happen. As young researchers they describe how they undertook thorough research, but then had to overcome the opposition of adults not taking their research seriously and not listening to them. They explain how this gave them determination not to give up. In order to address these dynamics, young people have to confront adult positions and also put effort into the research process through hard work and perseverance.

Ethical considerations run through all these chapters. Pickering et al. explore the tension between a controlling scientific protocol and a child's right to choose. The practical manifestation of the tension between confidentiality and child protection in research with young people is discussed in detail by Radford and Ellis. In their chapter they demonstrate that involving young people in considering ethical issues was a helpful way to design how children could be asked to take part in research on sensitive topics such as abuse. Carefully reviewing how the research would be conducted, alongside expert consultants including young people and young survivors, helped them to design and conduct research in a way that was respectful as well as effective and robust.

Information collection methods need to be appropriate to the young people, and some have used creative methods. An important example of the care to be given to choosing methods is given by Pickering et al. in their work with disabled young people. They found methods needed to take into account the limited measures that have been validated with disabled children and young people, and that the interviews may not be suitable when children may not have the cognition, verbal language or the vocabulary to describe their experiences. Practitioners often are well placed, with their knowledge and skills from working with children and young people, to develop activities for children and young people to facilitate their participation in research. Chester et al. describe how when developing material around diabetes research, the ideas put forward by the professionals were dismissed as 'boring' by young people. Young people wanted to generate positive messages and did not want any materials that emphasised 'down sides' associated with diabetes. Gaffney and Munro make a similar point: that by treating young people as experts in their own lives they were able to provide the adults involved with useful information about where to focus the evaluation. They also stress the importance for young people of having choices, which became a strong theme for the group of young people.

Data analysis can be an intensive period of group activity and Thomas allocated considerable time to working with young people on this. Their approach to data analysis was very practical, as they had a large amount of data and limited time available. They shared the tasks, with analysis of some of it completed by an adult researcher, whilst the thematic analysis of the interview data was done by the whole group.

Overall, authors assert that young people contributed richness and a unique dimension to the research. This, coupled with a willingness to be pragmatic, as well as a commitment to children's participation, is seen as essential to a successful participatory research project.

9 Young women researching access to sport

Leah Fletcher and Melissa Stamp with Liam Cairns

Introduction

Investing in Children is an organisation that promotes the human rights of children and young people. Founded in the mid-nineties by a partnership between the local authority and health authority, the organisation has developed a range of practices designed to support children and young people as they attempt to intervene in public decision making (Davis 2007; Williamson 2003).

One of the organisation's earliest attempts to do this focused on children and young people's experience of public transport. A group of young people had expressed dissatisfaction with the local transport services. Investing in Children brokered a meeting to discuss this, between the young people and local transport managers. However the meeting was unproductive, largely because the transport managers were not really interested in what the young people had to say, and used their superior technical knowledge to brush aside the young people's criticisms. For example, a manager from one of the bus companies demonstrated that the fares policy (full adult fare from the age of 14) was economically inevitable, by outlining a complicated formula, based upon the semi-rural nature of the county, the large number of small settlements (pit villages), the average distance between settlements and the price of fuel. The young people were unable to challenge his detailed knowledge. Later on, in the course of their research, the young people discovered that the same company, operating in an area with a very similar socio-geographic profile, had a fare structure that provided reduced fares for young people until they left school.

Undeterred, the young people resolved not to give up. They decided that, in order to effectively challenge the adult position, they would need to acquire sufficient technical knowledge of their own. They decided to *research* public transport, in order to develop a more robust argument for change. They spent the next 12 months gathering information about the provision of public transport, and young people's experience of this, in other parts of England and Europe. In their resultant report *Fares Fair* (Card et al. 1999), they argued that public transport in the county was environmentally unsustainable as it encouraged high levels of private car use and was socially unjust as it discriminated against low-income families.

A further meeting with transport managers was arranged, and the group presented their report. This time, the outcome was different. The county council were persuaded by the group's arguments, and agreed to introduce a new concessionary fare scheme for children and young people. (For more detail on the Transport Group, see Cairns 2001.)

Since then, it has become part of Investing in Children's practice to support young people who want to influence public policy, by assisting them to research issues in order to develop well-informed arguments for change.

Young women and sport

Investing in Children was approached by a local primary care trust (PCT) and Sport England after concerns had been raised about the relatively low level of engagement by young women in organised sporting activities. The PCT and Sport England wanted Investing in Children's help to explore why this was the case.

Investing in Children invited local young people to become involved. A number of groups of young women took up the offer. Leah Fletcher and Melissa Stamp were members of one of these groups. As is explained below, we were two 12 year olds attending our local comprehensive school. We were not selected, but volunteered to take part because of our interest in sport. We worked on this project for two years, and have continued to work with Investing in Children on a range of other issues since then. In total, we've worked with Investing in Children for over six years.

This is our story

We first became involved when it was announced in a school assembly that there was going to be a project about young women and sport. One of our physical education (PE) teachers encouraged us to attend a meeting about this in the gym at break time. The Investing in Children worker told us about the project. She explained that the National Health Service (NHS) and Sport England were concerned that lots of young women our age weren't taking part in any physical activity, and said she needed our help to find out why this was the case. She was down to earth and approachable, and was more interested in listening to our ideas than telling us what she thought.

We were aged 12 at the time, and we were both into sport, so it seemed like an interesting thing to do. We agreed to attend another meeting after school to talk about what we could do.

Eight of us turned up at a meeting with Investing in Children at our local leisure centre. It was really good. We felt like we were being treated as important people – like the way grown-ups expect to be treated all the time – and we felt what we said actually mattered. One of the most important things was it was different from school. We felt that we were in charge, and it very quickly became *our* project.

There was something important about the overall approach. Our Investing in Children worker was not deadly serious all the time, but we could all see that this was a serious issue, and we needed to get down to serious business.

Our Investing in Children worker told us that if we agreed to work on the project, we would get paid for our time. This made it even better – it felt like we had a proper job and that we were being taken seriously. (Since then, we've talked about this, and we think we would probably have agreed to become part of the project even if we hadn't been paid, but there's no doubt it gave us a real buzz at the time, and helped to make us really keen to do well.)

We spent quite a long time discussing what we could do to investigate the issue. At the time, it felt like we were getting together every couple of weeks, drinking pop and eating crisps, and talking, but, looking back, we needed the time because none of us had ever done anything like this before. Eventually we agreed that the first thing we needed to do was to try and find out *why* young women weren't taking part in sports.

We looked at different ways of doing this. We thought of surveying other young women's opinions by using a questionnaire, or doing interviews. Our Investing in Children worker told us about 'Agenda Days'. Investing in Children had been doing these for a number of years. Basically, an Agenda Day is an event where young people can get together without adults, to talk about issues that need discussing, and decide what to do about them. This seemed like a good place to start, so with Investing in Children's support, we decided to organise a young women's Agenda Day on young women in sport.

The research

We booked the hall in the local leisure centre one Saturday. We sent invitations (through schools) to all young women from our area. We explained what the project was about and what we wanted to achieve. We said that we wanted to find out why lots of young women weren't taking part in sports, and what we could do about it. We also said that everyone who turned up would have a chance to have a say, and receive a payment for their time.

On the day, almost 100 young women turned up, which was more than we expected, but it was great. The Agenda Day wasn't on a school day, so everyone who came had made their own choice to attend. There was no selection either – we had issued an open invitation.

It was a bit daunting, standing up in front of so many young people, and explaining what we were going to do. But we had talked about it and we were well prepared.

We quickly divided into smaller groups, and we and the other members of the project group worked in pairs. It was still quite challenging, because a lot of the people were older than us, but it helped that we were well organised. There was a great atmosphere and everyone got really involved.

Here is what we found out.

- Generally, everybody knew about how important exercise and healthy eating are – we get all that in school. We hear about it in personal and social education (PSE), but also in science and information technology and communication (ITC).
- One of the problems about leisure centres was that lots of young people didn't fancy the activities that were on offer, such as badminton and judo. There was plenty of football for young men, but leisure centre staff seemed to think that all young women were into netball.
- Lots of young people said that they would like to use the gym. There were a variety of reasons for this. The fact that people can go on their own and work at their own pace was attractive. Organised clubs, with an instructor or coach, were a bit too much like school. The gym is indoors, which is an advantage given that this is the North East. But the leisure centres imposed an age restriction, and most of the young people weren't allowed in.
- Some young women felt self-conscious and didn't want to exercise with young men around – they felt embarrassed or intimidated.
- There was discussion about PE lessons in school – some young people asked why they couldn't wear tracksuit bottoms (especially if there were boys around).

We followed this up by having a stall at the gala celebrations in a local town – we gave out fresh fruit and health information, and also asked people to fill out questionnaires. On reflection, questionnaires aren't as useful as Agenda Days, and we didn't find out anything new, but the limited results built upon the data we already had.

Creating an argument for change

So far, so good. We were pleased with what we had found out. Our next step was to arrange to meet with the manager of our local leisure centre.

It was a difficult meeting. When we were in the Agenda Day, even when people were disagreeing with each other, it felt like people were listening and treating each other as equals. Here, it was different. We gained the impression that the manager didn't really see the point, and wasn't taking us seriously.

We asked him why young people weren't allowed to use the gym. He told us that he didn't have insurance for people under the age of 14 to use the fitness equipment, which was why there was an age restriction. He also said that he thought the adults who used the gym regularly would complain if young people were allowed in too.

We weren't very happy with this, but couldn't argue with the insurance information even though we thought that it was a bit odd. It was frustrating because we didn't feel that the manager was prepared to answer our questions.

Following this, we were asked to go to a meeting to present the findings of our research. The meeting was organised by the PCT and Sport England, and the other people who were invited were PE teachers and local leisure centre managers.

We told them what we had found out. A few of the teachers thought there was no reason why tracksuit bottoms couldn't be worn in PE class, and that could be sorted out quite easily. But they didn't really take on board the other things we said.

Instead, they complained that the leisure centres provided lots of activities, but nobody attends. They said that the way to get things changed was for young people to come to the sessions that were already available, and then make suggestions about other sports. They said that there were opportunities to attend badminton sessions and judo classes.

We argued that what was on offer wasn't particularly attractive to young people. We thought badminton was a game played by older people, and nobody fancied judo. We asked why the centres don't ask young people what they are interested in, rather than providing things that we haven't asked for, and then complaining when we don't attend. This was somehow seen to be unrealistic, and our suggestion was ignored. Again, we asked about access to the gym. We said we had a list of 76 young women who would attend the gym, if they were allowed. We also suggested that the best way of doing this would be to provide female-only sessions, so that women would feel comfortable and supported.

Again, we were told that there were insurance problems. We were also told that using gym equipment was harmful to the physical development of young people.

More research

This was a setback, but we were determined to continue. We decided we needed to do some more research, but not into what young women were saying – we thought we had done a good job of that, and nobody had questioned the results we had come up with. We decided to do more research into what the *adults* had said.

With Investing in Children's help, we contacted other leisure centres in the region to see if the situation was the same everywhere. We found a number of centres where young people aged 11 years old were using the gym. We visited some of these centres, and were told that age really wasn't a problem. Indeed a particular advantage of their approach was that whole families were able to exercise together. There was no suggestion that adults had a problem with the young people using the gym.

We also contacted Durham University, to ask about evidence of the harmful effects on physical development of using fitness equipment. We found out that there is no problem about using the gym (although it wasn't a good idea to use the weights – something that nobody had asked to do). In addition, students from the university said that, as far as they knew, no extra insurance was required for young people to use gyms.

Persistence

We took this information back to the leisure centre managers. We really felt that the results of our research had shot down all their arguments. Indeed, we felt that we had identified an important new market for leisure centre services – providing access to fitness equipment to young women – but they were unimpressed. We contacted the head of Leisure Services, and told him what we had discovered. We also spoke to an elected member of the local government, and the local newspaper, about what we had done and what we hoped to achieve.

We heard nothing for ages, and then, finally, the policy was changed. Now all young people over the age of 11 years are allowed to use gyms. It had taken almost two years.

Reflections

All of this happened some time ago, and we are both at college now. We have continued to work with Investing in Children, not only on other research projects, but also by contributing to staff development courses. We have spoken at conferences, and have had the opportunity to travel quite a bit.

We have had the chance to think back on our experiences. We have no doubt that, partly as a result of our involvement with Investing in Children, we are much more self-confident and outgoing. We are also not inclined to accept that the world is as it is and that nothing can be done about it.

We think we have learned the following lessons.

- Adults don't always know best, but young people need to be prepared to fight to have their voices heard, even when it's obvious that they have the stronger arguments.

- Young people are generally up for it, and will work hard on issues that affect them.
- Hard work is not enough – you need to be smart and think about what you are doing.
- Research is common sense really – it's a way of finding out what you need to know in order to put forward the strongest argument for change.

10 The transition from practitioner to researcher

Physiotherapists undertaking research with disabled children and young people

Dawn Pickering, Karen Visser, Lyn Horrocks and Gabriela Todd

Introduction

This chapter describes a research project in progress by new researchers who have moved from physiotherapy practice into research. It sets out the challenges faced by practitioners moving into research with disabled children and young people, and will describe some of the lessons learnt that may help others starting on such a journey. The authors all came to research from National Health Service (NHS) physiotherapy clinical practice.

As physiotherapists, our professional role is to enable children to achieve their potential for activity and participation. Physiotherapists are ideally placed with their knowledge and skills to bridge the gap between health care and social care, and many develop activities for disabled children and young people to widen their participation (Hunt, 2011). Coming from clinical practice, where there is limited scientific evidence for the effects of physiotherapy treatment, the team were keen to undertake research to explore both physical attributes, as well as quality of life (McBurney et al., 2003). Thus, the idea for the research project and the journey of writing a research proposal began.

Leisure activities for disabled children and young people are limited, and children with cerebral palsy are disadvantaged by the lack of suitable provision. The consequent impact for the wider family can be considerable (Connors and Stalker, 2003; The Children Act 1989, 2004; Read et al., 2006). Both our experience as physiotherapists and previous research made us very aware of the impact on families of having a disabled child, and the extra challenges this can present not only to the parents, but also to siblings (Pickering and Busse, 2010; Read et al., 2006). As well as the care children need, parents seek to offer their child opportunities for recreational activities with their siblings and peers, and participation in the wider community. However, there are limited recreational, leisure or sports opportunities for disabled children and young people and their families (Bevan Foundation, 2011). Taking into account the lack of opportunities for recreational activities for families with disabled children, the research team chose to look at a recreational activity that had the potential to involve the whole family and friends.

Adapted dynamic cycling creates an opportunity for disabled children and young people to enjoy cycling with family and friends. Pedal Power is a charity in Cardiff that provides a cycle hire facility and has a range of adapted bikes for adults and children with a variety of disabilities (www.cardiffpedalpower.org). The physiotherapist employed at Pedal Power initiated the research project with the academic team at Cardiff University.

This project was developed to explore the effects of adapted dynamic cycling for children with cerebral palsy. The study's research question looks at potential effects on muscle strength and length, as well as quality of life, thus utilising a holistic approach to the child. Our aim is to be involved in a collaborative project that combines both academic and physiotherapy practice. We are using a mixed methods approach (Creswell and Clark, 2007). It is a three year study and this chapter was written at the end of year two.

This chapter is divided into sections covering the issues that have arisen for us as practitioners becoming researchers with disabled children and young people. These are: applying for funding, the values and principles behind the research, research design and ethical considerations, including the NHS Integrated Research Application System.

Applying for funding

The research team were not experienced at writing proposals to gain grant funding. We understood that unless a research team member has a track record of achieving grant funding and already has several publications to its name, it is best to be very specific who you target for money. Therefore, in this instance, a specific charity was approached who only fund research with children with cerebral palsy, the Nancie Finnie Charitable Trust.

In our experience it is wise to ask for as much funding as you think the charity can offer and to carefully consider what all the real costs of undertaking the project might be. You might need to budget for administrative support time, travel expenses for the children and families, consumables, replacement of items lost, postage and printing and publicity costs, as well as 'thank you's' for the children and young people who have participated in the research. These were aspects the team were naive about and we had not anticipated these costs. The resultant financial pressure can add to the challenges of managing a research project. The dissemination aspects of the project can be important to funders, so consider including some conference fees in your application as promoting your work to the wider academic and public audiences is essential to maximise your impact. Again the team overlooked this aspect and have consequently been limited in this area. Before we started the project we were unaware of the importance of the research in the community, and after the start of this project the Cardiff University's

Community Engagement team have assisted us to raise its profile. Having adequate funding for your project is important for determining how you can approach putting your values into practice in the research design and so warrants careful consideration.

Values and principles of research involving disabled children and young people

The team aspired to the values embedded in the United Nations Convention on the Rights of the Child (United Nations, 1989) when developing the design of the research project. Three different categories of rights are identified: protection, participation and provision. These come under four guiding principles, which are: non-discrimination (Article 2), in the best interests of the child (Article 3), survival and development (Article 6) and respect for the views of the child (Article 12) (Webb et al., 2009; see 'Why?' chapters – Part 2). The right to play and leisure (Article 31) and the rights of disabled children to special care and support (Article 23) were also incorporated in the philosophy of the study design.

This project involved children with cerebral palsy with their families and carers, and investigated the active participation of disabled children in a leisure activity. The children came from a variety of cultures, including Somalia and Bangladesh; the majority being from Wales with several whose first language was Welsh. They were aged between two and 18 years old. They had all types of cerebral palsy; many experienced difficulties with learning and communication. The information sheet created to tell them about the research project was translated into Welsh and Urdu, and sometimes the participants required the support of interpreters or child advocates to assist with understanding.

Doing research 'with' children, as opposed to doing research 'on' children, requires more than just a tokenistic effort. Hart's ladder of participation suggests the ideal is to have children and young people designing and setting the research agenda (Hart, 1992; Chapter 1). At the time of writing the research proposal it did not occur to the researchers to ask for input from service users. Since starting the research we have developed a range of contacts that have facilitated more participant involvement than we had originally planned. We have made contact with Involving People, which was set up with the aim of actively involving service users in health and social care research (www.nischr.org.uk). As a result of this service, user input has been sought and provided on the design of the participant information sheets and consent/assent forms from a parent of a child with cerebral palsy, along with assistance in translation of these information sheets and consent forms into the Welsh language. Active involvement ensures service users are not just subjects of research but contribute to the planning, management, carrying out and presenting of research. For the future we would aim to engage disabled children and young people in discussing and setting the research agenda so that their priorities are included and explored.

Health and social care workers involved with children need to balance numerous demands and expectations when producing research that is ethical, child friendly and rigorous. Disabled children and young people are seen to be a vulnerable group and so we need to have evidence to support any research intervention (Chapters 1, 3 and 6). If this group of children are not given the opportunity to contribute to the research agenda how can one presume that their quality of life can improve? What researchers think is important is not necessarily the same as what is seen as important by disabled children and young people.

Research design

The team used the World Health Organisation's International Classification of Functioning, Disability and Health (ICF) (World Health Organisation, 2001, 2007) to design the methods of measurement for the children with cerebral palsy. The ICF incorporates the social model of disability which means the focus moves away from 'an emphasis on individual impairments towards the ways in which the physical, cultural and social environments exclude or disadvantage people labelled as disabled' (Barnes, 2003:5). This model illustrates that whilst a medical condition might limit a person physically, the wider social environment and attitudes within society can create more barriers to participation.

The delivery of health care in the past has been criticised for neglecting the wider aspects of activity and participation, not taking into account the personal and environmental factors, thus reducing the holistic approach (Jelsma and Scott, 2011). This ICF model is being used in the data analysis as a framework to explore the effects of adapted dynamic cycling on participation.

When designing a research study the danger is being too ambitious. In our experience, as new researchers, we had to play to our strengths so we chose to use methods of which we already had some experience of from our studies. Some on the team were more experienced with quantitative methods, others with qualitative approaches, such as interviews. Whilst elements of measurement and interviewing are used in physiotherapy practice, the transition to becoming a researcher needed some adjustment. In clinical practice, measurement may be used to set goals that are reviewed periodically and can motivate the child. The measurement tool for research is being used to measure the effect of the intervention, in this case adapted cycling.

Rigour involves efforts to control the quality of your research with honesty and integrity, as well as to avoid errors and minimise bias (Hicks, 2009). Producing real world research involving children poses many challenges, as it is not possible to maintain strict control of variables and standardisation in the implementation of procedures (Chapter 6). Children, by their very nature, can be variable from one moment to the next, being likely to stray from following set procedures and protocols designed to answer specific research questions. The complexity of the variables for the disabled child includes their mood, illness, tiredness or fatigue, pain, muscle weakness or tightness. Also outdoor leisure activities, such as cycling, add a whole new dimension to research compared to indoor controlled environments.

A researcher needs simultaneously to be able to maintain validity (the ability of the measurement tool to measure what it says it will measure) and reliability (the researcher measuring the same way every time) in the use of these measures to maintain an acceptable level of rigour in their research methodology. There are limited measures that have been validated with disabled children and young people. The authors did not always find specific ones that exactly met the objectives for our study, so measures were adapted. This must be clearly justified.

Children with cerebral palsy have difficulties with balance and coordination. We used a hand-held dynamometer which measures muscle strength. The literature suggests it is a valid tool to measure muscle strength in children with cerebral palsy (Taylor et al., 2004). Younger children, however, did not always fully understand how to coordinate their leg to generate a specific movement at a specific joint, which sometimes resulted in variable data. The outcome measure further relies on the strength of the researcher (measurer) to counteract the child's movement, resulting in the potential for different results when taken by different researchers. In order to minimise this unreliability in measurement, the same researcher was used, where possible, for each child's set of measurements. This is supported by the research evidence on the reliability of this measure (Taylor et al., 2004). As children are likely to respond differently as a result of numerous variables and confounding factors, the researchers recommend the use of a single researcher when measuring outcomes in children.

The use of outcome measures would appear to be a particularly contentious issue that needs addressing prior to starting the research process. It is important to ensure whether the outcome measure remains valid and reliable, producing comparable data when implemented in a variety of child friendly ways and by more than one researcher. Using the research pilot study to test multiple ways of implementing outcome measures while maintaining reliability, prior to the implementation of a larger research project, is recommended when working with children, due to the variability that this could involve. Researchers have the responsibility of using outcome measures compatible with children across a variety of ages that can also be implemented in a variety of not overly intrusive ways.

A researcher also needs to be ready to be flexible and adaptable in implementation, and readily able to identify the slightest sign of a child's unwillingness to consent or assent at any stage of the research process. Health and social care workers can be well placed for conducting research involving children, as these are skills they regularly use when engaging children and families in their everyday professional practice.

For the interview data, disabled children and young people may not have the cognition, verbal language or the vocabulary to describe their experiences. Creative mosaic methods are described as a variety of ways to gather data, and can include drawing, walking and talking, sticker and collage work (Clark and Moss, 2001; Chapter 6). These methods can increase children's capacity for participation in research. The children in our study had limited mobility and some could not carry out dual tasks, such as walking and talking at the same time. Additionally, limitations with coordination, such as holding a pen to draw, meant their true responses were hard to discern. For example, one 10 year old was fully engaged with using stickers about cycling but, when asked to draw, as part of the data collection, her pen control was weak and it was a challenge for her to express herself in this way. Pictures and demonstrations were used to illustrate the measurement tools to explain to the children what would happen. Some younger children were not able to grasp what this meant and so alternate ways of explaining were tried. This could be demonstrating the tool with a brother or sister or on a doll/action man. This replicates what would happen in clinical practice. The team used kicking a ball to help the children to understand which way to move their legs. For the interview data, the team used pictures and photographs of cycling, to evoke an emotional response from the children. The eye pointing, gesture, smile or expressions of happiness were interpreted as recognition of something they enjoyed. In some instances, the child did not respond to a stranger and so the description of how he/she responded to cycling had to be accepted by proxy of the parent or support worker (Booth and Booth, 1996; Morris, 1998).

The whole process from recruitment to data management, analysis, publication and dissemination would benefit from the involvement of children and young people themselves. This process should be beneficial to the child in the first instance, rather than primarily the researcher. Tisdall et al. (2009) suggest that the format and context of communication is the key to gaining the best data and should not to be restricted by the choice of methods. As novice researchers, we approached this from our clinical backgrounds and adapted the methods as we went along, in response to the style of communication of the child and where we were collecting data. The understanding or motivation for the child to participate in research may be limited, and so the researcher needs to be motivating about its potential benefits.

There have been some withdrawals from our research, which is always disappointing. However, we consider these to be expected; the researcher must always respect the child's wish to withdraw and resist at all costs any temptation to put pressure on children to take part.

Whilst available guidance was helpful in the design of our research, the reality of our experience is that the research team reflected on their action and responses, and adapted the research process as the project developed (Silverman, 2006).

Ethical considerations

The Medical Research Council Ethics Guide for Involving Children in Research states that 'participants interests must prevail over those of science and society where there is a conflict' (Medical Research Council, 2007:5). There is a tension here between a controlling scientific protocol and a child's right to choose. A child is more likely to be able to provide consent and assent to research procedures if they are explained and implemented in a child friendly way (Medical Research Council, 2007). This in itself will impact on research rigour, as one method of explanation or implementation could be child friendly to one child while not being appropriate for another child of similar age. Methods of implementation acceptable to a young person aged 13 may not be acceptable to a child of three years, and vice versa. This can create a dilemma, as introducing a variety of methods in implementing research procedures can reduce the scientific rigour of the research (Hicks, 2009).

The parents of children with cerebral palsy that we came across seemed to believe that being involved in research may bring more awareness in the long term of their child's needs and how their needs may be met. Parents are often the gatekeepers for access to children; the child's own ability to be actively involved in research will vary, depending not only on their motivation and age, but also on their ability to understand and consider all the options presented to them. Some of our participants had expressive language limitations, requiring a carer to assist in the consent process. This meant we needed to have very clear processes for consent and assent for our study (see Chapter 6). In some cases children participated because the parents thought it was a good idea for the young person to be involved in the research and they were willing to do so, but other young people refused to participate, despite their parents' willingness. In such cases the children's behaviour was considered by the research team as not giving assent and they were not included.

Informed consent implies that a person understands fully what they are agreeing to, and they indicate that they agree to a variety of conditions, such as having their photograph taken and the data being used in publications, whilst assuring them of confidentiality and anonymity. The words involved can be difficult for younger children to understand, so information needed to be presented to them in a simpler way. It can be difficult to know if children really understand cognitively and, as in our study, they may have expressive language difficulties. If their behaviour and non-verbal communication indicated they were willing to take part, this was deemed assent. Assent is defined as the child's 'affirmative agreement' and is presumed as a positive choice to be involved, even if their written consent cannot be obtained (Kodish, 2005). Separate consent/assent forms were offered to the children. For disabled children and young people, the ability to give consent or assent to take part in the research can be difficult, and the person with parental responsibility may need to give consent on their behalf (Cullen and Lane, 2003; Renold et al., 2008; Chapter 6). Although the parents sometimes gave written consent, they were not always the people who attended subsequent measurement data collection sessions with the child and sometimes the accompanying relative or carer did not understand the research objectives. On these occasions, the physical data collection was not always completed successfully and had to be repeated or remained incomplete. Coming from practice in the NHS, we were surprised to find that the university had only a draft child protection policy for safeguarding children and no lone worker policy. Within the NHS these essential policies had long been established, and had to be adapted for our research purposes in this case.

In our experience doing research with disabled children and young people takes more time than with adults. Involving children in research and assuring consent and assent at every stage of the process needs the investment of extra time. It cannot be rushed, and adequate time must be allowed for the explanations and procedures involved. Children may sense if the researcher becomes anxious or stressed due to time pressures and may become anxious and distressed themselves. Transferring practice skills and techniques, such as using visual aids, photographs and role play with toys can greatly aid this process. Verbal encouragement and congratulations, as well as a reward, are vital. We neglected to budget for thank you gifts to show appreciation to the children for taking part. Due to this oversight, the research team created a certificate and gave a small medal upon the completion of data collection. This was something some of the younger children could take into school for their 'show and tell' opportunities.

We had to apply for ethical approval via the Integrated Research Application System (IRAS); this is the online process to enable access to patient data in the National Health Service (https://www.myresearchproject.org.uk). This is an onerous process that can take months to complete, and may require many amendments and revisions which have to be submitted to the IRAS with up-to-date versions of documentation, including a summary of the project. The lead doctors for the NHS Trusts need to be contacted for their agreement for you to approach their Trust for data access. In our case we approached four NHS organisations: two in England, two in Wales. The university provided us each with a research passport and an enhanced Criminal Records Bureau check, but by the time the IRAS process was finalised these were out of date. They are required to be within the current year and therefore the processes had to be repeated by the relevant NHS organisation. We were further required by the NHS organisations to have up-to-date Level 3 child protection training, which is a requirement for carrying at out research with children. This in-depth multiagency training enabled the researchers to remain current with their knowledge of legislation and practices for safeguarding children. This is essential as part of the research governance for conducting research with children.

A date must be planned for review of the project by the local Research Ethics Committee. Attending this committee needs careful preparation for questioning by approximately 30 experts in research. Expect some revisions and amendments. If you know your project and are experienced in your field you will be able to justify your decisions. In this case we had to make minor amendments, including simplifying the language in our patient information sheet for the Pedal Power study. For the advice to simplify the information sheet, we were advised to use the guidance on the IRAS website, which was 196 pages! The National Institute for Social Care and Health Research (NISCHR) Involving People organisation arranged for a parent of a child with cerebral palsy to comment on our participant information sheet and this helped us to simplify it to meet their requirements.

The letter giving final acceptance from the Research Ethics Committee is the beginning of the process to gain NHS access. The various Trusts' Research and Development Committees also have their processes for approval; this can involve setting up honorary contracts and occupational health screening before starting to recruit participants, so allow several months before you wish to start recruiting children from the NHS.

Role of researcher

We were a team of practitioner researchers, and parents knew this. As a result we found that during research interviews parents might raise issues to do with school or therapy that, as a practitioner, we would respond to in a certain way. As a researcher the response may need to be different (Chapter 17). There were a few occasions where specific topics came up related to sitting postures, surgery and future schooling for the child. As researchers we felt we could not comment as part of the interview record, but did so afterwards, once the interview process had been completed.

We have found the most valuable transferable skill from practice to research is having the confidence to communicate with disabled children and young people and their families. Thus enabling and empowering disabled children and young people to increase their participation and maximise the possibility that they can achieve their potential. To engage disabled children and young people in research we have found that we must be able to adapt our communication style to suit their needs. This process can enhance their participation and enable them to make a choice to be involved in research.

Reflection

As we review our progress and consider what we might do differently in the future, we recognise that we have used our strengths to engage with the disabled children and young people and are still addressing our weaknesses in terms of publication and dissemination. There is never enough time or money; you have to learn to manage with what you have been given. Working as a team we have achieved more than each one of us as an individual could have achieved, and the international perspective has enhanced our critical thinking and problem solving abilities (Belbin, 2010).

The team completed a Strengths, Weaknesses, Opportunities and Threats (SWOT) analysis, part way through, which enabled us to view how to build on our successes and address issues (Chartered Society of Physiotherapy, 2005). One of our strengths has been how we have been able to engage with academic audiences when we have presented the work; it is very encouraging for novice researchers to receive constructive feedback from experienced and well-respected researchers to help us develop further.

We have learnt that the role of the team leader is crucial to keep the team focused on the objectives; the challenge here was to stop the team working too hard. We also found that research recruitment can be a long and lonely task and the efforts necessary to bring in more participants can seem endless; this is an issue that has threatened the study, as we are still recruiting enough children with cerebral palsy to both the intervention and the control groups. Our support networks (university and charity) have been instramental in filling unforeseen gaps in various ways.

Conclusion

This chapter has described our experience as physiotherapists being involved in a research project with disabled children and young people. Principles and values have been demonstrated, some of the challenges in terms of research design, ethics and the role of the practitioner researcher explored and the NHS online application described. It is hoped the reader will take what is relevant for their research project and develop their own ideas. The outcome from the adapted cycling study is not yet clear, but we hope we can make a difference for the lives of disabled children and young people, and offer them wider opportunities for participation in society. We hope in the future to give disabled children and young people a greater voice to determine and set the research agendas, thus ensuring they are listened to and valued in our society.

The research journey we are on has enabled each of us to develop further in our understanding of undertaking research with disabled children and young people. As we improve our track record, it will give the team greater confidence to aim higher next time with research grant applications. We would seek to do this in partnership with disabled children and young people in order to explore their research agendas. Ultimately, we would like to make a difference to the quality of life for disabled children and young people, and we see our contribution as providing evidence that a change in thinking to embrace participation can enable their voices to be heard and move the process of actively involving children and young people in research forwards.

11 Offering children confidentiality in research

What are the limits?

Lorraine Radford and Jane Ellis

Introduction

Confidentiality is a central tenet in the practice of health and social research. Whilst confidentiality should be given to research participants, there is often a condition to this in respect of particular groups of people and in certain contexts; the most frequently mentioned group is children and where a child may be experiencing harm. The conflict between confidentiality and child protection in research with children and young people is often acknowledged in ethical guidance, research methods literature and research papers, but it is rarely discussed in detail (Chapters 6 and 17).

This chapter aims to explore children's rights to participation and to protection in ethical research. Following an introductory section on the legal and policy frameworks shaping children's involvement in research, we examine the protection–participation debate in the context of a case study considering the complexities of involving 11–17 year olds as respondents in a study of child safety and victimisation, and show how young people can be involved in discussing ethical issues and informing ethical practice in research. The chapter concludes with suggestions for managing the ethical and practical difficulties of participation, and argues that participation and protection are interdependent.

Confidentiality and child protection – Legal and policy framework

A confidential relationship arises when someone shares private information with another person. A professional can owe a duty of confidentiality to both children and adults. There is, however, no statutory definition of confidentiality although guidance is provided in common (case) law, in the Human Rights Act 1988, covering 'rights to privacy and family life' as defined by Article 8 of the European Convention on Human Rights, and the Data Protection Act 1988 which covers the storing and sharing of personal data. Briefly, the case law and statutory guidance indicate that confidentiality is not absolute and it can be negated if this is in the public interest, to protect a person from harm or to prevent a crime.

Most ethical guidelines for researchers advise that confidentiality can be breached if researchers believe a child is in immediate danger. For example, the Economic and Social Research Council (ESRC) guidance states:

> Researchers working with children, families and vulnerable populations should, when eliciting consent, make clear the limits to confidentiality. If for example an interview reveals that a participant or another person identified in the interview is in significant and immediate danger, the researcher will be obliged to take action in response to that disclosure. Before starting a project involving children, families or vulnerable populations, the principal researcher should have established a procedure and the necessary systems and identified contacts to activate help and support in the event of a disclosure. If the researcher feels it is necessary to break confidentiality, the participant will normally be informed what action is being taken by the researcher unless to do so would increase risk to those concerned.
>
> (ESRC, 2010:24)

When researching with children, further information on managing the practicalities of balancing participation and protection is difficult to find in the research literature.

Asking about violence and abuse

Our case study highlights the tensions between confidentiality and child protection. The National Society for the Prevention of Cruelty to Children (NSPCC) began research to gather up-to-date information on the prevalence and impact of child maltreatment from a nationally representative sample of children and young people living in the UK and to compare the rates of childhood experiences reported by young adults interviewed with rates reported in earlier research (Cawson et al., 2000). The new research looked at the maltreatment and victimisation of children at home, in school and in the community (Radford et al., 2011). It was based on a survey of 6,196 participants, recruited from households randomly selected from the UK Postcode Address File. The participants included:

- 2,160 parents or guardians of children and young people under 11 years of age
- 2,275 young people between the ages of 11 and 17, with additional information also provided by their parents or guardians
- 1,761 young adults aged 18–24.

A number of standardised and validated measures were used to assess the prevalence of maltreatment and victimisation, and the impact on emotional wellbeing and behaviour.[1] Computer-assisted self-interviewing (CASI) and audio computer-assisted self-interviewing (A-CASI) techniques were used, as these have been shown to be effective methods of gaining information on sensitive research topics and are now the norm in UK victimisation research (Mirlees-Black, 1995). A social research company, TNS-BMRB, undertook the fieldwork interviews. The NSPCC research team designed the research, managed the ethical and reporting issues, conducted all the data analysis and produced the final research reports. The NSPCC and TNS-BMRB together designed the interview questionnaire, developed the training and monitored fieldwork interviewers. Preparations for the research began with a literature review, and consultations with a group of international research experts, NSPCC child protection practitioners, ChildLine service managers, children and young people, and parents. The research proposal was approved by the NSPCC Research Ethics Committee, which included practitioners and independent academic advisers recruited from universities. Due to the sensitivity of the research, the Research Ethics Committee, the Expert Committee and an Advisory Group (made up of key stakeholders) provided ongoing scrutiny. The survey was piloted with a sample of 318 participants before the main fieldwork began, and feedback from participants was used to improve the main study design and delivery. Further details of the research methodology and findings can be found in the research report (Radford et al., 2011). The ethical issues we consider here concern only the limits of confidentiality for the 2,275 young people aged 11 to 17 who completed the interviews.

While views are mixed about whether or not children should be asked about sensitive issues such as abuse, many believe that children have the right to give their own views and an account of their own experiences under Article 12 of the UN Convention of the Rights of the Child (Zolotor et al., 2009, see 'Why?' chapters (Part 2)). Indeed it could be argued that it is unethical to exclude children from maltreatment research, since there is also an ethical need for accurate knowledge regarding abuse and the nature of risks that children and young people face. The NSPCC is in the unique position of being the only organisation outside the state in the UK that has powers to initiate child protection proceedings and powers to remove the child from the family home (Parton, 1985). Asking children about experiences of maltreatment raised the possibility of the NSPCC knowing a child was potentially at risk but not intervening to protect. Could we morally do this? What would be the right balance between promoting children's rights to be safe from abuse and violence (by gathering accurate information on their experiences to inform what we do) and promoting children's rights to be protected from harm (by taking action to protect children at risk of harm when they disclose abuse in the survey)? What level of confidentiality could be promised when consent was negotiated with children and parents? A literature review and consultation with our groups of research and practitioner experts revealed three options.

Full confidentiality – full confidentiality can be given as the survey is anonymous and the participant's personal details are detached from the survey answers (Dawes Knight et al., 2006). Using the CASI interview method, the interviewer would not see the answers a young person gave, so would have no idea if the young person was living with abuse unless a disclosure was made directly outside the interview. Children in immediate danger would not be identified until the data set was passed on to the NSPCC for analysis. This was not likely to be until several months later. Can researchers ethically ignore the child at risk? What level of risk is it legal or morally acceptable to ignore?

Threshold-based compromised confidentiality – where the research team would clinically review the survey answers and refer on children at risk. This approach had been taken by Finkelhor et al. (2009) in a national study of child victimisation done in the USA. Finkelhor's research interviews with children aged 10 to 17 years were conducted by researchers over the telephone. A certain combination of responses to questions about experiences of victimisation triggered an alert which required the interviewer to refer the child's survey data to a clinician for review for a decision to be made about the level of risk and whether or not a referral to child protection services was necessary. When does risk override the child's confidentiality? How could the thresholds for referral be explained to young people aged 11 to 17 in a way that gave them enough information to make an informed decision about consent?

No confidentiality – refer all young people with any possible indication of a child protection concern. As the research asked about experiences of maltreatment and victimisation, then any child who had suffered this would be referred. All children and parents would have to be told that if they disclosed any abuse, child protection services would be notified. This would make the research ineffective as the thought of a child protection referral could well stop young people and parents from disclosing any experiences of abuse and neglect.

Confidentiality and child protection in the research process

To gain insights as to how to address these ethical issues, consultations with young people and parents were set up. A consultation with young people in a London school, consisting of two single-sex focus groups, was set up and involved eight young people aged 12–16. Another group was set up with three young people aged 17–18 who have experienced abuse and who were contacted through an NSPCC therapeutic service. A parent group was recruited from contacts in an NSPCC service and involved seven mothers of children aged between 0 and 9 years.

The young people were asked to rank nine scenarios based on the questionnaire in order of the likelihood of needing to tell someone about them; whilst the parents were asked to comment on mock answers to some of the questions. Young people had lower referral and breach of confidentiality thresholds than expected, but the approach was nuanced for the young survivors. The NSPCC young people's group thought that in every case where abuse is suspected the situation should be followed up, as they felt that the young person involved should be given the opportunity to report it. However, they saw this as still within the terms of confidentiality of the research, and were much more comfortable with the idea that if the young person did not want to report it at that time then they should not be pressurised or have action taken against their will. They thought it was important that the young person involved should be given a choice of what to do. For the school group, the consequences of telling someone moderated their willingness to do so. This appeared to relate to how much control they might have over what happened after telling. The idea that the child could be put into care as a direct result was an obstacle to passing information on. The frequency, nature of the abuse, relationship with the perpetrator and whether anybody already knew were factors both young people and parents thought were important in making decisions about risk and when to breach confidentiality However, as found in the school-based research described above, determining the threshold of risk for a breach of confidentiality was not straightforward.

Participants felt that adults and children should be told clearly what the research was about before they agreed to take part. Previous research on child maltreatment had been introduced to participants as a survey about 'family life' (Cawson et al., 2000) and some guidelines still recommend doing this (CAHRV, 2007) so as not to put participants off taking part. To get access to young people, consent in a household survey has to be negotiated through parents (see also Chapters 6 and 10). Parents may not consent, particularly if they themselves have abused or neglected the child, although not all child abusers are parents and parents do provide accurate reports on their children's experiences (Finkelhor et al., 2005). Our feedback from young survivors, however, told us that they would have been angry and upset if they had agreed to take part in the interview without knowing in advance that they would be asked explicit questions about experiences of rape and child sexual abuse.

We decided to choose a more open and honest route to consent and to introduce the survey to households as research on 'child safety and victimisation'. The term 'safety' allowed us to focus on the positive value of conducting the research, while the term 'victimisation' flagged up that the focus was also on harm. Participants were shown a laminated card at the point of negotiating consent that gave examples of the topics covered so that they understood that 'victimisation' covered things like bullying, sexual assault and rape, and domestic violence.

Consent was negotiated with the parent who was interviewed first and he/she was asked questions about family income, structure, health, levels of violence in the neighbourhood and child's school. Consent was negotiated with the young person separately and before the A-CASI interview began. The young person had an on-screen consent form and also a reminder of the instructions about how they could choose to skip questions, not answer or stop and escape from the survey at any point. The interviewer would not know which questions they skipped or answered, and would not know if they chose to exit the survey early because the young person interview section would close down before the laptop was handed back to the interviewer to complete the final section. The pilot study with 318 participants confirmed that the more open approach did not deter parents or young people. The consent rate for the survey was 60.4 per cent; similar to general rates of consent gained in UK household surveys.

Our approach can be described as 'threshold-based compromised confidentiality with escape options', giving young people options to not answer, and to opt out of the interview in confidence without anyone knowing at the time. We decided there needed to be a review of any 'risk of immediate danger', but the balance of control over decisions should be shifted so that young people had more realistic choices about what they agreed to tell us and what would happen if there was a need to take action. A series of questions were asked in the survey about whether or not the young person would like to talk in confidence about experiences they had disclosed. This maximised the opportunities for them to make contact with sources of support on their own terms. All participants were given a debrief/thank-you sheet afterwards. This gave telephone numbers and email addresses for free helplines, including the ChildLine telephone number and the NSPCC Helpline number.

An alert system and a red flag and review process were developed so that if a young person asked for support, or if there was a combination of answers in the survey indicating a possible immediate risk, a flag was activated when the interview was uploaded on to the data system. This meant that the interviewer in the household would not know at the time that an alert had been activated. Consultation with the NSPCC legal team confirmed that child protection responsibilities would override responsibilities for data protection, so we were able to ask the social research company not to separate contact details from survey answers for red-flag cases until these had been reviewed, in case further action was required. Strict protocols were agreed for managing the alert, review and referral processes. All interviews that had been red-flagged, or where the respondent had expressed the wish to talk to a professional, were sent to the NSPCC on a daily basis, reviewed by two members of the research team and cases requiring further action passed on the very same day.

The following were options with 11–17 year olds:

- No further action taken
- Refer to ChildLine
- Refer to the NSPCC Helpline, the route for cases regarded as in danger.

All questionnaires red-flagged or where participants asked for further support (3 per cent of all those interviewed) were reviewed. In most cases no further action was taken because it was apparent the risk was not current or was low. In total 85 cases were referred on, 35 to ChildLine, 44 to an independent counsellor and six to the NSPCC Helpline. The Helpline referrals were made because of concerns about the child's safety, even though the respondent had said they did not want to be re-contacted. In all other cases referrals were made with the young person's consent. The low rate of referral to child protection and of take up of offers of support is similar to that found within other studies (Dawes-Knight et al., 2006; Wolitzsky-Taylor, 2008) and indicates that the likelihood of having to refer cases of immediate risk to child protection services is smaller than researchers might expect.

All referrals were followed up to get information on the outcome. Some young people and young adults who asked to be re-contacted and gave contact details did not reply when contacted by ChildLine or the counsellor. It is possible that some may have contacted services and helplines directly, using the contact numbers and website addresses provided on the debrief/thank-you sheet. It may also be possible that some participants no longer felt they wanted to talk.

All six of the NSPCC Helpline referrals were passed on to the local child protection services. All but one of these concerned children and young people were already known to a social worker. Feedback from social workers on action they took on the referrals left us questioning whether the referral had been helpful for the young person concerned. In three cases, the social worker or another professional contacted the young person and their caregivers to ask if they had disclosed abuse in a survey. In two of these cases, the social worker told us the young person was asked this in front of the allegedly abusive parents. Unsurprisingly, in these cases the young person denied they had ever done an interview at all. Retraction of a disclosure is common as children are often fearful of the consequences of having told somebody about the abuse, as they fear getting themselves, and sometimes the parent, into trouble (Allaggia, 2004).

Feedback from participants

A complaints system was set up for the research, and participants were told how to complain in the advance letter given to them and when consent was negotiated. We received no complaints from young people or young adults. Complaints from adults were few and were mostly about strangers approaching their house. Participants were asked during the interview how they felt about taking part. Of the red-flagged participants, 103 (over 54 per cent) said that taking part in the survey had been very or extremely worthwhile (70 young people and 33 caregivers); 38 said they had been upset by the survey (33 young people and five caregivers). Of the 33 young people who reported being upset, 27 also said that taking part in the survey had been at least quite worthwhile. Our experience of conducting this research confirms that young people want to take part and want to express a view about their own experiences, even when this may be upsetting. Researchers have a duty to minimise the possibility of causing upset and we feel that this includes being honest about what we are asking them to take part in. Carefully reviewing how the research will be conducted alongside expert consultants that include young people and young survivors helped us to design and conduct this research in a way that was effective, robust and respectful.

Conclusion

It is crucially important that children and young people are not harmed by taking part in research. However, this should not mean that children should not be asked to take part in research on sensitive topics such as abuse. Our experiences gained from this research confirmed that young people can take part in sensitive research and often keenly want to do so to give their views. Balancing children's rights to confidentiality and their rights to be protected from harm is no easy matter. We hope that by being open and honest about how we approached these issues in our research that we will encourage other researchers to consider how respect for a child's right to participate in research and a child's right to confidentiality can be practically supported. Actively involving young people in the process and in the review of ethical issues was the most helpful way forward. Protection and participation are not opposed and researchers should be wary of paternalistic protectionism since in disregarding children's views we discount the ways in which they have protected themselves, their strengths and coping strategies. Policy and practice based on children's knowledge and experience might mean that more can be done to help children in ways they would find helpful.

Six practice recommendations

When reviewing research on confidentiality and child protection ethics committees should ensure:

- Researchers can demonstrate they know what to do if a child is at risk of harm
- There are agreed protocols with named persons for making referrals
- An appropriate level of support is offered to participants; as a minimum information to be provided on contacts where they can get help and support
- Children's participation in research should include their taking part in decisions about the ethical issues; including young survivors if the research raises issues about safety and victimisation

- Adequate opportunities for participants to withdraw their consent and that these can be implemented by the child safely and confidentially
- On-going ethical scrutiny is in place for very sensitive research.

Note

1 The main measure of victimisation used was the Juvenile Victimisation Questionnaire (JVQ) (Hamby et al., 2004a, 2004b). The main measures of trauma impact were age appropriate versions of Briere's Trauma Symptom Checklists: Trauma Symptom Checklist for Young Children, Trauma Symptom Checklist for Children, Trauma Symptom Checklist (Shortened Version) (Briere, 1996; Briere et al., 2001).

12 Getting the message across

Working with young people to change perceptions of health research

Paul Chester, Eleanor D. Kennedy, Lesley Lowes, Alexandra Greene and David R. Matthews

Introduction

Health care research is essential for improving the management and prevention of long-term conditions such as diabetes. To enable this, there is heavy reliance on the good will of volunteers who agree to participate in clinical trials and other research projects, but it can be a challenge to reach and inform potential volunteers about research and then to encourage their participation. Adults who take part in research have reported a very positive experience (Lawton et al. 2003; Chester et al. 2011), and we felt that their enthusiasm clearly made them the best advocates for encouraging others to get involved in research. We therefore developed materials to capture this message using video and web-based media (Matthews et al. 2009). We found that the use of video captured a very personal perspective that could not easily be presented using any other medium. The material we produced comprised a series of interviews with patients and health care professionals, which were then available as a DVD or through the internet. However, although these were extremely well received by adults (Matthews et al. 2008), the response from a few young people was less positive. The indication was that the message was for adults and did not resonate with a younger audience.

It was clear that a different approach was required to engage young people with diabetes research. In the UK in 2010, 73% of households had internet access and 82% of people aged 16–24 years accessed the internet nearly every day (Office for National Statistics 2010). This, then, seemed the ideal way to reach and engage a large audience of young people. But what sort of material would appeal to this age group? Clearly young people needed to be involved in the process of developing age-appropriate material (Kirby 2004), and, considering the focus on diabetes research, young people with diabetes seemed the most appropriate to be involved as advisors and co-workers.

It was evident from an early stage in the project that the young people had clear views about what would and would not appeal to their peers and that this could be very much at odds with the ideas of the organisers. Therefore we aimed to involve young people in the development of a small pilot website using the video concept. The website would need to be attractive to young people and encourage an interest in diabetes research and research participation.

This chapter describes the involvement of young people in the design, production and review of materials designed to engage young people with diabetes and encourage them to consider the importance of research and subsequent participation in research. Challenges experienced are discussed and the chapter concludes with reflections arising from this work.

Getting started

A project plan was prepared, in close collaboration with a professional film production company who had considerable experience in health care video material and in working with young people. The plan was used to seek funding, most of which was obtained in a grant from the Drug Information Association. The project also received two other small grants – one from Novo Nordisk and one from GlaxoSmithKline.

The University of Oxford Research Ethics Committee advised us that, because this was not a research project, ethics approval was not required, but that, because the project involved working with children and teenagers, all team members would need clearance from the Criminal Records Bureau (CRB). The project team also paid careful attention to any ethical issues that could potentially arise. One of the authors (LL) is a paediatric diabetes nurse/researcher, who acted as advisor on ethical and practical requirements throughout the project.

The plan was in three stages.

1. To identify what material would appeal to young people
2. To produce video materials and design the website
3. To gather information about the outcome of the project.

Identifying material that would appeal to young people

The first stage was the work with a group of young volunteers aged 16–20 years to identify material that would appeal to young people. Three paediatric diabetes centres were approached to invite past or current patients to take part. An information sheet was prepared explaining the project and what the team intended to achieve. Early advice was to make the project as attractive and as appealing to our target age group as possible in order to encourage participation. The volunteers were invited to a workshop in central London. The location was a film studio since we felt this would be a more relaxed venue for the young people to work in and because we did not want to 'medicalise' the project. It was also felt that a film studio setting might create an interest and encourage volunteers to take part. Each volunteer was invited to bring a friend or sibling within the same age range; it was hoped that this would take the focus away from 'patients' and make the material of a wider appeal. In addition, parents were invited to join the first part of the workshop, but were encouraged not to stay beyond the introduction in order to allow the young people to talk without feeling restricted. Only two parents chose to come. All participants, including accompanying parents, siblings or friends, were accommodated overnight in a hotel close to the film studio and all subsistence and travel expenses were paid. In some cases the travel arrangements took a lot of organising because most teenagers did not have sufficient funds to pay for a trip to London and then claim back their expenses. Therefore tickets were supplied in advance and taxis pre-booked on account.

Despite careful planning to encourage and motivate the participation of young people, only two centres were able to find volunteers willing to help. Six volunteers agreed that their contact details could be supplied to the project organisers. With the young people's permission, parents were also contacted to have the project explained and to answer any concerns they might have. These contacts often took place in the evening because parents would be at work during the day.

The agenda for the workshop was in two parts. First, the presentation of the project and, second, working with the young people to generate ideas about how to present research and create an interest among their peer group, especially using the medium of video. To stimulate discussion, some initial ideas were put forward. The young people were asked to identify design elements for a website that would host the material. No restrictions were placed on the group, although it was explained that the organisers would be able to implement only some of the ideas that were within budget and time frame. Each of the participants was invited to contribute some text for the website on a topic relevant to their own experience of diabetes, of research or of living with a friend or relative with diabetes. At the end of the workshop, email contact details were obtained and a private 'invitation only' social networking site (Facebook) was set up to keep all the participants up to date with progress and to ask for comment on the various elements of the project.

All the suggestions generated by the young volunteers at the initial workshop were discussed between the production team and the authors. Within the budget available and within the practicalities of the suggestions, it was agreed to produce two videos – one a documentary style film about a research project, the second a street interview or 'vox pop' regarding perceptions of diabetes. From this meeting the design elements for the website were also agreed.

Producing video materials and the website

The second stage was the production of the video materials and the final design of the website. Two of the volunteers from our initial group agreed to make the vox pop video. The filming was organised by the film production company who obtained all the necessary permissions for street filming. The questions were devised by the youngsters, with some assistance from the organisers. Again, parents were contacted to ensure that their sanction was given for this activity. In addition, LL agreed to act as a chaperone for the young people during the filming, which took place during school holidays in a busy shopping precinct in a large UK city.

For the second film, we approached a UK investigator who was undertaking a multi-centred trial investigating a structured education programme for young people with diabetes (Price 2011). One of the trial sites agreed to re-enact the study programme and invite the young people who had originally taken part to return for a day filming the essential elements of the project. Eight young people and two of the investigator team volunteered for this part of the project. All the volunteers were brought to and collected from the venue by parents, none of whom stayed.

A key element for attracting the volunteers was that this would be making a film with a professional film company and not a clinical day. In addition, the investigator team were all well known to the volunteers and their parents and already had good relationships with the volunteers. Much of the organisation for this stage of the project was undertaken by the two volunteers from the investigator team.

Each of these video days was edited and condensed into a short film of a few minutes duration for the website. The website was designed as far as possible using the suggestions put forward at the initial workshop although it proved difficult to get the young volunteers to review and comment on the stages of the web development. It proved equally difficult to obtain written materials from the young people, despite the fact that they had initially agreed to write much of the content. Follow up through personal email and in some cases phone calls was used to encourage these contributions, although we did not want to put the volunteers under any pressure or make unwanted demands, especially at a time when some of them were studying for exams. Finally some additional materials were obtained from the extensive video bank generated from the original adult project which included interviews with several young people with diabetes.

Gathering information about the outcome of the project

The third and final stage of the project was the gathering of information about the outcome. Would the material appeal to the target audience, – the young people in their mid- to late teens? We used qualitative methods and ran a focus group to look at the website before it went live. To do this, we wanted to find another group of young people independent from stages one and two of the project and invite them to a focus group.

This posed a number of issues: we did not want to ask the centres that had already been closely involved with the project, so we had to find another way to identify potential participants. We decided to invite young people aged 18 years, since this made the approach far easier because we did not need parental consent (Chapter 6) and the respondents would still be within our target group. We approached two charities involved with diabetes; one was unable to help while the other identified a single person willing to take part. We identified two further participants from a database of people who had expressed an interest in diabetes research. Once again, each participant was invited to bring a friend or sibling of the same age. All expenses were paid, but there was no payment for participation.

We chose to run our focus group discussion in a rented meeting room that was not associated with health and social care, and in central London because it was accessible to all the volunteers. The session lasted two and half hours with a short break for lunch, which was provided. The discussions were tape recorded and videoed so that different dimensions of the group dynamics could be included in the analysis. The three facilitators had worked in diabetes research for a number of years, which helped them to understand something about the scenarios the young people spoke about and to follow the significance of these in relation to the material that the team wanted to evaluate.

The focus group was divided into two parts. Part one involved asking the participants to reflect on what research meant to them, whether they thought young people in general knew about research, whether or not they would want to get involved and what sorts of thing would encourage or discourage them from getting involved in research. The second part involved watching the website material, including the vox pop and research videos, followed by questions about whether the material had changed their views about research and made them more inclined to volunteer. They were also asked if they could advise us on how to make the material (information, design, content) any clearer. The participants had not seen the website or video material before the event.

The website, www.researchforme.net, was completed and went live 18 months after the initial stage one workshop.

What we found

At each of the three stages of this project, the group of young people involved were enthusiastic and willing to help. In the first stage, six people (four with diabetes, one friend and one sister) between 16 and 20 years of age participated; and, at the second stage, eight young people, all with diabetes, volunteered to take part (age 13–16 years). The authors consider this to be very successful since this was not part of clinical care and we were asking participants to take part in a project that would require time and commitment. It was interesting to note that at the initial stage 1 workshop the 'discussion' ideas put forward by the organisers were all rapidly dismissed as 'boring'; this included young people interviewing health care professionals. It was also clear that our volunteers wanted to generate positive messages and did not want any materials that emphasised the potential complications or 'downsides' associated with diabetes. They also had strong views about some of the design elements of the website, including the use of photos and an orange and purple colour scheme. It was interesting to the team there was no call for cartoon or graphics materials.

The young people involved in the project seemed to enjoy their participation. As one young person with diabetes (involved in the workshop and street filming) said:

> It was fun … it showed that lots of people knew a lot about diabetes … everyone knows someone that's got it … it was also nice meeting people my age with diabetes and hearing their stories … it's good to know that there's lots of research into diabetes, maybe a cure one day. Yes, I enjoyed doing it but I worry how much awareness it [the website] will raise.
>
> (17 year old, female)

Thus, despite the subsequent difficulty experienced in sustaining interest and enthusiasm, the young people appeared to feel a sense of ownership of the website, as demonstrated by this young person's concern. Given the many demands on this age group, for example A levels and applying to university, the reluctance for on-going involvement is perhaps understandable.

For the focus group, five people aged between 18 and 20 volunteered. Three of the participants had diabetes and the other two members were a friend and a partner. Two of the young people admitted that coming to London, free of charge, had encouraged them to volunteer for our research. The number recommended for a focus group is between six and eight. We did not see the low number of participants as a disadvantage because fewer speakers generally allows more time for in-depth discussion than might ordinarily be possible with a larger number of attendees. In our case, the smaller number made it possible for us to invite a mix of young women and young men so that any explanations and descriptions of similar common-sense assumptions might be instigated and made more explicit. This also allowed us to invite the volunteers to bring along a friend or partner.

After the initial introductions, the lead facilitator (AG), a qualitative researcher who was familiar with focus groups and diabetes research, invited the young participants to speak about why they had decided to volunteer for the group discussions. All three of those with diabetes said that they had come along because the topic looked interesting, it was a chance to meet others with diabetes and they wanted to be part of helping others with diabetes.

> I came because I wanted to help other people with diabetes that might be going through what I'm going through.
>
> (A female participant)

The accompanying partner and friend explained their reasons in the following ways.

> It's good to feel you're helping. (Friend)
> I wanted to learn more because I don't have it and I wanted to be able to help him. (Partner)

Feedback from young people

When asked to describe what research meant to them, none of the participants had appreciated that taking part in a focus group, commenting on a website or vox pop material qualified as helping with research.

> I thought it was all about sort of rat experiments and test tubes ... or taking drugs. I didn't know that this was research and talking about things in a group was news to me.
>
> (A male participant)

All believed that it was highly likely that other young people felt the same way and would probably be put off research because of its association with laboratory experiments.

> I don't think young people know much about research. It was only when I went to university and learnt about research and ethics.
>
> (A female participant)

The second part involved the young people looking at the website material (an educational research project (www.kick-off.org) that included sessions with children learning about diet, exercise and carbohydrate, managing hypoglycaemia, measuring blood glucose, a quiz, and young people commenting on aspects of their lives with diabetes and what they thought of being involved in research). This was followed by examples of the vox pop, and some short interviews all of which involved young people. The general view from the group was positive.

> It's nice to see people with diabetes talking because when the docs say it, they can make it look easy, but it isn't.
>
> (A female participant)

All believed that the material had changed their view of research and made them more open to volunteering for research.

> The video was good because it makes research more accessible ... you know it's not something that happens to other people like Frankenstein.
>
> (A male participant)

Two participants commented further.

> There are some things about diabetes that I didn't know so it's always going to be a learning curve as long as you're helped along the way and it benefits you. (A male participant)
>
> Yeah, it's good to feel you're helping (others by joining in research) but it also gives you more time to think about your diabetes and that's a good thing. (A female participant)

Several felt that the website was too geared towards children and would have preferred to have seen material that was more relevant to all the different age groups. In particular, it would be useful to have the different ages speaking about the pros and cons of joining research projects. A couple said they would have liked to have had more information about other research projects and the results of these.

To ensure that generalisations about research could be made effectively, two qualitative researchers with experiences in diabetes research reviewed the tape and video data repeatedly to identify potential categories into which specific headings might emerge that highlighted young people's views on the material they had seen, as well as their general views on what would encourage young people to volunteer for research.

Discussion and conclusions

The aim of our focus group was to elicit the views of five young volunteers on the website and video material the organisers had developed with the support of young people, all of whom were unknown to our members of the focus group. The website developed for adult advocacy receives approximately 10,000 hits per month (Chester et al. 2011) and this could be used as an outcome measure for this kind of project. We felt, however, that it was important to try and find out what the intended audience thought of the material. We chose the focus group as the method to evaluate our research because this method has been used successfully to access hard-to-reach populations, such as young people (Rosenfeld et al. 1996).

Focus group data are not usually generalisable. However, generalisation does seem appropriate in this case because our five participants provided us with data that helped us to make sense of how young people in similar situations might interpret the website and video material. Before seeing the research material, all the participants felt unaware of the variety of research being undertaken and for this reason felt that most other young people would be reluctant to take part in research. Most of the group members were positive about the research material, believing it encouraged them to feel more inclined to get involved in research, although they felt the material was more geared towards children and would have preferred it to have been more relevant to older age groups under 25 years of age.

This project lasted approximately 18 months from the first group of young people designing the project to the final focus group. While the project delivered the original goal, and we know from the focus group that the video and website were generally well received, there are some useful practical points and learnings that can be drawn from this work.

- Young people are generally very positive and they like to have positive messages about their condition. This was also found when working with adults with diabetes. It was clear therefore that to engage young people we needed the materials to be constructive in nature.
- Young people can work very well together in groups, but the groups can take a while to get going. Time should be allowed for this, and researchers working with young people may need to be prepared to give a 'kick start'.
- Recruiting volunteers is extremely difficult when working through third parties. Recruitment through health care professionals requires that you first engage the professionals before they can support your project. We relied heavily on the goodwill of colleagues working in paediatric diabetes to identify and invite young people to participate.
- Engaging young people over a long (18 months) period of time is difficult. While the participants were able to give fruitful and active input when gathered together, it was much more difficult to get contributions once the meetings or activities were over. It was almost impossible to get comments on the video or web design or to get the participants to provide any materials, despite the fact that they had given commitments to this effect. It is clear, therefore, that it is preferable to conclude the involvement during the meetings and not to expect much further contribution outside the organised events.
- Email is not a good media for contacting young people. Social media (Facebook) was of limited value for obtaining responses from the participants, although it was a simple way to provide information. Mobile phone seemed to be the best method for direct communication, although clearly this could be used only on a one-to-one basis. (See also Chapter 18 for use of such media with young people.)
- Which age group are we aiming for? The initial plan was aimed at mid-teenagers (around 16). Views and tastes change quickly during the younger years, so be clear which age group materials are aimed at.
- There were many practical issues to think about that are not perhaps required when working with adults. For example, making sure that parents were fully aware of the project and what was being asked of their children. Logistics such as organising young people to get to venues can be more difficult as they rarely have sufficient funds to pay and then have

expenses reimbursed. A chaperone may be required, and in the case of diabetes it was important to consider medical issues such as hypoglycaemia that may occur during the meetings and activities. For the latter, at each meeting we had available drinks and sugary food at all times.
- Recruiting young people to help with research is easier if there is some element of the participation (for example, the venue) that may be of interest to them.

Reflections

There were numerous lessons learned during this project and these are described in this chapter. Having an experienced paediatric advisor on the project (LL) was invaluable in identifying and resolving issues before they occurred. When recruiting young people to help with research, particularly older teenagers, it should be remembered that these people have very full and demanding lives, and so you will be competing with school or college work, socialising, sports and hobbies for their time.

To attract the volunteers it proved useful to offer something for them. Some of our volunteers were interested in a career in the media and so the opportunity to work with a professional film crew was appealing, while for others the chance for a day out in London was attractive although this was never used as an incentive to encourage participation.

It is worthwhile noting that ideas that we initially thought would appeal to young people were quickly dismissed, although they did serve to start the discussions. This clearly shows the importance of engaging young people at the earliest possible stage in a project before any commitments are made.

Working through third parties to find volunteers is not easy and we relied heavily on the goodwill of colleagues in paediatric departments. However, we found that once the participants were engaged, their enthusiasm and motivation was contagious. Keeping the young people engaged over a long period proved difficult. This may reflect the disparate nature of the group or, perhaps more likely, the changing circumstances of the people involved. Gap years and university were looming for some of them as we approached the mid-stage of our project.

Despite the practical hurdles, working with the young people in this project was an interesting and highly rewarding experience.

Acknowledgements

We thank all the young people who made this project possible.

We thank Dr Julie Edge (Oxford) and Professor John Gregory (Cardiff) for their help in finding volunteers.

We thank the organisers of the KICk OFF project and, in particular, Dr Katherine Price, Karen Robson and Julie Knowles.

We thank JOOSE TV for the video production and web design work.

One of the authors (PC) is an employee of Novo Nordisk Ltd. We gratefully acknowledge and thank the funders – the Drug Information Association, Novo Nordisk Ltd and GlaxoSmithKline.

13 Young people's participation in service evaluation

Michael Gaffney and Jenny Munro

Introduction

In this chapter we will describe the process of including young people in service evaluation. After we have described something of the process we will review the various elements of this undertaking with a view to highlighting a number of challenges that adult researchers and evaluators may encounter along the way. Developing children and young people's skills as researchers (Bland, Carrington and Brady, 2009) and evaluators (Johnson, 2010) is an expanding topic in childhood studies. We are now considering how to stretch the boundaries of this activity to include those who would not usually get a chance to participate, yet have much to contribute to adults' understandings of young people's lived realities.

Context

The Otago Youth Wellness Trust (OYWT) is a charitable organization operating for 15 years in Dunedin, New Zealand. It provides a free community-based service to young people aged 11–18. The integrated service or wrap-around service (Bruns et al., 2004) is delivered by a professionally qualified multi-disciplinary team of caseworkers using a modified HHEADSS assessment (Cohen, Mackenzie and Yates, 1991) case management model that is outcomes focused. HHEADSS in this modified form is an acronym for 'home, health, education (or employment), adolescent offending, drugs and alcohol, sexuality, suicidality'. The young people who are referred have complex and multiple needs, and do not easily access mainstream health and social services. The service is responsible for truancy in the city and this is a key means of referral for young people.

The organization was able to secure funding from the New Zealand Lottery Community Sector Research Fund to conduct a two-year evaluation. The aim was to develop an evaluation framework to ensure that the integrated service was delivering improved outcomes to all stakeholders, including: those in key government youth policy positions; government funders of the service; referrers of young people to the service; other service providers, who are working with the same young people; those who work for the organization; and, most importantly, the young people and their families who are service users.

The key evaluation questions with respect to the service were: 'Are we doing the right thing?' and 'Are we doing it well?'. All stakeholders had a view on the answers to our questions, and the aim of the evaluation was to make sure that each had the opportunity to provide their answer. A steering group of seven people (four employees and three external academics) was overseeing the project, with the two authors having responsibility for accessing the voices of young people and their families. The voices of others within the evaluation framework were relatively easy to access and as adults they tend to be relatively articulate. Our challenge was to think of ways to make sure that the voices of young people were not lost in the midst of a broader chorus. The steering group had decided to work with the well-established notion that evaluation is used to *improve* not *prove* (Shufflebeam and Shinkfield, 1985). For our evaluation methodology we were drawn to empowerment evaluation (Fettersman and Wandersman, 2005), appreciative inquiry (Cooperrider and Whitney, 2005), transformative evaluation (Mertens, 2009) and developmental evaluation (Patton, 2011).

In New Zealand there is growing recognition of the United Nations Convention on the Rights of the Child through the New Zealand Office for the Children's Commissioner, which has its own young person's advisory group. The Ministry of Youth Development has promoted Article 12 of the Convention within its *Youth Development Strategy Aotearoa* (Ministry of Youth Affairs, 2002). One of the goals is for adults to create opportunities for young people to actively participate and engage in community life.

> Youth participation is about involving young people in having a say in developing, evaluating and reviewing decisions that affect them, their family, schools and tertiary institutions, their community and their country. It is more than just consulting young people.
>
> (Ministry of Youth Affairs, 2002:25)

These ideas are very much aligned to the philosophy of OYWT as an organization and the theories of practice used by the caseworkers, which has then flowed on to how questions for the evaluation were framed, determining the instruments and methods that were employed, and shaping the analysis. Our challenge was working out how to make this process accessible and meaningful for the young people who might participate as co-evaluators in the project and for the young people who would provide feedback on the service as evaluation participants.

A key concern included paying close attention to the ethical issues as they arose throughout the process of evaluation. We did this by trying to promote reflection, while acknowledging the power differentials between adults and young people. We also looked for a range of participation techniques that would diversify the viewpoints within the research. The aim was to support collaboration and inclusion as we went, but never being sure what it would actually look like.

Setting up a young people's advisory group

The steering group for the project saw an opportunity to include the voice of young people within the evaluation. They did this by setting up a young people's 'advisory' group, which did not have a prescribed role other than seeing where the young people's interests lay and following them. It was envisaged that those interests might lie within the categories of 'youth as consultants' and 'youth as partners' (Checkoway and Richards-Schuster, 2003). The defining element is that we were asking them to help us with 'our' project, but with a view to making it theirs as well. Caseworkers within the service were asked to nominate young people they had worked with, or were working with, whom they considered had a level of confidence and competence to promote their ideas within a group setting. A total of nine were nominated of which six took up the offer, four girls and two boys. At the time of their nomination four had recently finished with the service and two were current service users. One person came along and then decided that it was not for them. There is always an element of uncertainty about how things are going for the group members, and there were no guarantees that life wouldn't take a turn for the worse so that someone might have to withdraw for a period. With six young people signed up we felt we had sufficient in the group to get us started.

We endeavoured to provide enough information about what was being asked of them on joining the group, but this is less meaningful than creating an experience that young people want to come back to. Until one has been involved in research and evaluation it is very difficult to know what you are letting yourself in for. Evaluation is so diverse that being involved in one project is not necessarily preparation for the next. When asked what sort of things they would be doing we said it was about supporting OYWT to improve the way it worked with young people; it would be an opportunity to express your views and tell us what you think; you would get to help with, and learn about, an evaluation project; and it was about being part of a group of young people who had experiences of the service. We would achieve this by coming up with ideas about how to tell if OYWT was doing a good job; by developing plans about how to include young people in the project as participants when collecting 'data'; and coming up with ways to share the project findings.

Getting the group together

The caseworkers brokered the relationship with Jenny Munro to see if the young people were interested, but right from the start we had to emphasize that their participation was voluntary. It was always difficult to tell if a willingness to participate is based on some sense of obligation. We learnt later that this obligation in terms of 'paying back' for the support they received, elsewhere referred to as an ethic of reciprocity (Holland, Thomson, Henderson, McGrellis and Sharpe, 2000), was a major theme and motivator for many of the young people who took part in the evaluation as participants. Our job was to make sure we did not abuse that goodwill.

The first challenge was to get the young people together so that they could get to know each other and us. Nobody had met before and so it was about starting relationships from scratch (see also Chapter 8). Some were more confident than others, and with an age range of 14–18 we found the older ones were happier to contribute, whereas others liked to spend more time listening to the direction of the conversation. We did things like generate some rules for the group, such as listening to the views of others without being critical and keeping things that were shared by others confidential to the group. We reviewed the options for how we might like to work together and let them know about the broader context of the evaluation project as well as providing the opportunity to meet others in the project through social gatherings. Their interest very much remained with how to answer the evaluation questions from the perspective of young people as clients.

One of the group practices that we worked with was covering tables with large pieces of plain paper that people could then draw on with maker pens and crayons. This seemed to become quite popular, and created for young people the space for doing and listening while others were talking. Not talking was okay too, and over time the group became comfortable with each other to the point that all were willing to share ideas. The drawing and 'doodling' were also a visual reference point that was a springboard into further dialogue with others and therefore acted as a medium for connecting young people within the group.

We always provided food and drink to start the session as most were scheduled for an after-school period. This time also created a point for sharing what was happening in-between meetings and gauging the feel of the group on the day. Given that research is usually a new experience for young people, opportunities need to be given for them to manage their commitment and establish how comfortable they are with the process (Hill, 2006).

Managing the commitment

We agreed as a group how often we would meet and for how long. The project would cover any costs, such as transport, and would recognize their time as a valued contribution to the evaluation by providing store vouchers. In the end we wanted to be flexible enough to let the young people determine their level of their contribution. In the first six months we met 10 times. This was quite a commitment and not everyone could make it every time, but many did. They got better at letting us know what would work as we negotiated the evaluation timetable together.

One of the challenges of running a project over such a long time frame is maintaining interest. Jenny Munro found it was a delicate balance between fostering enthusiasm, usually by texting or phoning young people in the lead up to the meetings so they did not forget, and coercion to participate. Smith (2008) calls this balancing act 'responsible advocacy' whereby individuals are protected from exploitation while their self-determination is maximized. Once the group got to know each other it did not matter if we did not meet as regularly as we did in the first half year. Sometimes opportunities to meet after school became difficult when the young people got busy – there might be issues at home and school, or health problems might arise. Generally a core group, with one or two changes and new entrants, was sustained. At times it was easier to meet during the school holidays when people were more flexible.

Developing the engagement

Young people, like the majority of adults who are not familiar with evaluation practices, needed a starting point in which to engage. Our central question was 'What is the service doing well?'. So, in line with assuming that young people are 'experts' in their own lives, we asked them what came to mind.

A young women started the discussion off by describing how having *choices* was important. For example, the way she got to spend time with her caseworker and choosing which activities they did together, and where, was very effective. This facilitated developing a liking for the caseworker in a context that made it easy to spend time together. One person liked someone who was chatty and could show understanding. Another liked getting outside, so going on walks in the bush were enjoyed. One person liked ending their sessions in a coffee shop, whereas for another she liked having a caseworker who was okay about spending time with her in an interior design shop. This helped develop relationships defined by respect, sharing and being listened to, rather than the intense professional-type relationships based on meeting someone in their office that most had experienced and rejected in the past.

Even though the types of thing they liked to do with their caseworker were quite different, the young people realized that having choices, especially about the spaces where they met, were important. This led to a question about how caseworkers were assigned to young people in such a way that they seemed to have such a good fit. We did not have the answer to this, but it made us as evaluators look again at the important role of assessment and realize that maybe more was happening in this process that we first thought. Thus by treating young people as 'experts' in their own lives, they were able to provide us with useful information about where to focus the evaluation within the organizational processes.

As the group got to know each other, the young people gained in confidence. In part this was from us as adults in positions of power providing enough leadership to give some structure to the sessions, but at the same time being ready to follow suggestions as they emerged from within the group (Walker, 2009). There were a number of ways that we could tell if this was happening; for example, the young people did more of the talking, they were responding to each other's ideas without reference to us as adults, and they became involved in planning. For example, we had planned to run through some interview questions by having the young people interview each other. But a young person suggested they would like to interview us, the adults. Thus we were now more vulnerable and they were in control as the interviewers. Sharing power like this is a form of reciprocity and an important means of equalizing power relations, which then supports the development of relational respect (Holland et al., 2000). It also gave the young people the opportunity to understand better the challenge of generating meaningful interview questions.

We should not oversimplify the notion of power as a dichotomy between adults and young people. The older group members had a lot more confidence than those who were younger and we saw it as part of our role to support them in becoming involved. In this sense, even though we are trying to increase young people's autonomy, we always found ourselves retaining an element of paternalism and 'knowing what is in the best interests' of young people.

Developing methods for use

At the beginning we had not determined how we were going to collect data from former and current young people who used the service. So, as the group progressed, we could ask questions of the young people about the best way to collect data. 'If these types of thing are important to you, in what sort of scenario would you be willing to share your experiences with someone you have not met before?' We started to identify the types of data that the group saw as important and it was agreed that it would have to be gathered within the context of an interview. This did not mean that we could not use other methods for other purposes, but if we wanted to hear more about what worked for young people and record the diversity of that experience, then we would need to speak with them in person.

We worked with an appreciative inquiry approach (Cooperrider and Whitney, 2005) that aims to have people start with a positive experience and explain its importance within the context of future possibilities, rather than set off to immediately begin with problem analysis that tends to work within a deficit orientation. We offered examples of this approach and asked if they would be comfortable with this style of interview. The advisory group drafted and refined the shape of questions, and a number of the young people offered to run through them as a practice for the interviewer. We had explored the idea of offering young people the opportunity to tell their story through other means, such as photos or music, but, in the end, while these were offered, the young people said it was more important to have someone listen to their stories.

Choice became a strong theme for the group, and one of the ideas that we developed for the interviews with current users of the service was to provide different starting points in the interview. That way if the young person was uncertain about the whole process they could have some control by deciding where to begin their story. One of the sessions became art focused while the group drew and painted cards that could be used as prompts. The young people came up with the metaphor of being on a journey and so used images of a train moving along the tracks. For example, for the question 'What are your hopes for the future?' there was a picture that showed a train moving off into the distance. They suggested using these as something tangible that young people in an interview could look at and 'play with' as a legitimate means of taking time to reflect and consider their answer without feeling so awkward in the context of an interview.

The questions about the process or experience of having a caseworker were more important to the young people than the outcome questions. They all thought a conversation style to interviewing was a better approach. They were able to identify key elements that happened in the caseworker relationship that made things better. For example, they appreciated having someone listen without passing judgement, or having support to get along better with their family and with people at school. They noted how it was good to have a caseworker to talk with while having some fun, they liked having their confidence built up, they talked about staying at school and having hope for the future. In this sense they were identifying the importance of the caseworker, and the relationship, as the 'intervention' and an important outcome in its own right. Having been attuned to these elements, we were then able to integrate these ideas within the data we sought from elsewhere and the analyses we conducted. The young people are placing more importance on the caseworker relationship as a 'process outcome', rather than focusing on the longer-term outcomes as defined by policy and funder stakeholders.

Those within the group who had finished with the service understood the importance of the questions about how things had improved. There was a sense of validating the HHEADSS topics and exploring these within a couple of sessions. The initial decision was to place the questionnaire online. This was based on the assumption that it would be easier for young people to interact with. We modified the phrasing of the questions and sequencing as a result. The diversity of the group was of benefit. In one discussion, a young person still using the service talked about how he would not be able to answer many of the questions as it asked him to look back as though he was now finished and in a position to evaluate the value of that time. The end result was confirmation that we should separate the young people into two groups, those who were current users and those who had finished with the service.

There is a tendency to think of such decisions as one-off points in a series of decisions. Instead, what the young people were doing were creating discussions that were iterative and cyclical. As evaluators we could take these ideas and explore them with other groups such as caseworkers and the broader project steering group.

Ethics

The process of selecting young people for the advisory group described earlier improved the likelihood of positive involvement in the evaluation process. But young people do not come into the service unless they are viewed as 'at risk' or vulnerable in some way (see Chapter 1). The evaluation proposal was reviewed by a health ethics committee, which had required that systems of support were available if problems arose. However such reviews cannot anticipate all the problems that might emerge. For example, when working with this group of young people we were not to know what might be evoked in discussions that would bring back memories of a painful time in their lives (an issue we will return to later). To this end, two of the group's rules were to keep confidences shared and only disclose what you are happy to share with the group. Smith (2008) says vulnerability is difficult to define and thus researchers and evaluators are making constant judgements between facilitation and paternalism, benefits versus costs of participation and the right to autonomy (for example, withdrawal from research), against the principle of justice in seeking service user involvement. These tensions operationalize an ethic of care between evaluator and vulnerable participant. For us this involved 'checking in' with the young people by phoning or texting them between meeting dates. This ongoing communication was a means to assess their level of engagement and to offer support where needed.

One person left the group when we got to the analysis stage of looking at interview transcripts. Some of the material had evoked memories about school so we talked about how she might be supported. One of the advantages of being in a practice setting was that professionals were available to follow up with the young people if this might be supportive (see Chapter 11). This event did raise concerns about whether this part of the process was doing harm rather than good. But others in the group were positive about being involved in this part of the evaluation where we were asking if the analysis framework we were developing made sense in the light of two initial interview transcripts. There is a fine balance to be achieved when taking young people into new territory like this, and it suggests good preparation is required and some understanding of what the young people are struggling with.

These types of challenge have been raised by Mudaly and Goddard (2009). While their article is specific to children who have been abused, the more general question is when would it be appropriate for children who have been in difficult circumstances to be involved in evaluation on that topic. The key question they raise is how to make sure young people are not re-traumatized by evaluation and research participation, in our case by reading other peoples stories. Giving young people the discretion about what to disclose will only go so far. We can see that we have a responsibility as evaluators and researchers to anticipate and forewarn where possible, but there are limits to what can be predicted in advance. In the end the young people must be supported to manage their own (dis)comfort level as we engage with the process. The young person mentioned above who left the group wrote a letter that shows how she managed her own comfort levels and autonomy rights. 'I've gotten past it but it's still very hard when I'm reminded of the past and high school. ... The advisory group brings up too much of the past that I'm still trying to move on from completely. The future is what counts now and that's what I want to put all my energy into. I'm going to accomplish great things.'

The young people were keen to engage in ethical discussions. One of the aspects of the evaluation was asking families what they thought about the service their son or daughter was engaged in. However, the young people could see that as a service user (rather than the family) they would want some control over who else may be spoken to as part of the evaluation. Rather than just family members being spoken to, the category was widened to include significant others. In line with the theme of choice, it was decided that the young people would have the right of veto over whether a significant other was interviewed or not and who that might be. We ended up speaking to about two thirds of 'significant others'; while most were parents, there were also school or course personnel nominated, as well as siblings.

We then had discussions about the impact of such decisions on the evaluation. Because we did not want to provide an analysis on matched pairs, the impact was not as significant. The benefit was that more young people were likely to participate by knowing they had control over this aspect of participation. In the end we also decided that parents do have an experience of the service in their own right and so sought these independent of young people in order to increase the numbers we were getting feedback from.

What have we as adults learnt from this process?

What have we been learning from our time with the advisory group? At the time of writing we are nearing the end of our project. The young people's advisory group is not meeting as regularly during the writing-up phase, but they are keen to be involved in the dissemination of the report, something we have already had discussions about. This has been quite a positive experience for the organization, which is now in a position of thinking about how to include young people in other ways within the service.

Running a group over such a wide age range was challenging for this group in particular. Those who had finished with the service tended to have more experiences to reflect on and discuss when 'looking back', which those who were still in the service could not. Thus keeping a balance in the group so that all young people felt they were contributing was important and at one stage we had to bring some new people in to achieve this.

From the examples given we think our evaluation was richer for the contribution made by this particular group of young people who are so often marginalized and excluded. Short-term evaluations make this type of involvement more difficult to achieve and still remain true to the notions of young people's participation. It takes time for a group to come together and develop a working relationship just as it does for adults. There was a benefit for the young people in their participation. They were learning about a specialized practice that developed their skills. One young person has already moved on to wider forum opportunities beyond the organization. For some of the young people, who were going through difficulties during their time with us, the group became an important and consistent place for them when other things were not going well at home or school.

Conclusion

This group of young people was able to make a positive contribution to this evaluation because, as 'experts' in their own lives, they have particular perspectives to draw on that we did not have available for ourselves as evaluators. Having the time to build relationships with these young people and step them through the process meant that they were able to see the links between their own experiences and the evaluation questions and the various elements of the evaluation process: method development, ethical dilemmas, analysis and dissemination. An ethic of care and responsible advocacy was important in relationship building so as to support their capacity and competence in a meaningful manner. In return we had to be prepared to value their knowledge and experience, and grant it the respect that it deserved within the process. For example, we started to explore the importance of choice as a result of our learning in the advisory group. We think that the young people who took part as evaluation participants were better off as a result of including the advisory group within the evaluation. For example, we developed the idea of offering young people some control within the interview process by offering them a choice about where to start.

The evaluation was not without its challenges and, in the area of health and social care, evaluators and researchers must be mindful of the experiences that the young people have had. A careful selection process was undertaken to identify those who are better prepared for the process, but, as we saw, there was still uncertainty. Yes it did mean that some voices may not have been heard, but those included in the advisory group were still voices from the margins compared with how research and evaluation in the past has tended to draw on young people from the mainstream (Prout and Tisdall, 2006). We did not always get it right, and in any area where young people have been in difficult circumstances we need to be prepared to notice, recognize, respond and review as each challenge arises.

We found that young people want to participate in these types of project when they can see that their views and perspectives are acknowledged by adults as valid and valuable in their own right. To accomplish this requires developing relationships over time that demonstrate a sharing of power within a scaffolding of experience. This is especially important for the particular group that is with the OYWT, because their experience of institutions is largely one of being on the social margins – a position from which they often find it difficult to live up to the expectations of adults. They come to OYWT feeling judged, shamed and angry. Yet when given the opportunity, young people can demonstrate their own competence in evaluation activities such as those described in this chapter. This can be achieved when young people are supported by adults in their engagement and feel their voices have been heard. An ethic of reciprocity allows trust and respect to build over time. The result for the young people on the advisory group is an experience of success, a sense of contribution and greater optimism about their future. Evaluation and research projects that do not allow time for such things will set young people up for either failure or for stressful participation that is frustrating rather than engaging.

Adults can create positive experiences for young people when they understand and address power relations within the evaluation process and seek to respond to the challenges of responsible advocacy – advocacy that is defined by its reciprocity and power sharing. That reciprocity was established by the young people's initial experience of the service that created a context for them wanting to 'return the favour'. This project had the benefit of a group of vulnerable young people guiding us in where to look for the key elements of a wrap-around service. Something they had direct experience of and of which the significance to them we could only imagine, until we asked and listened.

14 A long-term partnership

Adult and young researchers working together on the evaluation of the Children's Commissioner for Wales

Nigel Thomas with contributions from Hannah France, Joanne Hillman, Cerys Jenkins, Ben Sawyers, Josey Cook, Jamie Richards, Rhodri Pugh-Dungey, Toby Pearson, Mathew Taylor, Anne Crowley and Mandy Cook

Introduction

> I was lucky to be involved in the evaluation for the Children's Commissioner from one of the earliest points – I was involved in the interviewing process appointing the researcher, Mandy. This set up the level of young people's involvement which was carried on throughout the research – full participation equal to that of Nigel and Mandy. Since I went on to university it was hard for me to keep meeting dates and be as fully involved as some of the young people, but coming back to a meeting recently was wonderful. Seeing how far the group had come was amazing; the young people being so involved in the research and the group getting on so well and being very comfortable with each other. Mandy and Nigel have been amazing at involving every member and it was wonderful seeing the relationship that has emerged between them and the young people. Doing my own research on the group I found that the young people had very positive views of the group and I myself have loved being involved. I hope that the success of the group encourages other individuals and organisations to include more young people, as I feel the group has proved that young people and adults can work together.
>
> (Hannah France)

Children and young people can take an active part in research by contributing to adult projects, by directing their own research with support from adults, or by working together with adults on joint projects. This chapter is about a project where young researchers worked in partnership with adult researchers. The research was an evaluation of the Children's Commissioner for Wales. It took three years, with mainly the same young people involved throughout.

The Children's Commissioner for Wales was established in 2001, with the responsibility to 'safeguard and promote the rights and welfare' of children in Wales. The duties include monitoring policies and services for children, making representations about matters affecting the rights or welfare of children in Wales, and being available to children and taking account of their views. The Commissioner has powers to inspect premises and demand reports from service providers, and to investigate and assist in individual cases. The project was conceived in discussion with Peter Clarke after his appointment as the first Children's Commissioner, and was funded by him on the understanding that children would be actively involved in the evaluation.

This was the first systematic study of a children's commissioner or ombudsman anywhere in the world. Because the aim was to involve children and young people at every stage, a detailed research plan was not worked out in advance, beyond a statement of aims and broad approach. The aim was 'to evaluate the effectiveness of the work of the Children's Commissioner for Wales, and in particular its impact on children and young people'. The approach would involve working with a group of children and young people to review the objectives of the Commissioner's office and identify the focus of an evaluation, and then conducting the research in partnership. A full account of the context and background to the research, the methods used to conduct the evaluation, and our findings and conclusions, appears in Thomas et al. (2010). The focus in this chapter is on the process of working together as a group of young people and adults with a shared commitment to completing an effective evaluation, to give a 'feel' for what it was like to undertake research in this way and how we tackled some of the challenges that arose. The chapter explains how the research group was formed and operated, and what happened in the three phases of the research (planning and design, data production, analysis and writing), followed by an evaluation of the model of working.

The steering group

> I was involved in this project right from the beginning. It was a good experience for me and I learned a lot from being involved with Nigel and Mandy. I also learned a lot from the other young people involved. It was good to see young people so dedicated to something. I also had a lot of fun getting to know everyone and would like to thank all the members of the group. We shared plenty of laughs, had a few disagreements but we all came together in the end. Plus it gave me a sense of satisfaction to know what we achieved.
>
> (Joanne Hillman)

The involvement of young people in the project began with the appointment of the paid researcher on the project. A small group of young people were involved in the recruitment process on an equal basis with adults, through an advisory group which wrote the person specification, shortlisted, interviewed applicants and was represented on the formal appointment panel (see also Chapter 5). The first task for the appointed researcher, Mandy Cook, was to recruit a bigger group of young people to help plan and direct the research. A leaflet was distributed to young people's organisations, and the group was joined by a further 10 young people from two local youth forums and a young worker from a care leavers' organisation. Members were aged between 12 and 22 years at the start, and the average age was 16.

There were 13 meetings of the steering group over the three years of the project. Initially planning of meetings was done by the adult researchers, but as the project developed young people took on more responsibility for this. After each meeting Mandy wrote up what had happened and circulated it to everyone. There was a brief evaluation exercise at the end of each meeting, and at the end of each year the young people met with two facilitators to evaluate the work in more depth. On the first occasion the young people indicated a strong wish to contribute more actively, and requested residential meetings. With additional funding from the European Social Fund, we arranged three residential meetings in the second half of the project, which provided extra time and space, enabling stronger relationships to develop in the group and giving us more opportunity to work together to analyse and discuss our findings.

Of the original 16 members, 10 were still involved at the finish. Group members were involved in designing the research, carrying it out and writing the final report. Members were not paid for their work, but meetings and activities were made as enjoyable as possible. At the end of the research each member received a certificate from the two universities acknowledging their work, and everyone was given book tokens at a final celebratory lunch.

Year 1: Planning and design

> I went to my first meeting in August 2005, and only knew one or two people. It's now been nearly three years and my confidence and knowledge of the subject have grown. I've loved every minute of being on this group, from meeting two of the best friends I could ever make to learning interview skills and actually using them for the evaluation. The residentials gave me a chance to get closer to my friends and these last three years will be an experience I shall never forget. I've met people from all walks of life, and got to understand their situations more, and also their wisdom has developed me as a person and changed me for the better. It has been an enormous honour to be involved with evaluating such a figure for children, and I hope we have done a good job, and hope to be involved in the next group. The staff, or adults aiding with the evaluation, have been amazing to us, letting us hold the reins and steer the project and also providing a good input too, helping us if we

> didn't understand and also sending out fifteen ba-jillion questionnaires to be filled. I've totally enjoyed my time on the group and as I said above would do it over again. The people I have met and friends I have made will hopefully stay with me the rest of my life, and I am grateful to have met such an amazing group of confident intelligent young people and am honoured to have shared my time on the group with you.
>
> (Cerys Jenkins)

In the first year the focus was on planning, design and pilot work, as envisaged. There were four meetings – a half day followed by three whole days. At the first meeting we had a presentation from the Commissioner's communications and participation team, to ensure that we all had a basic understanding of what the Commissioner did. Although the young people in the group all had a background in active participation of various kinds, their awareness of the Commissioner's role was quite limited.

We then started by looking at the Commissioner's functions and objectives as set out in the law. We broke them down into categories, looked at each task and asked: (i) What are the indicators of success – that is, what would we expect to see if the task was being done well? (ii) What data would we need in order to establish these indicators? (iii) What methods could we use in order to collect such data? We worked on this exercise in small groups. This was a challenge, as members found some of the concepts difficult to understand. We repeated the exercise at our second meeting, having simplified the descriptions of the Commissioner's tasks, and finished the session with a clear statement of what enquiries we needed to pursue in our evaluation.

To use these questions to build a research plan, we needed to understand something about research methods. The approach we took was to share knowledge within the group, using brief lectures, presentations and discussions to develop our understanding (see Chapter 7). We looked at generating research questions, identifying appropriate methods, and ethics. We agreed an ethical framework for the research, designed to safeguard the well-being of group members and of everyone who might help with the research, adults or children and young people. This was later approved by the appropriate university's research ethics committee.

Having identified the tasks and the methods we needed to use, we put this together in a plan for the evaluation, drafted by Nigel and Mandy from the notes of the first two meetings, and taken back to the group where it was discussed and agreed. We realised it was not possible to do everything at once, and identified two tasks to work on first: 'tracking', or observation of the Commissioner's team at work with children and young people; and a survey of children and young people to find out how much they knew about the Commissioner and their rights.

The next stage was to design the tracking and survey instruments; for this we worked in two subgroups. One produced a form to record observations and a plan for which events or processes to track. The other produced a questionnaire aimed at children and young people and a plan for using this with a sample of school pupils across the country. It was realised that both the tracking and the survey would require a pilot stage. By the middle of the year our focus had therefore begun to move on to data collection; it was clear that most members of the group were keen to take an active part in this.

This was a critical moment for the project, which could have gone in one of two directions: the paid researcher doing the work and consulting the young people from time to time, or concentrating on facilitating the young people's direct engagement with the research process. Hitherto the group had only been willing to stay on task for limited periods, and it was necessary to build a lot of play and relaxation into the sessions to sustain interest. However, over time, all members became increasingly committed to the project and contributed actively to the design of research instruments (see also Chapter 18). Because members were now keen to be 'hands-on', the accent was much more on work to facilitate their involvement. However, with limitations on the young people's availability, most being full-time students in school or college, in practice Mandy Cook still had to do most of the data collection. This had implications for her workload, and constrained how much we could achieve during the life of the project. However, this was outweighed by the value of young people's active engagement with the whole work. Although we continued to call the group a 'steering group', from this point on it effectively became a research team.

Year 2: Data collection

> The Children's Commissioner's evaluation group was the best project I have ever taken part [in]. I joined when I was 12 years old, not really realizing the scale of the project. I came along to the first meeting in Swansea and I have loved the project ever since. I had so much fun doing the project but as well as that it was a lot of hard work too. Nigel and Mandy – without these two people this project would have been impossible. Baskerville Hall was our second home throughout the project, the place where all the work got done, and all the fun was had. I loved every minute of this project, from all the writing and interviewing to the Domino's pizza.
>
> (Ben Sawyers)

There were five meetings during the second year, including one residential. This was the main phase of data collection, beginning with the tracking and survey, but going on to encompass interviews and documentary analysis. It also saw significant developments in the group process, with meetings used to review progress and plan the next stage of work, and increasing contact among group members between sessions. All members were involved in some work between sessions, to varying degrees.

Observation and survey

> It's been a long three years, but every bit has been worthwhile, if I could go back I would still have joined because it has been an amazing experience. I can remember my first meeting being scared and nervous to our last meeting feeling entirely comfortable to talk and have my opinion heard. Throughout the three years we have all flourished from what we have learned, I know personally my confidence has grown and so has my self-esteem. Without this study I wouldn't have been aware of the problems the children commissioner's office face and just how much there is that needs to be done for young people across Wales. I cannot imagine how much we have covered over three years, it sounds a long time but it accounts to about 12 meetings which I think is pretty amazing. The residentials have been great, it's weird because from the start it felt like a team and I can't remember not talking or laughing with everyone. I've just enjoyed this whole experience so much, and I would love to give my thanks to all the people involved for making it great. It's going to be something I'll never forget, and I know everyone else feels the same. I know we have achieved something and that's what I am most proud of.
>
> (Josey Cook)

The '*tracking tool*' was used in a series of observations of the Commissioner's team at work with children and young people, some conducted by Mandy Cook and the remainder by younger members. Also, one member was appointed to the Commissioner's young people's advisory group and took the opportunity to invite advisory group members to complete questionnaires at the beginning and end of their term of office. Later we evaluated materials that the Commissioner's team produced for children and young people; a small group looked at a range of materials and rated them for content, style and presentation, again using an instrument designed for the purpose. Because members had been involved in designing all these tools, we found them easy to use and the results were not difficult to collate.

The *survey* was a much bigger job. We put a lot of work into planning it, because we wanted to make sure we got the questions and presentation right, so that they could be used again in the future. Group members piloted the questionnaire using personal contacts, and then we ran the survey in schools in eight local education authorities; in each area we identified a 'virtual school' comprised of class groups from Years 3 to 11 (aged 7–16) in different schools. We produced an information pack for each pupil who completed a questionnaire, with a summary of the United Nations

Convention on the Rights of the Child and leaflets about the Children's Commissioner and other organisations.

Interviews, documents and individual casework

> I have thoroughly enjoyed my time spent on the CCfW evaluation committee. I've learned a lot about interviewing techniques, analysing documents and most importantly what the commissioner's aims and goals are! I've made many new friends, and had many fun days with the committee, from eating pizza, to playing cricket and having water fights! I will now in future spread the word about the Children's Commissioner in far more detail and understanding than before I was part of this group, something I'm quite proud of having achieved.
>
> (Jamie Richards)

Once the observations and survey were underway, we considered the best way to pursue the rest of our research plan. We agreed that most useful would be to *interview* 'stakeholders' – people who had contact with the Commissioner or were affected by his work. We thought long and hard about who to interview, listing categories of people and targeting individuals in each category. We also thought about what questions to ask, focusing on people's understanding of the Commissioner's role and assessment of impact. We did pilot interviews, then revised the questions to produce a 'cue sheet'. Within the group we trained ourselves in how to interview and record what people said, while respecting their rights. We conducted 67 interviews with participants across Wales. Most group members were involved in interviewing, although the majority were conducted by Mandy Cook. All were recorded and transcribed.

We also interviewed 13 people referred to initially as 'big cheeses', later more politely as 'key players', who had a role in the decision to appoint a commissioner or an important relationship with the office. For these we developed new questions, focused on expectations of the Children's Commissioner and how far these had been fulfilled.

While this work was continuing, we were also looking at *documentary* material. Some of this was done by Mandy Cook and Nigel Thomas and fed back; some was done during group meetings. The documents included all major reports produced by the Commissioner, leaflets on consultations with children and young people, annual reports and reviews, planning and strategy documents and records of policy and consultation work.

We were not able to study *individual casework*, as originally planned, by talking to recipients of the service, because of concerns in the Commissioner's office around consent and confidentiality. We suspect that this was related to the participation of young people in the research (the Commissioner was on sick leave at the time).

Year 3: Analysis and reporting

> During my time as part of the Group I have made numerous friends, learnt many new skills and techniques, shared many fun times with people on residentials and meetings and generally had an amazing time over the past three years! I have learnt many new skills including interviewing techniques, communication skills, organisation skills and generally bettered myself as a person and now have a wider perspective of life. The people younger and older that I have worked with no longer seem like colleagues or peers but friends that I hope to see again in the near future! After reading the report it has amazed me how much work we have actually done, not to seem modest but the meetings and residentials that we went on were amazing fun and didn't seem like work as the activities we undertook were enjoyable and we learnt something from them and got the work done as the report shows, much has been done!
>
> (Rhodri Pugh-Dungey)

At our first residential meeting we trained ourselves in how to analyse and interpret research data. This enabled all members of the group to take part in analysing results during the final year, which was an intensive period of group activity with four meetings including two residentials. Some members dropped out for personal reasons, but others were increasingly committed to the project. Young people began to take a lead in planning sessions, and the work rate increased.

Our approach to data analysis had to be very practical, because of the amount of data and the limited time available (see also Chapter 18). Analysis of the survey data was completed by Mandy Cook, with some help from others. The thematic analysis of the interview data was done by the whole group, using a template to summarise key points in responses to particular questions, and looking for patterns of responses. We analysed the tracking data in a similar way. We analysed the documentary material in a variety of ways; some documents were read and discussed in the group to get a sense of the range of activity.

Much of this analysis took place in group meetings, particularly at the residentials, where it was easy for a pair or small group to work on a particular piece of analysis and bring it back to the whole group, or the adult researchers, for checking. Other work was done by group members between sessions, but with the overall direction set in the group meetings. In this way everyone 'owned' the analytical process and had a sense of what we were doing and why. It was a young researcher who suggested we rate different professionals' confidence in their understanding of the Commissioner's role as evidenced in the interviews, which produced one of our more significant findings.

As we progressed with the analysis, we began to pull together emerging findings in our group discussions. We used a range of methods to identify key issues and questions for further enquiry – including a formal debate in which two teams attempted to persuade each other that the Commissioner was effective/ineffective using data from the evaluation, which helped to clarify our thinking about the large amount of data we had gathered. We also had a series of meetings with the Commissioner's team, to discuss emerging findings and queries from the group.

The final report (Thomas et al. 2008a) was produced collaboratively, although most of the writing was by Nigel Thomas. Together we agreed a set of headings for the report, and then a complete report in note form. Drafts were circulated between meetings, and the final draft read through and approved by the whole group. The young researchers were keen to take on writing particular sections, but other demands on their time, including academic workloads, meant this was not practical. Instead it was agreed that each member would have a page in the report where they could write their own reflections on the project.

The report was welcomed by the new Commissioner, Keith Towler, who took office in the final stages of the project, and used in a strategic review in which many of our recommendations were implemented (see Thomas et al. 2010). We have also presented our research at a major international child welfare conference, with younger members of the group playing a full part in this (see, for example, Thomas et al. 2008b).

Discussion

> Working in this group has been a fantastic opportunity, I'd just like to thank Nigel and Mandy for all their hard work preparing the meetings and residentials as well. I think I speak for all the young people on the group when I say this has been one of the most interesting projects I have ever worked on, the work of the Children's Commissioner's office is never ending and it is extremely important, I'm proud to say I've worked with them and the other members of the group, all of whom have talents that will help them in the future, as one of the oldest young people on the group I've noticed the changes in the younger members over the last three years. Keep an eye on this lot they will be the politicians of the future. After three years it's going to be strange not having meetings anymore but I hope that we will all keep in contact as we have really created some special friendships, some of us more than others but I will miss them all I've had a great time and I've learnt so much.
>
> (Toby Pearson)

This was an ambitious project: a systematic investigation of the effectiveness of a children's commissioner (not done anywhere else) with the full and active participation of children and young people, on a small budget. There were tensions between our commitment to including young people fully in the research and the expectation that we would carry out a thorough evaluation of the Commissioner's office. There are many things that we might regret not having done more fully.

However, the project was a success in the sustained commitment shown by the young researchers, their genuine interest in the topic, the understanding of research and critical enquiry which they were able to develop, the social value of the project and the sense of personal growth. It was also a success in that the research was grounded in young people's priorities and perceptions, and the report was well received by the Commissioner despite being critical.

Challenges included: the tension between getting the research done and working in a participatory way, the practical limitations on young people's involvement (time commitment, issues of travel and distance, and young people's lack of freedom of movement) and the extremely limited resources available. Combined with the fact that the evaluation was conducted at a difficult time in the work of the Commissioner (see Thomas et al. 2008a), this meant we were unable to complete all parts of the plan as originally anticipated.

However, we are satisfied that the involvement of children and young people in this project has been real, pervasive and sustained. By 'real' we mean not tokenistic, in that young researchers have had a real influence over the planning and operation of the project, and it would have been unimaginably different without their contribution. When we were planning our report, the younger members wanted to emphasise strongly how they always felt included, their views taken on and responded to, and a sense of ownership of the project. By 'pervasive' we mean that young people have been directly involved in every aspect of the research. They took a full part in overall planning and design, in shaping the methods and instruments used, in collecting data, in the difficult processes of interpretation and analysis, and in producing and disseminating the final report. By 'sustained' we mean that most of the young people who joined the project in 2005 were still there at the end, and keen to continue. They were all involved, not only through our regular discussions and activities, but in taking on work individually or in pairs outside the meetings – interviewing, observing and analysing the resultant data. They all contributed a huge amount to this project, and we all, young people and adults, learned a huge amount from being part of it.

Conclusion

> Evaluating the office of the first Children's Commissioner for Wales is an experience I'm not going to forget in a hurry. Coming from a care background myself I felt there was so much more the office could be doing on behalf of children and young people looked after or leaving care. As the research went on it became apparent what a huge role the office really had to fulfil, they were the first established children's commissioner's office in the UK and were viewed by some as the saviour to

> all things related to children and young people. This really was a big expectation to live up to. Being part of a group with members from a range of backgrounds and with different experiences helped us in conducting a fair and honest piece of research. Opinions were able to be aired and discussed in a way where everyone was able to contribute, followed always by a group conclusion. Mandy and Nigel did a great job in facilitating and keeping us all on track when we began to waffle! It is my opinion that this report has reached a balanced conclusion on the impact of the children's commissioner's office and we have made some excellent recommendations, which if implemented will further enhance this impact.
>
> (Mathew Taylor)

This research did not follow a predefined model; rather the approach taken was exploratory – 'let's try this and see where it goes'. However, this example shows that it is possible to engage young people in a research project over an extended period, and for them to develop a sense of ownership. There were issues around confidentiality and confidence, which we have not been able to explore fully here. From the point of view of professional academic researchers with external expectations to meet, handing a share of responsibility for a project to young people is risky, but we are convinced that it is well worth taking that risk. Even with a limited budget and no opportunity to include a representative sample of young people, the experience for all involved was worthwhile, and the young people contributed a richness and a unique dimension to the research. A willingness to be pragmatic, as well as a commitment to children's participation, was essential to the project's success.

Acknowledgements

The research was conducted under the auspices of the University of Wales, Swansea and the University of Central Lancashire. We should like to express our gratitude to all those who assisted with the research, especially Mike Jenkins and Jan Weaver for supporting the young researchers and the late Peter Clarke, without whose confidence in young people the project would not have taken place.

Part 5

Reflection

The five chapters in this final part offer *reflection* on the authors' experiences of working with children and young people on research projects. The chapters reflect on various research projects and the authors highlight different aspects within them. Newman et al. reflect on how the Medicines for Children Research Network (MCRN) enhanced consultation opportunities for children and young people to improve the quality of clinical research. Mackie reflects on a very specific form of involvement, peer research, and considers its impact on insight, innovation, investment and interest. Uppal discusses some of the ethical issues inherent in carrying out research with children and young people, focusing on role tensions and issues of power and reciprocity in the interview process. Boeck and Collin are particularly interested in bringing their reflections on their roles as adult researchers into dialogue with those of young people. Finally, Carter et al. reflect on their experience of being Associate Research Assistants and reflect as researchers on various aspects of research.

Whilst each has their own focus, the chapters also raise some common issues – many of which have also arisen in different ways in the previous parts of this volume. These include: partnership and dialogue, the need to carefully consider roles and, within this, power and control, ethical issues, the impact involving children and young people can have on all aspects of a research project from design to analysis, and the link between young people's involvement in research and change in service delivery or outcomes for young people.

Mackie asserts that the general principles of young people's participation in research demand that their involvement is through choice. Young people highlight (in Boeck and Collin) that being able to determine and increase their level of participation was important to give them a sense of ownership over the research. Boeck and Collin emphasise that, as adult researchers, they became participants in a dialogue with young people and facilitators of spaces and processes in which young people participate and come together in dialogue about the way research is done. An awareness of how power is exercised is necessary for such dialogue to occur. An emphasis on trust and reciprocity with young people aids awareness of how power is exercised and redressed.

Boundaries between the roles of researcher, friend, practitioner, therapist and clinician can become blurred in health and social care research. Uppal reflects how some of these roles came more easily than others, based on her own anxieties, experiences and knowledge. However, adults not only have to explain concepts that may be hard to grasp for children, but also have to ensure that messages from young people were effectively taken on board by researchers (Newman et al.). Mackie and Carter et al. found power needed to be considered not only as exercised between young people and adults, but also between young peer researchers and the young people researched.

Both Mackie and Uppal consider important ethical issues, and highlight how often these are linked with power and control. Ethical guidelines and codes are important, but, as Uppal highlights, they will not be able to inform researchers how to negotiate particular dilemmas or situations within the minutiae of doing research. In her frank account she reflects on the importance of building reciprocity through, not only asking questions, but also giving information if young people ask for this. Mackie considers the issues, which might be experienced by the young researchers themselves and may require on-going support during the research project. Other ethical issues include the payment of researchers and whether an exit strategy has been considered with the peer researchers.

Several chapters stress the important contribution young people make to all stages of a research project. Gaining access to young people and children in the research process was highlighted by several authors. Carter et al. assert that when accessing other young people they are able to break down barriers by talking about shared interests. They also point out that the training of young researchers becomes a crucial part of the participatory research as highlighted throughout this book. Importantly, Mackie highlights that the logistics to prepare and deliver good training has cost implications and can affect the research timetable.

The ability of young people to innovate, particularly in the development and application of research methods, is a common theme. Newman et al. write about how young people were responsible for a major change in research techniques. Mackie asks: Who knows how to engage young people better than young people themselves? Mackie and Boeck and Collin emphasise the involvement of peer researchers, and call for projects to be both well-defined from the outset, but also to be flexible. Flexibility in the research design can accommodate spontaneous improvement, recognising the positive impacts of the ability of young people to innovate, particularly within the data collection phase.

The positive impact of young people on the research is not only during the data collection, but also in the analysis and interpretation of data. This lead to alternative insights (Mackie) and challenges to adult assumptions about young people's lives (Boeck and Collin). Carter et al. suggest that combining young people's and adults' opinions makes the findings more holistic. Critically one of the Associate Research Assistants (ARA) asserts that it is not only about the data they gather, but that young people also interpret it differently to adult researchers.

All the chapters consider that a participatory approach to research enhances the quality of the research and value of what is found. Boeck and Collin emphasise building cycles of reflection and evaluation into research projects ensures that critical reflection is not a one-off activity, but an on-going process of critical examination of each stage of the research.

15 Medicines for children

Reflecting on how young people improve research

Jennifer Newman, Claire Callens, Carly Tibbins and Nicola Madge

Introduction

Historically the use of off-label and unlicensed medicines for children has been common, with only a limited number of paediatric clinical trials conducted and few age-appropriate formulations authorised for babies, infants and children. Children have been described as 'therapeutic orphans' who are denied access to effective medicines because of a lack of research (Shirkey 1968). A review of studies of off-label and unlicensed medicine prescribing in children showed that it ranged from 3.3% to 56% of prescriptions in community practice and 36% to 100% in hospital settings. This may be linked to an increase in adverse events (Cuzzolin et al. 2006). The requirement for more paediatric clinical trials, better age-appropriate formulations and more authorised medicines for children has been recognised and supported by regulations in the USA and the European Union.

In the UK, the government has adopted a strategy to improve medicines for children by producing the British National Formulary for Children (bringing together information on licensed, off-label and unlicensed uses), improving extemporaneous formulations and developing a research infrastructure for paediatric studies. The research structure was set up in 2005 and is known as the Medicines for Children Research Network (MCRN). The MCRN is funded by the Department of Health and is part of the National Institute for Health Research (NIHR) Clinical Research Network. The MCRN provides researchers with the practical support they need to make paediatric studies happen in the National Health Service (NHS), so that more research takes place across the UK and more patients can take part.

This is in line with a more general rise in patient and public involvement within health research (Department of Health 1999; Boote et al. 2002; Telford et al. 2004; the Research and Development Directive, DoH 2005). Our view within the MCRN is that high quality research, good accrual and retention rates and improved outcomes for children, depend on listening to the voices of families and carers and, most importantly, children and young people themselves, and taking account of their experiences, priorities and perspectives. The MCRN has recognised the emerging national patient and public agenda by appointing dedicated personnel to ensure that patients and families play a central role in influencing the design and delivery of research into medicines for children.

The main aim of this chapter is to reflect on how the MCRN enhanced consultation opportunities for children and young people to improve the quality of clinical research through the forum of a young person's advisory group and topic-specific focus groups. We also focus on how we promoted the involvement of young people in schools to raise awareness of clinical trials and medicines, and utilised this resource for eliciting views of the wider public. The chapter highlights how engaging and involving young people can have many benefits including greater understanding of young people's perspectives, enabling young people's voices to be heard and providing an invaluable resource for researchers to improve study design. However, involving young people effectively means having the available resources in terms of time, funding and expertise, as well as the ability to convince researchers of the importance of involving young people as partners in the research process.

For the purpose of this chapter we refer to young consumers as those between the ages of eight and 18 years who may have experience of a particular medical condition requiring medication, or who may not have a current illness but are able to represent the views and perspectives of young people more generally. We use the terms 'consumer liaison officer' and 'consumer team' to refer to those with a specific responsibility to involve young people and their families in the design and delivery of research into medicines for children.

Establishing a young person's advisory group

Whilst there is plenty of literature on the role and benefits of patient and public involvement in relation to medicine and healthcare planning, there are fewer examples for health research, particularly with young people. Without a sound evidence base we faced the challenge of how to involve young people in a way they felt comfortable with and would enable them to contribute effectively. We also wanted to make sure they were not placed in a predominantly adult environment where their contribution might be minimal. Involvement in research can take the form of consultation between professionals and patients and the public, it can involve collaboration between professionals and service users, or it can take the form of user-led research (Chapter 1). We were led by the principle that our activities should transform users from research subjects into partners with researchers (Hanley et al. 2003).

After much discussion it was decided to adopt a strongly participatory approach and set up a pilot young person's advisory group. This group would provide a forum for young people to learn about, and comment on, various aspects of the research cycle from the identification of research questions to the dissemination of research findings.

The next task was to recruit young people to our group. We confronted the issue of suitability and representativeness in considering whom we should involve. How could we take account of the great diversity of young people likely to be involved in clinical studies, as well as the varied medical conditions that affect young people in the UK? We realised, however, that group members could not be representative of all young people, and determined that membership of the group should be open to any young person between the ages of 8 and 18 years who had some knowledge of taking medication, might be involved in a clinical trial, or had experience of using hospital services. Nonetheless we did not want to discriminate against young people who felt they did not fit the inclusion criteria; for example, those with a personal ambition to study medicine.

As discussed in previous chapters (Chapters 6, 10 and 11), recruiting young people requires the cooperation of gatekeepers such as parents, legal guardians, teachers, and perhaps local education authorities and doctors. With this in mind, the recruitment process began with over 150 letters and information packs distributed via primary and secondary schools, voluntary organisations, out-patients clinics and health centres in Liverpool, UK. An Open Day was organised and attracted seven young people aged between 8 and 17 years. Six other young people expressed an interest, but were unable to attend this meeting. Twelve of these 13 young people were from three local secondary schools and learned of the group through the head teacher or the science teacher. The other young person found out about the group through an advertisement in the hospital. These young people comprised four boys and nine girls. One member had been involved in a clinical trial, five had chronic conditions, some had experience of hospital admission and all had taken medicines. The group was predominantly White British with the exception of two members who defined themselves as White Arab and Black British.

Prior to joining the group, young people received written information about membership, an application form and a parent information sheet. On receipt of this information, young people and their parents were contacted to ensure clarity about their roles as members, sign consent forms (for those under 16 years), and organise practical arrangements, such as travel, dietary requirements, access issues and emergency contact details. Appropriate transport was organised and all members received a high street voucher as a thank you and to encourage their initial and continued commitment.

The group in progress

Once recruitment was over, the group was set up with the intention of holding approximately six meetings per year during weekends or school holidays. During this time members would take part in activities to gain knowledge and skills to enable them to: learn about the MCRN and clinical research into medicines for children; have an input into the design and delivery of research, such as adapting and disseminating documents on clinical trials to maximise their suitability for children and young people; discuss and comment on aspects of research that might be important to outcomes of clinical trials and research; contribute to the design of monitoring tools and schedules for children involved in clinical studies; contribute to research ideas and priorities; and disseminate information about the group and become young ambassadors for the MCRN.

At each meeting young people were given training on various aspects of clinical research to equip them with appropriate skills to participate to the best of their abilities. We worked with the National Children's Bureau and Health R&D NorthWest, whose remit was to support, provide training and advise NIHR networks, such as MCRN. Almost immediately, however, we found that the wide range of ages within the group meant difficulties in accommodating the different interests and learning abilities of members. We also found that the concepts of research and clinical trials and the remit of the MCRN were hard to grasp, particularly for the younger children. There was, too, some difficulty in ensuring that messages from young people were effectively taken on board by researchers due to lack of feedback from researchers. Overcoming these difficulties required careful planning in partnership with the young people. Identifying what worked and what did not through the monitoring and assessment of each session was crucial. We concluded that more hands-on activities were required to maintain an interest throughout the group, with split age groups for learning sessions. We planned learning and teaching activities for the morning and more physical and interactive activities for the afternoon, tapping into the creative/artistic/visual skills among the group, avoiding jargon and, most importantly, inviting researchers to the sessions so that young people could ask them about particular studies. Members of the group felt important if the researcher took the time and effort to speak to them directly. It also enabled young people to obtain written feedback from researchers as to what happened as a result of their input. For example, if they had suggested changes to a patient information leaflet, were their comments taken on board and how did the ethics committee regard these changes?

We seemed to have found a successful formula as six months later membership increased to 21 members, with an average attendance of 14 per meeting. We realised that recruitment is a continuous process and facilitators had to expect natural drop-out and accommodate new members as they joined the group. Gatekeepers, and in our case individual teachers, were also an issue as some appeared to tell only the most confident or forthcoming young people about opportunities for joining the group. This became clear when three young people became interested in membership when told about the group by an existing member. The lesson we learnt was that ideally we should present to school assemblies, or provide information for every pupil in a school, if we wished our recruitment strategies to be fully inclusive and provide equal opportunities for all young people.

Three years on, seven of the original 21 young people recruited remain active members of the group. With new recruits membership is currently at 20. Furthermore, and due to the success of the pilot group and the lessons learnt, the group has expanded to form a national group with an overall membership of 82 young people based in four MCRN local research networks (LRNs): East, West Midlands, London and South East, and South West.

Achievements of the group

Group members work alongside healthcare professionals and have become involved in a significant number of research projects over the last four years. One of the biggest contributions of the group has been the assessment of the appropriateness and effectiveness of research instruments and tools, such as patient information leaflets, consent and assent forms, questionnaires and interview schedules. To date the group has reviewed approximately 30 patient information leaflets for both publicly funded and industry funded studies, commenting not just on the style of the information but on the practical issues of the study such as taking blood samples, lengthy hospital stays, frequency of hospital visits and so on. The group's contributions have proved invaluable, enhancing acceptability to the target group through improvements in design and child appropriate phraseology. In one study the group was responsible for a major change in how a saliva sample would be collected from children, as highlighted by the study coordinator.[1]

> As a result of the young person's comments we changed the information sheets accordingly, for example we changed the font size, reduced the writing and inserted more relevant pictures. We also made a few changes to the study procedures, for example how it made us reduce the number of saliva samples and have a look at other methods for collecting it. Partly because of the children's concerns we changed the methodology to use a very small swab on a stick instead of chewing on cotton wool – children got on very well with these and they are about to be used at another site routinely for this procedure.

Reviewing information was not a task the group always relished due to the length and incomprehensible nature of some of the information they were given. It was not unusual for the group to be faced with 16 pages of information that was full of medical jargon, lacked colour and pictures and was sometimes patronising. To overcome some of these issues the group developed a simple yet concise guidance document for researchers on how to design patient information leaflets for children and young people. Researchers found this advice very helpful. One stated:

> We have received excellent advice from the group on our information sheets for children and young people, in particular the suggestion that we include some pictures. The group has also given us invaluable feedback on the questions we hope to use when interviewing children, pointing out pertinent issues such as the fact that some children might be uncomfortable talking about trial staff in case they got them into trouble. Overall the group has enabled us to make the study more child-friendly and we are extremely grateful to its members.

Feedback has not, however, always been received, much to the disappointment of the young people. One of the biggest challenges we have faced has been to encourage researchers and healthcare professionals to access the group at an early enough stage to give them sufficient time to obtain feedback from the group. Sometimes members have received information only a few days before researchers planned to submit an ethics application.

Young ambassadors

In addition to the many tasks carried out by the Young Person's Advisory Group, group members expressed a desire to get involved in much bigger projects with potentially greater impact, such as involvement in designing a study prior to obtaining funding. Forging links and raising awareness amongst healthcare professionals are crucial to make this happen. One of the best strategies is for young people themselves to act as ambassadors for the MCRN.

Young members are given the opportunity to attend all MCRN- and non-MCRN-related conferences to promote MCRN messages and the work of the group. These activities have increased awareness of the group and led to opportunities for young people to influence the design of paediatric research. They have, for example: carried out lay reviewing for the NIHR Research for Patient Benefit Programme; worked with the Medicines and Healthcare Regulatory Agency (MHRA) to advise on early access to medicines; worked with the National Research Ethics Service (NRES) on how best to design information leaflets for children and young people; contributed to MCRN guidance for researchers on involving children in the design and delivery of research; produced DVDs to promote the work of the group; and contributed to debates surrounding the involvement of children and young people in trials, touching on issues such as deferred consent in emergency situations.

Researchers have given very positive feedback and are extremely impressed with the level of knowledge and understanding of the group members. A research and development innovations manager who visited one of the groups stated:

> Many of our research for patient benefit applications relied heavily on the ideas of the young people to inform the consumer-involvement sections. As a result of their involvement the protocol, patient information leaflets and questionnaires were all changed dramatically.

Group members felt that they had benefited personally as well as having had the opportunity to contribute to the research process. One young person, for example, said that she had gained more confidence to speak up in groups. Others expressed how important they felt because their opinions mattered.

Setting up topic-specific focus groups

The MCRN Young Person's Advisory Group is an excellent resource for researchers but there are some situations or studies that require speaking to a more targeted group of young people with experience of taking medicines for a particular condition or illness.

Those with personal experiences of certain illnesses or life-changing conditions can be invaluable members of focus groups. Their views about priorities for research, the safety of old or new medicines and the best design for a clinical trial could be vital to the success, or even initial development, of a study. As an example, one doctor had safety concerns about a new oral medication that had been trialled only with adults with multiple sclerosis and not yet used with young people. Although he queried whether or not a paediatric trial was required, other colleagues thought it was safe to allow young patients to go onto the new medication if they were closely monitored. When initially exploring these concerns with the young person's group, members strongly agreed that it was safer to do a small-scale trial first. Their views were presented at a European meeting where, as a result, doctors and commissioners recommended much wider consultation, including with actual patients, before steps were taken to develop a clinical trial. This example shows that young people's views can have a lot of influence not only in swaying the development and design of trials, but also in changing the perceptions of researchers on the value of listening to young people.

Another example was a focus group set up for young people and families affected by cerebral palsy to inform the design of a clinical trial to compare the efficacy and safety of two currently used drugs to assist with spasticity. Issues under discussion included the trial design, methods of involvement and the practicalities of involving children. One of the suggested trial designs, involving the use of a placebo or a washout period of one month, sparked an immediate reaction from one young person. She pointed out that the research team might struggle to recruit to such a trial: she herself notices a deterioration in her condition after missing just one dose and would not take part in a trial that expected her not to take drugs for a month. It seemed that this was something the researchers had not considered. The outcome was a joint research proposal for a trial that everyone agreed with and is currently being worked up into a full proposal in partnership with the group, with key input from young people.

Both these examples illustrate how important such focus groups can be. Nonetheless they can be expensive and time-consuming to plan and run. Recruitment strategies need to be effective, and our experience suggests that sending out invitations via members of staff known to patients and over-recruitment, increase the chances of attendance. It is also important that there is absolute clarity on the role of young people in the focus groups, emphasising that their role is to input into the design of a trial and not to participate in it. Resources, staff, expertise and, most importantly, consensus among all those working in collaboration with young people and their families, are essential components of a successful focus group consultation.

Raising awareness of clinical trials in schools

From the outset the MCRN recognised the need for a systematic effort to raise awareness amongst young people about the importance of paediatric research and how clinical trials are carried out. One way of raising awareness with young people is through the medium of school. Medicines receive minimal attention in the National Curriculum, often only as a small part of education about drug abuse. Clinical trials receive even less attention and, unfortunately, Frankenstein-like preconceptions about what is involved may become fixed and difficult to shift, such as 'using children as guinea pigs'. School provides a perfect opportunity for young people to learn about medicines and medical research and their importance. The young people can be given a chance to respond to specific information, and researchers can learn more about young people's worries, views, needs and gaps in information from the questions they ask and comments they make. Messages delivered in lessons can also filter through to parents and carers via letters sent home before and after lessons.

The consumer-involvement team embarked on several initiatives visiting schools in and around MCRN regions. One initiative involved teaming up with a science-based artist to run creative workshops on the topic of 'where do medicines come from?'. Another initiative that is still running today in schools in the West Midlands and Trent regions focused specifically on medicine compliance, adherence and safety, as well as displacing myths about clinical trials. This work was led by the consumer-involvement coordinator at the MCRN local research network.

For this initiative, and before any work was undertaken in schools, the consumer-involvement coordinator forged partnerships with agencies such as the local educational authority, Healthy Schools teams and school nurses. Meetings were held with all these agencies to ensure they were in agreement on content of lessons and how messages should be delivered. The consumer-involvement coordinator also undertook similar training to that provided by school nurses for teachers to ensure consistency. Lessons were then developed in line with young people's knowledge and understanding skills as prescribed by key learning objectives outlined in the National Curriculum for science and for physical social health education (PHSE) classes. It soon emerged that school lessons had to be presented in the curriculum's standard format, integrating key learning objectives, to make them attractive to teachers. At the same time, it was equally important to listen to on-going feedback from young people and their teachers to determine how best to make the sessions interesting and interactive. Other factors taken into account when planning lessons were ethnic diversity, cultural barriers, learning abilities, short lessons to accommodate the short attention spans of younger ages (4–8 years), development of group-based activities for older children (8–11 years), and having a question and debate format for secondary-aged children (11–16 years).

Benefits of engaging with schools

Having access to large numbers of young people in one setting is extremely beneficial, and allows researchers to carry out work with young people in a systematic and organised manner. Two particular examples of our work stand out.

First, the MCRN worked in partnership with a formulations team from a local university as part of a project to ascertain the views of young people on flavour and formulation preferences for medicines. The views of children between the ages of 4 and 14 years from two schools were collected systematically, and age-appropriate interactive sessions on clinical trials were designed alongside a formulations questionnaire. Seven sessions were delivered in one day and the views of over 300 children and young people collected. These data are of interest to formulations professionals concerned with improving medicine formulations for this population. This initiative provided a good example of how a large amount of data can be systematically collected, over a short period of time, from young people in a safe and familiar setting.

A second project that evolved from working within schools and gaining information from young people addressed concerns about asthma medication and a lack of understanding on the importance of access to reliever inhalers. Cross-agency working between MCRN, primary care trusts, school nurses and an asthma nurse specialist at a tertiary centre led to the idea of developing posters to be displayed within schools. A local secondary school was approached and asked if pupils would participate in the design of the posters. Consequently, two extremely powerful posters for primary and secondary schools were produced. This cross working between the various agencies and young people led to all schools displaying posters. It also generated radio and press coverage about the project and gave the young people involved a sense of achievement and self-worth. This illustrates the powerful impact that involving young people in projects for young people can generate.

Our work in schools not only educates our future adult population, it may also potentially help find more effective ways for healthcare professionals to engage and communicate with children and young people from diverse backgrounds about their medicines and lifelong health choices. There is scope to empower young people to be more responsible for their healthcare, especially as we know that many childhood diseases such as asthma, allergies, diabetes and obesity are on the increase. In turn, improved understanding and health management in childhood may lead to better health in adulthood and hopefully a reduction in overall healthcare costs. Working in schools can also be beneficial for communities that are less likely to engage with healthcare services.

Conclusion

The MCRN has had a substantial amount of success in engaging with children and young people. The formation of the MCRN Young Person's Advisory Group, topic-specific focus groups and engaging with young people in schools has enabled young people to become more involved in the research process by giving them the confidence, information and opportunities to be able to contribute at all levels. To achieve the greatest benefit from the involvement of young people, participation should be integral to the entire process from the outset rather than an 'add on'. It is also important that researchers considering involving young people in their studies should seek guidance from those who have substantial expertise in the field. The MCRN is an organisation that assists healthcare professionals to undertake paediatric research in partnership with young people. Involving young consumers in research is a massive investment for all, and particularly so for young people who volunteer their time and efforts over a long period of time.

Note

1 All extracts are from feedback forms from study coordinators.

16 Peer research with children and young people reflecting on the impact of adopting a rights-based rationale

Peter K. Mackie

Introduction

The participation of children and young people in all areas of society has increased rapidly since the almost universal ratification of the United Nations Convention on the Rights of the Child (see 'Why?' chapters in Part 2). In research terms, this participatory turn has translated into a shift from research *on* children and young people to research *with* children and young people. Hence, an abundance of studies in the last two decades have sought to gather the views of children and young people, rather than assume that statistics and the views of adult gatekeepers will necessarily reflect their reality (Brownlie et al. 2006; Christensen and James 2000; Hallett and Prout 2003). More recently, researchers have moved the participation agenda forward by engaging children and young people in all aspects of the research process, including the design, undertaking, analysis and publication (Kellett 2005a; Smith et al. 2002). As Schäfer and Yarwood observe: 'such involvement recognises children as social agents, cultural producers and experts of their own lives' (2008:122). Most notably, children and young people have been involved in the research process when the subjects of the research are their peers (Gong and Wright 2007; Fleming 2010; Kellett 2005a; Murray 2006).

Peer research is based upon one key principle: the researcher belongs to the same peer group as the research subjects. The peer research approach has predominantly been adopted in studies where the subjects of the research are perceived to be particularly hard to reach or vulnerable, such as migrants (Radcliffe and Campbell 2010) or prison leavers (Sheffield Hallam 2011) but the group most frequently involved in this type of study is children and young people (Campbell and Mackie 2011; Gong and Wright 2007; Fleming et al. 2009; Mackie and Russell 2009). The growing trend of children and young people researching their peers will be the subject of this chapter. The chapter begins with a reflection on the evolving reasons for using a peer approach: commenting first on an early rights-based rationale before setting out an emerging impact-based rationale. With reference to the author's examples and to existing literature, the author then reflects upon some of the major obstacles that must be overcome when adopting this participatory approach, before finally commenting on why researchers might choose to use peer research in future health and social care studies with children and young people.

An early rights-based rationale

Early adoption of peer research approaches with children and young people appear to be underpinned by rights-based motivations. The United Nations Convention on the Rights of the Child set out an expectation that children should have the opportunity to participate as competent members of society (Chapter 1). Whilst participatory research with children and young people existed before this time, the Convention on the Rights of the Child led to more widespread adoption of participatory principles in research and in all areas of society. Within a relatively short period of time, there was an expectation on researchers to adopt participatory approaches, and studies that failed to do so were perceived to be ethically unsound and of poorer quality. The unquestioning adoption and prioritisation of participatory research with children and young people led Smith et al. to claim:

> One of the emerging issues for research of this kind is that its merits are proclaimed by its proponents, rather than demonstrated effectively through its implementation.
>
> (Smith et al. 2002: 194)

This concern is discussed in more depth by Smith (Chapter 3), who reflects on the process by which the participation of children and young people in research can become routinised, with no critical examination of the evidence to support such an approach. With researchers beginning to question the impacts of the participatory turn, a growing body of evidence has emerged which demonstrates the significant value of participatory research. The next section of this chapter contributes to this debate by reflecting on the consequences of adopting a peer research approach.

An emerging impact-based rationale

Reflecting on the author's experiences and existing literature, it is possible to identify four key areas of impact resulting from the adoption of a peer research approach. In this chapter the author refers to these impacts as the 'four Is': insight, innovation, investment and interest. The nature of each of these is discussed.

Insight

Relationships between the researcher and the subjects of the research are complex and are significantly influenced by notions of power (Brownlie et al.

2006; Gong and Wright 2007; Schäfer and Yarwood 2008). In most cases, the researcher adopts the dominant position in the relationship. Societal norms will also influence these power relations – where the research subjects belong to a marginalised group within society, they will naturally adopt a subservient position during an interview. In the majority of studies with children and young people the interviewer is an adult and a clearly hierarchical relationship emerges, with adults occupying a considerably higher status. This unequal relationship between adult interviewers and child interviewees can have significant implications for the insights achieved in the research. First, there is a tendency for child interviewees to say what they believe the adult interviewer might want to hear in an attempt to conform to expectations of the dominant adult. Equally, child interviewees may choose not to discuss particular experiences because they either feel the issues are not important enough for the adult interviewer, or they may relate to illegitimate or illegal activities, which would potentially leave them vulnerable to punitive action by an authority figure. In a study which used peer-led focus groups with young people who had never committed a criminal offence, Murray (2006) raises these concerns, questioning whether an adult-led focus group would have revealed the fact that so many of the participants had contemplated vandalism.

As in Murray's (2006) study, the peer research approach is often advocated because it addresses common concerns about uneven power relations that exist between adult researchers and young interviewees (Gong and Wright 2007; Schafer and Yarwood 2008). The assumption is that, despite the remaining hierarchical interviewer–interviewee relationship, young people will discuss issues more freely with their peers than with adults, and it is argued that this open and frank relationship will lead to a greater insight into the experiences of children and young people (Chapter 19; Kellett et al. 2004; Schafer and Yarwood 2008). Murray states:

> The value of peer led groups lies in providing discourse which potentially provides fresh insights … that an adult's presence may have precluded.
>
> (Murray, 2006: 277)

Much of the existing literature on peer research has commented on the insights the approach provides into marginal and potentially illegal activities. Whilst this is certainly the case, the approach also frequently provides new insights into everyday activities and concerns. In a peer-led study involving the author, exploring the perceptions of homeless young people towards standards of temporary accommodation, the young homeless interviewees reported concerns, such as a lack of access to kitchen facilities during the evening and the invasion of privacy by support staff (Mackie and Russell 2009). These are both concerns that were not previously reported to the author in a study exploring a similar topic, but conducted by adult interviewers (Mackie 2008). It is likely that such everyday concerns were perceived by the young people not to be important enough to report to the adult interviewers. Peer research clearly has an impact on the insights gleaned during the interview phase of a study, but it should be noted that the involvement of young people in the analysis and interpretation of data may also lead to alternative insights.

Innovation

The involvement of children and young people at all stages of the research process can lead to considerable innovation. Kilpatrick et al. (2007) worked with a team of peer researchers in their study with disaffected children, and they acknowledge that they were at least partly motivated to pursue this approach because the young researchers would help to develop appropriate and engaging methods of data collection. The ability of young people to innovate, particularly in the development and application of research methods, is one of the key attractions to using this approach; after all, who knows how to engage young people better than young people themselves?

Innovation in itself does not constitute a positive impact on a research study. However, the author's experience of research involving peer interviewers (Mackie and Russell 2009) demonstrated how spontaneous innovation by a peer researcher whilst in the field led to the identification and use of a more comfortable research setting, which consequently prolonged the involvement of the interviewee and led the interviewee to talk more openly about his experiences. In this example, following a brief and uncomfortable start to the interview at a table in the kitchen of a homeless hostel, the interviewer and interviewee decided to move outside where they both smoked and discussed the research topics. An interview that might have ended within five minutes, having collected superficial data only, finally ended after approximately 30 minutes with much richer interview data. The intention is certainly not to promote smoking as an innovative and replicable approach; instead it is to recognise the positive impacts of the ability of young people to innovate, particularly within the data collection phase. Such innovations were commonplace during the author's research with peer interviewers.

Investment

Whilst one of the most prominent critiques of the peer research approach is the additional time required to recruit and support peer researchers, it must also be recognised that this approach can lead to a reduction in the cost and duration of the research. For example, Murray (2006) describes how young peer researchers speeded up interviewee recruitment, improved retention rates and contributed towards interview transcription.

> Firstly, once the peer was contacted, it was largely their efforts that resulted in the recruitment of participants. Secondly, because the focus groups comprised young people drawn from the same friendship circles and they were (presumably) encouraged by the peer leader to attend, absences were minimal. Thirdly ... one of the peers offered to transcribe their focus group, with the added benefit that the peer was able to identify the participants with ease.
>
> (Murray 2006: 278)

Studies involving the author have resulted in similar cost and time savings in some cases (Clapham et al. 2010), but not in instances where the peer researchers have less social capital to draw upon. This relates closely to the second finding under this broad heading of investment benefits: in addition to the project benefits, the peer research method always makes an investment in the researchers (Kellet 2005b). Whilst investing in the training and experience of researchers may not constitute a benefit to the project, it does contribute to wider social goals, particularly where the researchers are vulnerable. The author has seen an unemployed homeless young person become involved in an early study as a voluntary and inexperienced researcher, before getting involved in later studies as a paid researcher, and then moving onto paid employment in the homelessness sector. Such investment in young researchers must be perceived as a positive outcome of the approach, although it does not constitute a positive impact on the research itself.

Interest

The general principle of children and young people's participation in research demands that their involvement is through choice. Consequently, children and young people tend to get involved in research when they have a keen interest in the topic and this interest appears to impact in two ways. First, the interest translates into enthusiasm, which impacts positively on the morale and motivation of others in the research team (McLaughlin 2006). Second, the keen interest of children and young people can result in an environment in which the peer researchers will frequently challenge the assumptions of adult researchers. For example, in a study involving the author and five peer researchers, the adult members of the research team, drawing upon the good practice literature on participatory research with children and young people, identified a venue for interview training that was familiar to the young people and was easily accessible. At the end of the first session the young people challenged the adult members of the research team, suggesting that they would like to attend a session in the university building as many of them had never been into a university and might not otherwise have the opportunity.

Research adopting the peer approach not only benefits from the high levels of interest of the children and young people who get involved; their involvement, particularly during the dissemination phase, can significantly influence levels of interest amongst policy makers and those who might act upon the research findings (Brownlie et al. 2006; McLaughlin 2006). The author has regularly observed the heightened engagement of local and national government officials when the findings of studies about young people are presented by young people themselves.

It is clear that adopting a peer approach to research with children and young people has positive impacts upon the research project and there is a growing literature that supports this claim (Clacherty and Kistner 2001; Kellett 2005a; McLaughlin 2006). The author suggests that this growing evidence-base is leading to a shift from a predominantly rights-based rationale for the adoption of the peer approach and participatory research more generally, towards an impact-based rationale, in which researchers follow the peer approach because of the considerable benefits it brings. This is particularly relevant at a time when the impacts of academic research are under high scrutiny.

Overcoming obstacles and achieving impact

As researchers increasingly pursue peer research with children and young people, they must recognise and negotiate the considerable challenges inherent within the approach. With reference to literature and the author's experiences, the key challenges are identified and discussed in the remainder of this chapter. In broad terms, the challenges are considered in the order in which they are likely to be encountered.

Researcher engagement

One of the key benefits of this approach is that it enables researchers to gain insights into the lives of marginalised and hard-to-reach groups. Consequently, peer researchers must be identified and recruited from within these marginal populations and this constitutes the first challenge (Chapters 1 and 3). These children and young people will rarely be contactable through typical avenues such as schools and youth clubs; instead, alternative recruitment mechanisms must be pursued. In the majority of cases researchers will recruit peer researchers through organisations which work with these groups. For example, a study involving the author had previously recruited from a charity which provides accommodation and support to homeless young people. Similarly, Smith et al. (2002) recruited young peer researchers from groups organised by the Children's Society. According to Smith et al. (2002: 195), this recruitment mechanism is convenient and it is likely that 'positive relationships with young people would already be in place'. It is also beneficial to recruit young people through support organisations because these organisations are often able to provide comfortable interview locations with support staff on-hand should they be needed. Whilst the recruitment of peer researchers through support organisations may make hard-to-reach groups far more accessible and in some ways, easy to reach, the young people being recruited may not share the same experiences as those who have failed to engage with support organisations. Consequently, the peer researchers might find it difficult to identify or interview young people who have not engaged with support services. This remaining challenge must be considered carefully when designing the sampling strategy.

Training and skills

> Natural empathy, even if it exists, cannot be assumed to be a straightforward or appropriate substitute for training in interview techniques or analysis.
>
> (Smith et al. 2002: 196)

Smith et al. (2002) quite clearly recognise the need to ensure that peer researchers receive appropriate research training, which is likely to include interviewing skills, ethics and child protection training at a minimum (Chapters 7 and 8). The need to prepare and deliver this training obviously has cost implications and it affects the research timetable and can therefore act as a barrier to adopting the peer research approach (Kellet 2005a). However, researchers must recognise that peer researchers bring with them an ability to relate to their interviewees; an ability and skill that cannot be taught to interviewers who do not belong to the peer group. Balancing the need for and cost of highly trained researchers with the need for empathy, understanding and insight must again be considered carefully during the design of the research.

Access

Peer researchers are afforded different levels of control and independence in research projects (Brownlie et al. 2006); even within projects, the author has worked with one peer researcher who was responsible for arranging, undertaking and transcribing interviews, whilst another researcher requested support at all stages. Peer researchers who choose to take significant responsibility for identifying interviewees and arranging interviews can face difficulties in gaining access to potential interviewees via gatekeepers. For example, in a study involving the author but led by a homeless young person, the young peer researcher reported difficulties in gaining access to talk with other young homeless people because homeless hostel staff were unsure of the peer researcher's motives and status. In this instance, the author was only required to make one phone call in order to provide clarification, but this incident does highlight a key challenge that young peer researchers may face. It appears that the validity of requests made by young peer researchers is questioned to a greater degree than the requests of adult researchers. This perhaps reflects power relationships which place young peer researchers in a marginal position relative to adult gatekeepers. As more peer research is undertaken, it might be expected that organisations will increasingly recognise the validity of requests by young researchers, but currently the research team must be prepared to support their peer researchers in accessing some interviewees.

Power and control

It can be difficult to determine who should have control at various stages of a peer research project; for example, who determines the research questions and the methodology. The literature on children and young people's participation in research strongly advocates their control over the entire research project. However, peer research is often incorporated within projects that have been funded by research funding bodies who expect research questions to be clearly articulated and methods to be outlined in the proposal, and this raises a key challenge when peer researchers are then recruited onto a pre-defined project. The author has been involved in peer research projects at both extremes of this participatory scale; in a study of temporary accommodation standards for homeless young people the young peer researcher took control at all stages, whilst a study funded by a major research funding body required the peer researchers to work within a broadly pre-defined interview agenda and with groups of young people representative of particular characteristics. In both studies the approach has impacted positively in the ways outlined earlier in this chapter and neither approach is advocated more favourably here. Researchers must recognise that the peer approach will offer varying degrees of power and control to the peer researchers, and it is essential that the young researchers are aware of the limits of their control from the outset.

Concerns about power relations do not just exist between the academic and the peer researchers, it must also be recognised that power inequalities persist between the researcher and the researched, albeit to a lesser extent than between an adult interviewer and child interviewee. It is well recognised that power relations between young peer researchers and their interviewees may be unequal, due to differences such as gender or ethnicity (Gong and Wright 2007).

> The matching of interviewers and interviewees by researchers according to pre-determined criteria may not necessarily facilitate a closer relationship in the interview.
>
> (Schaffer and Yarwood 2008: 123)

Chaotic lives and chaotic research

Any academic who has undertaken research with vulnerable children and young people will be very familiar with the frustration of arriving at the venue for a prearranged focus group or interview only to find that the interviewee has not turned up. Such frustrations relating to delays in the research timetable are more frequent when the researchers themselves are experiencing fairly chaotic lifestyles. The author has experienced significant delays to research projects because the peer researcher has been unable to work due to problems at home or due to ill-health. Whilst the benefits of heightened enthusiasm and commitment, discussed earlier in this chapter, certainly stand true, the chaotic nature of the lives of some peer researchers has implications for the project timetable (Fleming et al. 2009). Perhaps the most basic consideration, particularly in research with mobile groups of young people such as migrants or homeless people, is to allow significant amounts of time for Criminal Records Bureau checks to be processed.

In light of the additional time and cost involved in working with peer researchers who live chaotic lifestyles, Smith et al. (2002: 194) make an important recommendation. They suggest that potential funders should be prepared to recognise these additional requirements in their assessment and support of research proposals. When such considerations are made it is likely that further studies will be pursued using the peer approach.

Ethics and social care

> As well as the practical difficulties in involving young people as co-researchers, and the methodological challenges of achieving valid and reliable findings, a series of ethical issues also arise.
>
> (Smith et al. 2002: 199)

Research with children and young people raises a plethora of ethical issues (Chapters 6, 10, 11, 17 and 20), many of which are discussed later in this edited volume. However, peer research raises at least three additional concerns. First, and most significantly, peer researchers will frequently experience health or social care issues themselves and may require ongoing support during the research project. The issues faced by peer researchers will be extremely diverse, ranging from an ongoing but managed health problem, to an unexpected and immediate social care issue such as the loss of accommodation. The research team must expect problems to arise during the research project and appropriate support must be made available; this is most frequently achieved by working closely with the organisation from which the young person was recruited. Above all, research teams should allocate time for unexpected problems associated with peer researchers and, where possible, more than one peer researcher should be recruited to a project. This will not only ensure that the peer researchers can reflect on their experiences together, but it may enable the project to continue during a period when one researcher is unavailable.

The second key ethical issue is the payment of researchers (Chapters 5 and 7). The decision to pay peer researchers or not divides academics, although most would recognise that where peer researchers are making a significant time commitment there must be some form of reimbursement (Brownlie et al. 2006). The author advocates payment of researchers on the premise that an adult researcher would quite reasonably expect to be paid. Research teams must question why the time of a young researcher should be valued any less than that of an adult. It is perhaps most appropriate to discuss the form of payment with the peer researchers themselves.

The third and final ethical consideration is whether an exit strategy has been considered with the peer researchers. The researchers will have been engaged for a fixed period of time on an issue that interests them, but what happens at the end of the project? The academic will continue in their paid role, so too will staff at support organisations, but the young peer researcher is unlikely to have a clear direction of travel. France (2000) recognised this significant issue, claiming that this was one of the major shortcomings of their Joseph Rowntree Foundation funded project:

> Young people's exit from the project was difficult. Not having a strategy created difficulties in moving some of the young people on.
>
> (France 2000: 1)

The author's experience suggests that this issue is rarely addressed by research projects, perhaps because it does not impact on the outcomes of the research and funders are unlikely to support activities that seek to address this challenge. In studies involving the author, it has proved to be possible to involve researchers in subsequent projects, and on each occasion the improvement in skills and confidence have been noticeable. This would constitute one exit strategy. One peer researcher successfully moved from his role as a peer researcher to a job in one of the supporting organisations and this might constitute a second exit strategy. More generally, research teams must consider the exit strategy of their peer researchers, which may involve a session exploring employment options and CV writing, or it might lead to further research proposals. It must be recognised that supporting young people at the point of exit from the project is ethically important, but it is also time consuming.

Conclusion

Set in the broad context of increasing involvement of children and young people in health and social care research, this chapter reflected on a very specific form of involvement: the peer research approach. The chapter first considered why this approach is used, tracing the shift from an early rights-based rationale, in which very little was known about the actual impacts of children and young people's involvement; to a rationale based upon the apparent impacts of peer research on insight, innovation, investment and interest. In the contemporary research environment, where impact is given considerable prominence, it is likely that researchers will increasingly consider adopting such methodological approaches.

The final section of this chapter reflected upon the author's experiences and the experiences of others in order to identify the key challenges of applying peer research approaches. In summary these relate to researcher engagement, training provision, access to interviewees, power and control, chaotic lives and ethical concerns. It is anticipated that as funders and the research community become more aware of the positive impacts of this approach, the associated cost and time implications of undertaking peer research will be recognised and resourced and that more research will be carried out in this manner.

17 What is it really like to be the researcher?

Dilemmas, role-conflict and reflections on interviewing children and young people

Shruti Uppal

Introduction

Embarking on a social work qualification a year ago has brought me back to issues I grappled with when I worked as a researcher, albeit now couched differently. Clearly, themes of oppression, power and anti-discriminatory practice are as equally relevant in health and social care research as they are in practice, and critical reflection (an exercise strongly encouraged in social work practice) has a significant role to play in both these domains. Having had to document my own values, anxieties and prejudices in relation to my practice in the last year has made me reflect on the extent to which this is similarly encouraged in my previous work – research. In part this contribution is therefore an attempt to generate some debate as to the role that such critical reflection in the sphere of research with children and young people can play, drawing on accounts of the 'messiness' of the research process.

In the last 20 years, there has been a growing body of literature on the practical, methodological and ethical issues related to carrying out research with children and young people (e.g. Morrow and Richards, 1996; Mayall, 2002; Fraser et al., 2004; Christensen and James, 2008). Whilst I will not summarise it here, it is encouraging to note the growing significance now apportioned to this area and the increasingly favourable climate in which to discuss the minutiae of the research process. However, there exist relatively few contributions that do just this or rather, do only this. Discussions of the intricacies and inherent difficulties in carrying out research with children and young people are rarely merited as pieces of work in their own right, instead alluded to, mentioned in passing, or, instead, their absence justified due to the limits of academic publishing. As Boman and Jevne (2000, taken from Duncan et al., 2009) point out:

> [B]y the time research is presented or written up, all the perils and pitfalls of the research experience have been omitted or smoothed out in a

> tidy report outlining what went right rather than what went wrong in a research endeavour.
>
> (Boman and Jevne, 2000: 547; Duncan et al., 2009: 1692)

In this chapter I discuss some of the ethical issues inherent in carrying out research with children and young people. Two themes are explored: first the role conflict that arises as a result of our enquiries versus our respective professional backgrounds, especially pertinent in health and social care research; second, issues of power and reciprocity in the interview process, drawing on some feminist perspectives as well as those from working with children and young people. It concludes with a discussion of the impact that we have as researchers on the children and young people we work with and how we can further this debate.

Throughout the chapter the underlying question of whether, and how, these themes differ with respect to research with children as opposed to adults will be examined, as well as drawing on the experiences, anxieties and feelings of the researchers involved. It is argued that providing greater space for dialogue about these very reflections – on how we behave as researchers, and what this means both for our own practice and for the participants we work with, will ultimately shape how we can more ethically grapple with similar dilemmas in the future.

Role conflict in the research process

Whilst there is a certain degree of role conflict in playing the part of the researcher, versus other roles, e.g. friend, advisor or practitioner, in all spheres of research, in qualitative health and social care research this is even more pertinent for a number of reasons. There are increasing numbers of researchers who have practice experience in health or social care, resulting in two or more sets of 'professional expertise' to draw on. Even for those researchers that have no frontline experience of their research topics, the nature of their enquiry often means that they are asking about sensitive and personal issues, and children's and young people's expectations of their knowledge and expertise may therefore extend to these areas. As Duncan et al. (2009) note in relation to a disclosure made by a young person reagarding their recommended and actual self-medication regime:

> This potential for disclosure can be further enhanced by the fact that researchers are professionals and, notwithstanding the framing of the research process, participants may perceive the encounter as an opportunity for expertise or help, or perhaps even a safe space to debrief without the repercussions and uncomfortableness associated with regular contact afterwards.
>
> (Duncan et al., 2009: 1694)

A one-off research encounter may be more inviting for a young person to disclose something to a researcher (rather than, for example, to a medical professional) because that researcher presents as a peripheral actor in their social world and therefore any risks from disclosure may be minimised. In the example above, the young man during the course of his interview disclosed that he was going against his doctor's advice for his condition (which required daily self-medication) and was experimenting with his dosage. Moreover, it became clear during the interview that he had not disclosed this to anyone else. When he directly asked the interviewer if she would relay this piece of information to his mother, she replied that she would not and that confidentiality would be mintained. However, this presents a conflict within ourselves: as researchers on one hand and health promoters on the other.

> Thus, boundaries between the roles of researcher, friend, therapist or clinician can become blurred. Morse (2007) discusses the potential for uncovering information through qualitative research that might need to be reported to a third party, specifically describing the tension that can arise when therapeutic goals and research project goals conflict.
>
> (Duncan et al., 2009: 1694)

I have faced such conflict in my own research experiences, where levels of my knowledge, expertise and, therefore, confidence to assume the various roles asked of me have ultimately influenced how I have navigated such situations. When carrying out research with unaccompanied asylum seekers about their sexual health needs (Sinha et al., 2006), a number of issues were raised other than just those pertaining to the primary research questions. This included me being asked to offer up knowledge of welfare rights, how to access a GP and therapeutic support in the face of disclosures of violence and torture in participants' countries of origin. Based on my own anxieties, experiences and knowledge, some of these roles came easier than others, and I found myself giving information about how to access free prescriptions and GP surgery registration with relative ease. However, providing emotional support over and above that which may 'naturally' arise during the course of an interview was something I felt much more uncomfortable about, at that point having had no previous practice experience of providing therapeutic or emotional support.

Within health and social care research, there is clearly the risk that children and young people may ask us factual questions about issues that we are not fully equipped to answer (Chapters 6 and 10). How do we then deal with these as and when they arise? Are we to simply signpost to other resources or professionals that can more accurately answer their questions? Or is there an obligation to provide some, albeit partial, information to correct misunderstanding, for example? The research with unaccompanied asylum seekers, an incredibly oppressed group of young people with little access to resources (otherwise reserved for 'legitimate citizens'), caused me to feel strongly that they should be informed of the few resources they had genuine recourse to. Whilst this also included signposting them to other agencies with greater expertise, I did not feel that it compromised the research process to inform them of what I knew on the subject of their health entitlements. Further, in the vein of reciprocity and not simply 'taking' from participants, I felt that it would have been unethical not to give some information immediately (in case they did not follow up the signposts they had been given).

Some would argue, however, that even these roles that I felt were relatively 'unproblematic' in taking on (e.g. the information giver) are inappropriate to assume as a researcher. Mahon et al. (1996) instead posit:

> Whilst it would seem appropriate for researchers to try to meet these expressed needs by referring the child to a local advice, counselling or support service, it is perhaps important that the researcher does not attempt to take on such a role him or herself. This is no different from many qualitative research scenarios where researchers come across situations (for example, failure to take up benefit entitlements) which may require expert advice from others.
>
> (Mahon et al., 1996: 151)

Reflecting on these interviews, and speaking to other researchers who have also experienced a conflict of roles within the research process, raises some interesting questions in relation to such dilemmas.

- To what extent do we implicitly favour those roles that we are most comfortable with over and above those which make us more anxious and/or which we feel less confident about adopting? For example, Mauthner (1997) also comments on simultaneously navigating between the role of 'teacher' and 'mother', when researching with young children, taking on disciplinary and caring responsibilities respectively.
- Are there some 'roles' (e.g. health promoter/child protector) that need to be adequately explored before the fieldwork stage has begun? For example, in the dilemma set out by Duncan et al. (2009), the interviewer afforded the young person complete confidentiality at the start of the interview and even at the point at which he disclosed information that potentially endangered his own health. The dilemma for health and social care researchers then is whether they have an adequate understanding and conceptualisation of risk as it relates to the well-being of their participants, and that they are confident about steps to take if they feel this is being jeopardised in some way. Whilst many researchers now advocate a *conditional* confidentiality[1] clause at the start of research with children and young people, the crux of this approach relies on researchers being able to professionally assess what constitutes sufficient and significant risk

of harm (Chapter 11). This may be an area where the blurring of protective responsibilities between health and social care practitioners and researchers means that the latter would benefit as much from child protection and safeguarding training as do the former.

- Moving away from concerns around child protection or health, some researchers would argue that there is still a duty on researchers to challenge certain views, misinformation and prejudices that may arise during the course of the interview (Kitzinger and Barbour, 1999), especially in group interviews where the dynamics between participants is not limited to a one-to-one researcher–participant model. In this setting, what the researcher does or does not do will affect all group members. By choosing to challenge potentially inflammatory or offensive comments, researchers can uphold the rights of the subjects of that prejudice. Conversely, by ignoring the same comments, they can be seen by other (potentially oppressed) members of the group to be condoning those views. In this case, silence can be just as powerful as intervention. In addition, some argue that there is a responsibility on researchers to correct any erroneous views held by group members if this is again potentially jeopardising their well-being. For example, Kitzinger and Barbour (1999) provide the example of misinformation about HIV transmission during a focus group discussion to justify when a researcher should intervene. Again, judgements about when it is appropriate to intervene (and draw upon roles other than 'researcher') come down to individual assessments, but there are clearly cases where some would argue it is ethically justified.

Following this example of Kitzinger and Barbour of when it may be appropriate to take on other roles (e.g. health promoter) during an interview process, it is important to consider whether these issues are necessarily any different when carrying out research with children and young people compared to adults. In this vein there are clearly some issues that are child-research specific (e.g. child protection). However, Hunleth (2011) in her research on HIV illustrates how potentially 'misinformed' participants in her research were viewed differently, dependent on whether they were adults or children. Reflecting on her own practice, she observed that she did not correct adults when coming up with a 'technically incorrect' answer. However, 'when children told me that "ARV" was a disease or that ARVs cure TB, I immediately wanted to correct them and I viewed the children as misinformed' (Hunleth, 2011: 91).

This is interesting, and given that Hunleth was carrying out parallel HIV research with children and their parents, she may have been more able to reflect on the differences in the ways she interacted with these groups. However, her reflections illustrate the different ways in which we understand the competencies of our participants: again, children and young people may be perceived to need more protection, information and/or guidance, whereas in this example Hunleth almost looks beyond what the adults are telling her in a literal sense to find symbolic meaning in their words. She in unable to do this with the children's accounts, and she further reflects on the unease this caused her:

> In reality, when the children started to give what in fact were wrong answers, I felt the same anxiety as Emily. Should I explain that ARVs (antiretrovirals) were not a disease, as expressed by some children? What if the children 'learned' incorrect information from my workshops and used what they learned to inform their understandings of illness and their interactions with sick individuals? ... My acknowledged concern that the children would see me as a teacher obscured my own rather subconscious understanding of myself as a knowledge producer.
>
> (Hunleth, 2011: 91)

Power and reciprocity in the interview

Oakley (1981) argues that traditional and positivist approaches to research set out the interview as an objective and straightforward exercise in data 'extraction' from the interviewee. In these accounts, there is an implicit hierarchy of the interviewer as 'expert' over the interviewee who is there to answer questions. Whilst this exchange may be facilitated by the build up of rapport, the interviewer must essentially remain boundaried throughout, not 'biasing' the data in any way. However, whether this truly objective exercise can ever be achieved is questioned by Oakley, and she rejects these 'male-stream' accounts of research (portraying the interview as simply a 'one-way' process). Instead she advocates a more reciprocal and equalising approach with her interviewees that tries to minimise the inherent power differentials in the researcher–researched relationship. One of the ways in which this is achieved is through responding to questions that interviewees may ask of the researcher, and Oakley argues that not to do so would be unethical:

> The dilemma ... could be summarised by considering the practical application of some of the strategies recommended in the textbooks for meeting interviewees' questions. For example, these advise that such questions such as 'Which hole does the baby come out of?' 'Does an epidural ever paralyse women?' and 'Why is it dangerous to leave a small baby alone in the house?' should be met with such responses from the interviewer as 'I guess I haven't thought about it to give a good answer right now', or 'a head-shaking gesture which suggests "that's a hard one"' (Goode and Hatt, 1952: 189).
>
> (Oakley, 1981: 48)

Other researchers have documented the issues in taking on a reciprocal approach to interviewing, being open to having questions asked to them as well as by them.

> In her early fieldnotes Denise describes one of many occasions when a participant sought such information from her, "He also asked me about my life – this was not inappropriate, rather it was a mutual exchange within the parameters of a 'getting to know you' conversation." Had she not reciprocated, she believes, she would have been given short shrift.
>
> (Russell et al., 2002)

Webb (1984, taken from Reinharz, 1992) goes further in arguing that not to answer questions and offer advice (as a qualified nurse) would have been grossly unethical and would have compromised the research process.

> As I continued to do more interviews after making these decisions I was convinced even more strongly that in fact there had been no choice. Either I could have adopted this kind of methodology, developed intimacy with the women, and invested my subjectivity in the research and in return learned in great depth and richness about their feelings and experiences. Or the project would not have been feasible and would have ground rapidly to a halt.
>
> (Webb, 1984, taken from Reinharz, 1992: 256)

Whilst Russell et al. (2002) describe this process as one which is relatively unproblematic, others have documented a much more anxiety-provoking experience when the lens is turned back onto the researcher.

> Panic invades … and one million alternatives to answering the interviewee's question flood my mind. I scrutinise the interviewee's non-verbal behaviour trying to read them like a magical book of answers. … The interviewee sits poised on the chair, leaning slightly forward waiting in anticipation for my response. Time is lapsing. Their eyes filled with self-doubt and a nervous laugh touches their lips. I try to remain calm even though I too, am filled with self-doubt.
>
> (Wright and Reid, 2003: 10)

In relation to interviewing children and young people, many have commented on the heightened power differentials due to the age (and some might argue competence or developmental maturity) between researchers and participants.

> Any lack of power experienced by young people has the potential to complicate research processes such as deciding to participate, feeling able to ask questions or seek clarification, having the confidence to withdraw from the project and in some cases, feeling able to provide candid responses to questions posed by researchers.
>
> (Duncan et al., 2009: 1695)

When discussing notions of reciprocity and how to minimise differentials of power during the interview then, is it that straightforward to disclose information about ourselves and our views during the interview, and what are the implications of doing so? Whilst it is relatively uncommon to find frank accounts of being asked questions from children and young people in the methodological literature, it is something that both I and colleagues have experienced during the research process.

Questions that have been asked by young people (e.g. Uppal et al., 2005) include:

- Age, background, ethnicity, having children, place of work/residence
- Personal opinions/behaviour on topics being discussed (e.g. being gay, safe sex, risky behaviour)
- Factual information about things being discussed (e.g. effects of drugs, alcohol, mental health problems)
- The research project (e.g. why asking these questions, what will happen to the results).

In line with earlier accounts of being faced with questions from interviewees, it can be a very unnerving process, and one which, when faced with for the first time, can put the researcher off course in the context of the interview process. Some of the role conflict that these questions generate has already been discussed in the preceding section. To reiterate, it is clear that researchers navigate these (and other) questions in line with their own notions of which questions are 'safer' than others, what impact to answer/not answer may have on both individual interviewees but also on the dynamics of the interview, and also how their responses may affect the way in which they are viewed by their interviewees. I have been much more open about disclosing information that I view as less 'intrusive' (i.e. age, ethnicity, where I am from) to participants, than personal experiences and views that may or may not be directly linked to the research questions being asked. Hill et al. (1996) support this insofar as differentiating between 'safe' responses and those seen as more influential.

> It could also be helpful to share a few details about ourselves (like pets, ages of our children) in order to reduce social distance. It was important, though, to avoid giving information which might influence what children said and we took care throughout the discussion to convey an accepting attitude and openness to any experiences shared with us.
>
> (Hill et al., 1996: 136)

The heightened differential of age, together with working in health and social care, arguably adds a certain complexity to these dilemmas due to the types of topic being discussed: if a young person asks us about our own history of risk-taking behaviour (e.g. substance use, sexual encounters, criminal activity), would a frank answer to children and young people be any different from revealing the same information to adult participants? There are consequences of self-disclosure, and when working with children and young people these can be amplified, given the additional power dynamics present, reflecting children's subordinate place in an adult-centric society. Revealing personal experiences of risk-taking behaviour may condone such activities to our interviewees. In the case of questions about substance use or criminality, researchers may find it easier to refrain from answering any such questions where the responses have legal (as well as ethical) implications.

During a focus group with young people around substance misuse, I recall an occasion when one of the members asked myself and a facilitator about whether we had tried any substances ourselves. The experience of being faced with such a powerful (and anxiety-provoking) question in relation to the research topic was one that not only reflected the young man's interest in our personal experiences, but also felt like a challenge to our 'authority' in facilitating the group: as a test, to gauge what our responses would be. Given that there were others present during the discussion, the dynamics at once changed, with the young people watching us in anticipation. Hood et al. (1996) have also suggested that questions from children and young people during the interview process may be attempts to regain control of the conversation or momentarily deflect the 'gaze' from themselves, and, in one sense, it did feel like this. In this example, we chose not to answer the question and the subsequent response of the young man was frustration at both our and other professionals' previous lack of disclosure. He suggested that harm minimisation messages that were being disseminated would be more effectively taken on-board if they were accompanied by personal experiences and anecdotes from associated adults. Whilst this specific question was asked of us only once during the course of this project, the theme of young people wanting to hear more honest accounts of adults' experiences is a common one (Uppal et al., 2009).

Dilemmas of this nature can arise not only when we are asked questions that fall into the grey area between those which are non-intrusive and rapport building, and those which we perceive as being out of bounds for whatever reason, but also when we unequivocally decide not to disclose. By not disclosing, we equally impact on the subsequent dynamics of the interview and, in this way, both our actions (and inactions) will always shape the social context of the research process. As Ribbens articulates:

> Ultimately we have to take responsibility for the decisions that we make, rather than trying to deny the power that we do have as researchers. While we may seek strategies to minimise this power, groups without power more generally in society are not in a position to *assert* power over the research process either, which is the essence of vulnerability. But what all styles of research have in common to my mind, is that they

> cannot escape the conclusion that our research is itself a social process, occurring within particular sorts of social contexts and structures, and that it will have our own thumbprints all over it.
>
> (Ribbens, 1989: 590–91, original italics)

Conclusion

It is clear that we cannot avoid impacting on both the research process and on our participants, whether this is through the way in which we ask questions, the roles we assume, what we disclose about ourselves, or by our very presence and how this is contextualised by children and young people with respect to their own realities. As Hill et al. (1996) point out, 'Even so, characteristics like age, gender and accent will inevitably have set up certain expectancies in the children which may have shaped their responses.' (Hill et al., 1996: 136). It is not simply our behaviour then that is being socially located by our young participants: verbal and non-verbal cues are constantly being assessed and assimilated into children and young people's worlds, and this inevitably affects their interactions with us.

Whilst ethical guidelines and codes can direct us to an extent, they will never be able to inform us in relation to how to negotiate particular dilemmas or situations within the minutiae of 'doing research' (e.g. Cree et al., 2002). As Gallacher and Gallagher put it:

> For us, research is fundamentally a process of muddling through, sometimes feeling lost and out of place, asking stupid questions, being corrected and having our preconceptions destroyed. In this way, we cannot deny our incompetence and vulnerabilities: our immaturity. And we do not want to.
>
> (Gallacher and Gallagher, 2008: 503)

It is these reflections on what it feels like to carry out research that become obscured in the process of academic publishing, and yet it is these very accounts that can prompt us to question our own practice, values and judgement when researching with children and young people. '[W]hat is needed, therefore, is honest acknowledgement and reflexive exploration of the ambiguous and dynamic nature of the research process.' (Cree et al., 2002: 49).

In line with Christensen and Prout (2002), this necessitates an academic climate that does not rely solely on individual accounts of researchers, but where they can come together to collectively negotiate what these personal experiences can tell us about developing ethical practice.

> Flexibility and sensitivity to children's interests by the individual researcher is necessary but, in itself, it does not provide, or help to develop, a collectively available set of ethical values. It does not

> recognize clearly enough the need for childhood researchers to debate and develop a shared ethical ground on which their work stands.
>
> (Christensen and Prout, 2002: 492)

I have attempted to explore two ethical issues that arise when carrying out research with children and young people, illustrating these with both my own and others' accounts of the 'messiness' of the research process. I hope to have added to the small, albeit growing, body of work in this area that gives primary attention to these issues. In doing so I hope to further the dialogue in how we, as researchers, can take forward ethical guidelines and enact them in our everyday research practices, and also document the processes by which we do this.

Acknowledgement

I would like to thank my first research supervisor Professor Helen Roberts for originally providing me with the opportunity and the encouragement to think about some of the issues discussed here, and in shaping my subsequent practice, both research and otherwise.

Note

1 That is, complete confidentiality is guaranteed *unless* something is disclosed that puts the participant or someone else at risk of harm.

18 Youth and adult researcher reflections on participatory research in Australia and the United Kingdom

Thilo Boeck and Philippa Collin

Introduction

It is clear to us that young people should be seen as creative agents who bring about change (Chapter 2; Sayer 2003). As researchers currently employed by universities, with practitioner backgrounds in non-profit, youth and community work, we believe that throughout the research process the relationship of knowledge to practice should be "interactive rather than passive" (Sayer 2003: 354). Young people's own subjective accounts and constructions of their social world lie at the heart of our studies (Morrow 2002; Prout 2005), and our work in participatory research has been oriented towards the productive and respectful inclusion of these subjective accounts in the research process.

We are aware that this approach does not come without criticisms. These include concerns about the danger of bias (Hammersley 2009), the mediation of young people's views by "adult" researchers (Jones 2004: 113) and the benefits to individual young people coming at the expense of quality research (Chapter 3). In this chapter we consider how health and social research involving young people can address these challenges. We will present some of the young people's reflections on their experiences as peer researchers in two projects in which the authors have been involved: one in Australia and the other in the United Kingdom. At the same time, we offer our own reflections as academic researchers in these projects. Through these reflections we hope to contribute to broader understandings of how to facilitate participatory research with young people that is meaningful and rigorous.

The two participatory research projects

Project Re:action – United Kingdom

Project Re:action was a participatory research project by the Youth Action Network and the Centre for Social Action (De Montfort University) funded by the Big Lottery Fund.[1] The research aimed to learn more about young people's volunteering experience, the impact it had on their lives and their communities, and how much difference full participation made to that experience. Thirty-five young people were involved in planning, and carrying out the research. Eight young people also volunteered to be part of the Re: action steering group. This group worked very closely with the specially appointed project worker and researcher over the three years, making an essential contribution not only to the running of the project, but also designing the research, conducting focus groups, formulating the survey questions, taking part in the analysis of data and producing an evaluation toolkit, thus the project was, as far as is possible, defined by the young people.

All work carried out was based on the principle of equal partnership with the young people, recognising that everyone (young people and adults in this project) had unique skills, knowledge, experience, and the capacity to be critical and creative. The project was based on the belief that everybody was able to learn from everyone else.

Inspire Foundation Youth Participation Evaluation – Australia

The Inspire Foundation Youth Participation Evaluation (Inspire YPE) project was supported by Australian Rotary Health. It examined the role of participation for promoting the mental health and wellbeing of young people. The research examined the role of youth participation for: (1) individual mental health and wellbeing; (2) service delivery; and (3) organisational culture and practice. The project had a number of stages in which young people recruited through Inspire Foundation programs (www.reachout.com; www.actnow.com),[2] directly participated in the development of the framework, pilot and review and research. Initially, two young people contributed to a steering committee advising the research team. Nine young people were researchers in the pilot, undertaking interviews, analysis and writing up case studies. They contributed to the review of the evaluation framework in a series of meetings and a workshop. Five young people then joined the research team to undertake the research. Peer and staff researchers worked together via mobile phones, emails and secure online forums, as well as in two face-to-face workshops that were facilitated by two young people. In the first workshop the team reviewed and refined the evaluation aims, framework and interview schedules; learnt qualitative research skills; identified forms and instances of youth participation at Inspire and key informants for interview; and planned the interviewing timeframe. The second workshop was focused on qualitative data analysis in which the whole team analysed interview transcripts.

In the write-up phase, two of the peer researchers reviewed the written report and provided substantive feedback on the findings, discussion and conclusions.

Reflecting on participatory research with young people

In both projects peer researchers were asked in short face-to-face or online interviews to reflect on their experiences. Existing analysis of the experience and impact of youth involvement tends to focus on the perspectives of young people themselves: the principles, values, methods and communicative practices that work for young people. We agree that this is of critical importance to the further development and deepening of young people's participation in social and health research. However, in this chapter we are particularly interested in bringing our reflections on our roles as adult researchers into dialogue with the views of young people. To this end, in considering their views, we have reflected as "professional, adult researchers" on our experiences of working with young people as researchers in these projects. We are also aware of the way the language can work to reproduce power, particularly in the case of youth and adult. Thus, in this chapter we use the terms "peer researcher" and "staff researcher" to distinguish between different roles and agents, although these terms were often used interchangeably in the research projects themselves.

Whilst there were some differences in the design and execution of these two projects, here we focus on the common themes and similarities that we believe provide important insights for successfully working with young people in health and social research: agency and power, communication and resources, peer researcher expectations and research quality.

Agency and power

Although egalitarianism in research is premised on the principle that the perspectives of each researcher are given equal value (Wilkins 2000), this is hard to achieve in research involving peer researchers as they are rarely tasked with the management of a project and their participation is often mediated by adults (Jones 2004: 113). Nevertheless, in our projects peer researchers expressed a strong sense of agency as members of the project team. For some this emerged through increasing opportunities to take a hands-on role in the research.

> Originally we were meant to be just the steering group ... but then they said that if we wanted we could be researchers as well and do it in our own organisations.
>
> (Katrina, Project Re:action, UK)

For Katrina, being able to determine and increase her level of participation was critically important because it gave her a sense of being valued and having ownership over the research. For others, this sense of deep involvement was achieved regardless of when they came onto the project.

> Other than the project scoping and methodology design, I was involved in the rest of the project – I had influence over the rest of the project.
>
> (Eric, Inspire YPE, Australia)

For Eric, having actual influence was the important part of his involvement. He reflected on the challenge of balancing out the boundaries of the research with enabling the influence of, particularly, the peer researchers.

> Everyone worked together as a team – the research team kept us up to date and the staff involved were very open to our input and working together supportively.
>
> (Eric, Inspire YPE, Australia)

There was a strong sense among peer researchers in both countries that they were respected, valued, and that their participation was purposeful.

> I liked the look of it (Project Re:action) – it was actually trying to find something out. And we weren't just being asked questions, it was like, "get your hands in there" and looking at it and learning about it – learning different skills. And the fact that it was all youth-led was really attractive. Often these projects are just adults saying "ok, do this, do that".
>
> (Chris, Project Re:action, UK)

These reflections challenge discourses of young people as passive, powerless consumers of civic life (Ginwright et al. 2005). Their participation as researchers resulted in these young people – who are frequently positioned as powerless in health and social research – gaining and building a position of power for themselves within the research. This required us to identify and work with the varying knowledge, skills, strengths and challenges that each team member – including staff researchers – embodied. The shared planning, skills and analysis workshops were particularly productive and participatory spaces for this work.

This process – learning new skills, engaging in discussion, making decisions and taking responsibility for different aspects of the research – impacted on the peer and staff perceptions of youth roles in these projects.

> The adults listen to what we have to say. If we've got something to say then we sit down and listen to and respect what each other has to say. We've all got individual opinions and there's no right or wrong answer, there are just different points of view and they try to bring all of that together.
>
> (Niral, Project Re:action, UK)

Niral felt her contribution as a steering group member and peer researcher was of equal importance to that of the staff researchers, highlighting the ways in which we might conceptualise children and young people's participation as the struggle over recognition (Fitzgerald et al. 2010). Recognition is understood as both a process in identity formation in which dialogue and *mutual recognition* are necessary (see, for example, Taylor 1995; Honneth 2004) and as a question of status (Fraser 2000). Conceptualised as a struggle over recognition, youth participation in social and health care research can be thought of as an effort to redress *misrecognition* by creating the conditions in which young people can assert themselves as citizens. As adult researchers we are agents in this process, participants in dialogue *with* young people, and facilitators of spaces and processes in which the ways in which young people participate come into dialogue with the way that research "must be done". An awareness of how power is exercised and redressed is necessary for dialogue to occur and, particularly, for young people's understandings of their own experience to emerge.

As researchers we have to ask ourselves very carefully if our own approaches to researching young people's experiences are grounded in research *on*, research *for*, or research *with* young people (Darbyshire et al. 2005; Oakley 1994). If we "research with" young people we need to perceive them as active agents, which departs from a deficit model (Arches and Fleming 2007). The challenge here was to confront our own understanding: "[S]potting limitations in our own understanding is a step towards further learning, whereas spotting deficits in other people's understanding merely confirms what we knew before. Avoiding deficit interpretations is an important aspect of 'anti-oppressive', 'anti-racist' and 'reflective' practice." (Winter and Munn-Giddings 2001: 212). However, adopting a strength perspective (Saleebey 1996)[3] needs also to be realistic about what kinds of skill and experience each member of the research team has. This means that roles need to be flexible and structures need to be built in to support everybody in enhancing existing skills or gaining new skills. This is not a linear, but a complex process.

Communication and resources

Approaching communications and resourcing with a view to meeting the needs of both peer and staff researchers was critical to both these projects. For many peer researchers, the provision of communication resources and flexibility in how they communicated with the research team helped them participate in the research regardless of their location, resources or personal circumstances. Both projects allocated resources to support internet and mobile-phone use, and funding for travel for face-to-face workshops. For example, in Project Re:action, email was a successful communication strategy in part because peer researchers were provided with a laptop and, in some cases, a subsidised internet connection. While these resources were initially described as supporting young people's participation, they came to be thought of as regular project resources to be used in order to support the team to deliver on the project. Practically, this meant that the emphasis was on ensuring that the research – and research process – was more fully shaped and informed by young people's involvement rather than the focus being on the benefits to the young people themselves.

Meetings that brought together steering groups of peer and staff researchers to design and review the projects, research tools, build knowledge and skills, and to undertake analysis were particularly important. They created forums for genuine input and exchange of ideas, and supported learning and skills building. These workshops required all researchers to be fully prepared.

> Generally they send us out material as attachments ahead of time, so Thilo will send us something and just ask us to read it before our next meeting. So I have been busy with university work, but I generally look at it and jot down some thoughts for the next meeting.
>
> (Niral, Project Re:action, UK)

Niral appreciated that staff researchers shared documents and encouraged her to engage with the theoretical and conceptual material underpinning the research. She felt more informed and therefore able to offer critical assessments, as well as reflect on her own experience. Being given sufficient time to access, read over and consider the material was also seen as a respectful way to work with young people.

In both projects a notable feature of the workshops was that they were designed and facilitated by young people.

> [T]he workshop facilitators weren't staff or peer researchers but the workshops were such an integral part of the whole process and their facilitation made up a significant part of its success.
>
> (Darren, Inspire YPE, Australia)

For the Inspire YPE, these facilitators were other young people who volunteered with the foundation. All members of the research team highly valued these facilitators for their skill, their unique style and the opportunity they provided for the whole team to learn, plan and undertake data analysis. The inclusion of peer facilitators was critical for shifting the traditional power and authority of the staff researchers. As members of the team we were reminded to respect the work of the group, to support our colleagues without taking on board the role of "expert". This was not always easy, but debriefs at the end of these workshops indicated that peer researchers greatly appreciated the respect and collegiality that staff researchers had shown, citing confidence in voicing their thoughts and opinions as specific outcomes of this approach.

The modes of communication were seen as equally significant as actual resources by many peer researchers, who noted the importance of regular communication, particularly via mobile phones, text messages, email, live chat and online forums.

> Heaps of that work is online – like the survey – and we use email and stuff to discuss things. Members of the steering group live all over the country so it's really important for that. So anyone can be involved.
>
> (Nathan, Project Re:action, UK)

While mobile phones and internet-based communication may now be obligatory for professional researchers, we would argue that their use in these projects was significant, primarily because of the ways that the young people's digital communication practices shaped project design and the ways in which the researchers worked together over the course of each project.

For example, peer researchers did not make a distinction between how they used different technologies to engage in the research and how they used it in their everyday lives.

> I think I could probably live without my mobile phone, but definitely not the internet! ... I think because it's easier to communicate on. For example if you're on live msn you can talk about a project you can agree on what needs to be discussed at the next meeting. ... And you can talk to many people at the same time!
>
> (Niral, Project Re:action, UK)

For Niral, using her mobile phone and internet to connect with the research team and to engage with the project brought the research closer to *her* everyday life, rather than requiring her to operate within an adult research world. In effect, the traditional boundaries between adult and peer researchers were more effectively broken down – in our opinion – as a result of significant use of mobile and internet-based communications in these projects. Furthermore, these technologies enabled peer researchers to stay connected to the project and opt in as much as possible. It provided the team with effective ways to review, problem solve and garner feedback on aspects of the research outside the planned or formal research team activities. Peer researchers were very proactive, and engaged in much more detail with the research and data – and in ways that were often outside of formal analysis. Indeed, years after both of these projects, we continue to exchange text messages and email with many of the peer researchers as we further develop our thinking on these projects and distribute the research findings.

Peer Researchers' expectations

The Inspire YPE and Project Re:action specifically exceeded the expectations of the young people (see also Chapter 14). Peer research contributions were substantive across all phases of the research projects, and the level and quality of their research was impressive to both staff and peer researchers alike.

> For me personally, I didn't know I'd be able to do these things, as a young person – for example, data analysis. I didn't know we'd be sitting in a room looking at questions that young people have answered and analysing it. We thought, oh we'll just do the focus groups and run the sessions, but the adults will do it [the analysis] after.
>
> (Niral, Project Re:action, UK)

Moreover, peer researchers expressed confidence in the relationship between their involvement and the research outputs.

> Decisions get made, things get changed, policy gets influenced. But it can be difficult to gauge what you do – I know that they take stuff that you say on-board and take notice of it.
>
> (Chris, Project Re:action, UK)

For some the skills and confidence gained translated into personal achievements that surpassed their expectations of what they would individually gain from their involvement.

> I'm going to University in September. That's something that I didn't think I'd do. That's the biggest thing that I've got out of it. I'm more confident, I've learnt a hell of a lot. I've met fantastic people from different backgrounds who I never would have even had the opportunity to meet a year ago.
>
> (Chris, Project Re:action, UK)

Chris had experienced interrupted education and employment. Thus his participation in Project Re:action and subsequent acceptance into a university course were, in his own words, life changing. Young people in Australia also spoke of personal insight and achievement.

> The first word that comes to mind is genuine. It was a great experience being on the project as a researcher from the beginning until the end ... On a personal level, it gave me a great insight into the diversity and complexity of the research and also all the findings.
>
> (Eric, Inspire YPE, Australia)

For Eric, gaining a greater level of participation than expected also resulted in unexpected personal gain.

Trust played an important role for both peer and staff researchers in extending the possibilities of the participatory dimensions of the research.

Peer researchers expressed a high level of trust in the process and the research team. As staff researchers we would echo these sentiments. As one young person in the UK put it:

> Cos they always keep us – what's the word? – keep us, informed. About everything that they're doing at the time and make us feel involved by always giving us things to do – not just telling us what they're doing, but asking if we want to be doing it too – "do you want to help with this – do you want to do this?".
>
> (Katrina, Project Re:action, UK)

In our experience, this often worked both ways. Peer researchers became proactive, assertive, and generous with the research. In the case of the Inspire YPE, several peer researchers contributed more interviews than required, mobilised participants in focus groups, organised venues, transcribed audio recordings, offered advice on drafting, and contributed high level feedback and analysis on research findings.

Research quality

Participatory research is beneficial both because of its values, such as empowerment and inclusion (Chapters 1, 3 and 4), but also because it improves our understanding of those most affected by research and policy. For these reasons a participatory approach to research enhances the quality of the research and value of what is found (Smith el al. 2002; Chapter 3). This has played out in two significant aspects of the research projects presented in this chapter.

First, the involvement of peer researchers called for these projects to be both well defined from the outset, but also to be flexible. This was recognised by peer researchers themselves.

> [W]e need to set some non-negotiables but this needs to allow enough room for influence from the peer researchers.
>
> (Eric, Inspire YPE, Australia)

In both projects this involved clearly defining the different phases of the research project: design, pilot and review, field work, analysis and write up. Each of these phases involved different young people although some remained involved the whole time. At each stage the team reviewed the research framework, including underlying assumptions, the methods and the timelines. The complexity of each peer researcher's life and the individual purpose with which each approached the research called for the project to flex and adapt without compromising the continuity and integrity of the research. Maintaining a clear purpose and reflection on the evolving evidence and findings was undertaken throughout the process in order to account for the high level of reflexivity in the research. This was also built into the analysis and conclusions of the projects.

Second, having young people participating in data analysis has contributed to the overall quality of the research as reflected by Niral.

> At these data analysis sessions, when Thilo and Jonathan say something, sometimes we think "no, that's not what they [young people] mean" … We can feed that back. I know Thilo says that this has really changed his view of young people. So I know it's having an impact on them and hopefully when this project gets out it'll affect other people too.
>
> (Niral, Project Re:action, UK)

In these projects we have not only aimed to understand the meanings and significance the social world has for young people, but also were able to look at and interpret these realities from different perspectives. These were generated and verified by and with the young people themselves. As one Australian peer researcher put it:

> I think we provided different data by being a different interviewer and altering the researcher–participant dynamic. We were also able to analyse the data from a youth perspective with existing knowledge of the organisation and its programs.
>
> (Darren, Inspire YPE, Australia)

That this is recognised by the peer researchers themselves, illustrates the level of reflexivity and self-awareness of the peer researcher – an awareness that brings rigour and careful consideration to the research itself. The following quote from a member of the Project Re:action steering group highlights how young people who have been part of these academic research projects grasp this and how the participative element of the research was crucial to achieve this understanding.

> It was an opportunity to contribute my opinion as somebody who has experienced volunteering with the members of the group. What I think I liked is the fact that I did make valuable contributions as a young person.
>
> (Nathan, Project Re:action, England)

When analysing data, as adult researchers, we needed to be aware of our interpretation of young people's accounts of their worlds locating our findings within conceptual frames that do not adequately reflect on young people's experience. We recognised that "our knowledge of the world around us will depend on the way that we look at it" (Agar 2005: 34), and that adult views of children and young people can differ from children's and young people's views of themselves (Waksler 1991: viii). Having young people as equal partners in the Inspire YPE and Project Re:action steering groups, involving them in the whole research process and having them participate in data analysis has not only made a difference to the young people, but also to the adult researchers, and has contributed to the quality of each research process and project outcomes.

Conclusions

In this chapter we set out to bring our reflections on our roles as adult researchers into dialogue with the views of young people. In both projects, we sought to create regular and on-going dialogue with peer researchers, building an environment of trust that allowed all of us to be reflexive and critical in our work. We argue that within this process, as staff researchers, we need to be honest. We need to ask ourselves, regularly, if we are imposing our own perspectives and methods, or if we are creating the space for young people to explore their own topics, questions and develop innovative methods, and thus unleash their own creativity. Treating young people as creative agents who bring about change means that they can determine their level of participation, bearing in mind that for many young people the actual influence is as important as the form and extent of their involvement.

Building cycles of reflection and evaluation into each research project ensures that critical reflection is not a one-off activity at the end of the project, but an on-going process of critical examination of each stage of the research. An emphasis on trust, reciprocity and dialogue *with* young people aids awareness of how power is exercised and redressed. However, whilst participatory research involves rethinking subject positions and how power operates, this is not in conflict with being realistic about what kinds of skill and experience each member of the research team has. The young people themselves reflected that roles should be flexible and project structures needed to support everybody in enhancing existing or gaining new skills.

We learned that good communication structures and sharing knowledge and ideas is important and was valued by peer researchers who felt more able to offer critical assessments as well as reflect on their own experiences. In our experience, using young people's own communication practices and preferences to shape how the team communicates enables young people from very different backgrounds to participate and engage with the theoretical and conceptual material underpinning the research. We believe that this, combined with the continued reflection on the research process and the emerging findings, supported the high level of reflexivity in the research and that this contributed to the overall quality of the research.

As such, we would encourage researchers involving young people in their projects to build into their project design regular opportunities to ask some important questions: Who are we as a research team? What makes us similar and different? What are our different skills? What is my role as a staff researcher? Can young people determine their level of participation? What are the young people telling me I must understand about their views on the way the research is unfolding? Am I listening? Am I imposing my views? How participatory is this research?

Acknowledgements

We acknowledge the work of all members of the research teams associated with the projects mentioned in this chapter. Inspire YPE – Ehon Chan, Kris Gesling, Belinda Eslick, Zenna Baxter, Tanya Pretila, Kitty Rahilly, Justine Stephen-Reicher, Jane Burns, Michelle Blanchard and Helen Herrman. Project Re:action – Niral Makadia, Chris Johnson, Nathan Cadogan and Hogar Salim.

Notes

1 The Youth Action Network is a membership organisation for youth volunteering projects across England. Re:action took place between 2006–2009.
2 The Inspire Foundation (www.inspire.org.au) is a non-profit organisation that provides online services that aim to improve young people's mental health and well-being. The inspire YPE was undertaken between 2009–2010. Peer researchers quoted in this chapter have been given pseudonyms.
3 The strengths perspective emphasises the individual's capacities, talents, competencies, possibilities, visions and hopes.

19 'I have always had a passion to be a part of something unique'

Young people reflecting on being researchers

Harrison Carter, Mayuri Chudasama, Susanna Dobson, Iman Dalenius, Pritesh Nathubhai and Ruth Taylor with Thilo Boeck and Jennie Fleming

Introduction

This chapter is based on a series of recorded conversations between six young people employed as Associate Research Assistants (ARAs) by the Centre for Social Action (CSA) at De Montfort University and two older members of CSA staff (see also Chapter 5). The ARAs have worked on a number of research and evaluation projects. These include the evaluation of a large national project supporting young people's participation, young people's involvement in museums, work with a local project offering training to young unemployed people, a young people's legal service, and a research project about young people's use of social media and its role. They have also identified their own research priorities and sought funding for these. Over time their role has developed and they are now also part of deciding what funding to apply for and involved in applications.

We have had a number of conversions based on reflecting on the ARAs experiences of research. We have also asked them questions about the views and concerns expressed by academics and practitioners regarding participatory research with young people.

The topics discussed include:

- Why do you participate in research?
- Do young people have better access to other young people, and a better understanding of their issues?
- The impact of research training on young people
- Can young people research any topic?
- The quality of research involving young people
- The impact of being researchers on the rest of young people's lives.

This is not an exhaustive account. We have edited the various conversions into a coherent piece, but hope to have kept the freshness of the conversation and reflection intact. All the young people have contributed to these conversions, but we have distinguished only when adults and young people are talking – a new paragraph indicates a new speaker each time.

Why do young people participate in research? First, what is your own motivation to be involved in research?

It's just something different; you don't really get many opportunities to be involved in this way.

I have always had a passion to be a part of something unique regarding young people. That young people as employees can go about doing this research and can be trusted to do that quite well, it's a unique opportunity. But also by us going out there it has an added benefit to the university as they are seeing a different side to what a researcher is.

Also it's good experience for the future, because I want to go into psychology it's good to learn research skills and learn how it works and to improve my confidence as well.

For me it's the same – it's interesting to get involved. I think it's wonderful that an organisation as big as a university would be so willing to involve young people. I guess that's the Centre's work, it might not be the university as a whole. Also in the future research may be an integral part of most of our careers in the sense that it's kind of furthering knowledge, it's being curious and going out there and finding things. And so it equips you to do it in the future as well.

Moving on, why do you think generally that young people should be part of research?

A lot of the things we research and take part in are very important issues for all kinds of people especially, but young people. I think it's important that through the research we get all sorts of different perspectives. Everyone should be included. You can't discriminate because of someone's ethnic background or sexuality or anything like that, so why discriminate because of their age? It's really important that all of the different kinds of people are involved in research.

Also the fact that we are young can affect what information we find out. For example if the people we are speaking with are young themselves, then they might feel more open to talk to us about it, which can add quality to the research.

People talk about service user involvement and young people being involved in services that affect them; our work is a part of that. We are being involved and talking to young people about the services that affect them. It is not just the data we get, we might interpret it differently when we look at it compared to when an older researcher looks at it. We may see different things. We may be able to apply some background knowledge, because of some past experience we've had to what they are telling us.

You have raised one of the other issues that is often discussed. There seems to be an assumption that young people have a better access to other young people and are better able to get their views. Do you think it's always the case?

I think it can be the case. At the museums it was nice because before the session started, we could talk about things like music with the young people there, so it just broke down the barriers before going into the research. Sometimes it is the case where those barriers can be broken down, but then others not, depending on how well you can communicate with that person.

There is also a lot to be said for just visually having young people there. I remember the first project we worked on, the young people said they were really surprised but really pleased to see that young people were part of the team. It validated what we were doing. They took us more seriously because, as a team, we were showing in what we were doing, that we were passionate about what we were there to find out about – that is young people's participation and involvement. I would say it helps the young people at the projects to see us being researchers.

I think it might depend on the subject. If there is something quite sensitive or upsetting, and they are quite emotional about that topic – say the research was about miscarriage or something – young people would probably want to talk to an adult more than they would a young person. Because they might think that a young person could regard them differently than an adult would. Also an adult might be able to empathise with them more than a young person would on that subject. But if it was something that they were quite happy to talk about they would probably be happier to speak with a young person.

I think it's definitely true that young people are not *always* the best. For quite a lot of young people, when they meet other young people they don't know, there can be almost a sort of semi conflict before people have built up a rapport. If they happened to feel threatened or intimidated by speaking to young people who are their peer group, then we might not capture as much good data.

That's why I think this group works so well because there is a combination of adults and young people. I think adults on their own or young people on their own aren't going to get as good a result as adults and young people working together. It's like when we went to do our group sessions at the projects, and you were really surprised that we were actually more scared about talking to the young people than the adults. I agree young people might feel people their own age might judge them more than people of another age.

Just because we are the same age group doesn't mean we have experienced the same things. Sometimes mutual experience can be a bonus, it can be really helpful, but other times we might be undertaking research on something that we have had no experience of. It is wrong to assume all young people have the same experience.

I think it definitely varies because I have been in situations where that's happened, and I have also been in situations where the young people respect you more because you are a young person. I think it varies.

Young people being researchers can make it look like the research will actually be used and used to implement change. If you yourself were taking part in research and just two adults came, you might think they were going to collect this information, take it away, and write a report. Whereas I think with young people being researchers it looks like, 'Oh they are working with young people so maybe there is going to be some kind of change'.

In my experience, adults were often more aware of me being young than the young people are themselves. Like simple things, conversation would be directed more to the adult researcher, it's like 'Hello I am here!' . So yes I think maybe the adults are more aware of age than young people.

You mean it was the adults directing the conversation to the adults?

Yes, although in a way I don't completely blame them for that.

They are always going to be there, I think, it's always going to be the case. That kind of feeling isn't going to change because as we grow up to be adults we will probably do the same thing. Without meaning to be horrible to people, it's just what happens.

There is sometimes the perception that there are certain topics for research that young people might not necessarily be the best people to research. You have already mentioned miscarriage or domestic violence or things like that. Are there areas that it is not appropriate for young people to research, because they are so sensitive?

Even if we might not be able to actually collect information on those topics, young people can still contribute to the research. Working on designing of the workshops or the analysis, something like that.

Obviously it's not quite as good but it's an improvement on no involvement of young people at all.

I think it depends on the person. It could be true for any researcher really, it's about how sensitive you are yourself. If you have to listen to traumatic things that have happened to someone, then young people can be sensitive to that. So it depends on what the research is and who the person is.

What do you think about young people being involved in research into issues that affect young people, but affect everybody else too? As a team we have looked at things like young people's involvement and participation. We have focused on services that were designed specifically around young people. But what about, for example, GP services that everybody uses?

I think it would be different, but it would be equally beneficial that young people are involved in research into such things, the same as it is that young people being involved in research into things specifically relating to young people. There is a common idea that there are these things called 'young people's issues' and these things called 'older people's issues'. But this is not really true is it? For example, speed limits may affect young people, bus services will undoubtedly affect young people and there are all sorts of things like that. These are services which affect everybody but they affect people in different ways, so young people should be involved in research into these things.

I think it affects the credibility of the research, like we were talking about earlier. I think there is this perception that it's alright for young people to do research with young people, but when it gets to young people researching things wider than just young people's issues its – they should maybe keep away from things.

I was at an event about young researchers recently. People were talking about training for young people undertaking research. Some people had the view that by training young people in research, we are forcing young people to be like adult researchers. They suggested that by training young people in research skills, we could lose the essential elements of involving young people in the first place? What are your thoughts about that?

That's a hard question.

Maybe that kind of natural empathy, just being normal and natural and not put together, not fake, that could be trained out of us. If we are talking about body language then you can start thinking, 'Oh how am I sitting?'. Things like at the museums at the beginning I was conscious of making sure it wasn't too confrontational. It's OK to be aware of those things but we need to make sure we are not too rigid in the way that we take information on board.

I think anything that you might lose in training, whatever it might be, is less than what you gain. I would not be able to do this work if I hadn't had the training full stop really. Simple things like conducting the interview, writing notes, probing questions, things like that, that if I had just been thrown into an interview and hadn't had the training I wouldn't be able to cope at all. Whereas I don't think anything we may have lost, whatever that might be, would compromise the research. Does that make sense?

What I most remember from training was the scenario where you played difficult people to interview, and we had to try and find ways around it …

I found that really useful. We were put into a situation of using the skills we learnt from the day before, how to re-phrase questions, things like that. Being put in that situation and actually interviewing, I thought that was a really good idea.

It was really useful for when we actually did the interviews and we interviewed real people. We did find some of the characters that were portrayed in the role play. If we had not had the training we wouldn't have known how to cope with it. Because we had that initial training, that initial awareness of how things can go and what people can be like – having training it was beneficial.

Also learning about how, for example if someone you were interviewing went off the point and you had to help them back into the actual question and what they were focusing on. I found that useful, we learnt that in the training as well. There are no negative things about the training; it's just a step up and more knowledge and skills.

I think the way the training was done made the team stronger. It was a nice time to get to know the team and just start to really bond. A strong research team makes for better research.

I would really agree with that. I think it was also a time where we found everyone's weaknesses and strengths. If you know some people are especially good at this and some are especially good at that, you can mould your workshops and your interviews around that. If someone is really good at note taking and another person hates writing but is really good at explaining the exercises, then it's important for everyone to know that and the training showed this to us all.

However, the training wasn't just about learning pure knowledge, teaching us all this stuff, the training was about us getting to know each other. It helped us be comfortable talking to each other and be comfortable to share ideas and thoughts and be confident in the group. That in itself is as important as learning things, that ability to form a rapport is very important.

There weren't times when you thought 'no that's wrong I wouldn't do it like that'?

No I wouldn't put it like that because nothing was imposed on us. There was nothing to say that's wrong, because it was all suggestions and ideas and everyone had an equal opportunity to be able to contribute to that. We were encouraged to give our own opinions and give our own ideas and suggestions. It created an environment where we can say, not that I disagree with that but, I wouldn't look at it in that way, I would look at it like this. That was good because then we get different opinions and perspectives on things, and that's really important to the analysis of the research for example.

I don't know if this is answering the question at all, but doing more interactive things was good. It didn't feel like we were at school and we were just being told or read these research methods or ways to do things. It was more actually doing those methods with demonstrations.

The training used the same exercises that we could then choose to use in the research sessions. That meant we had ourselves participated in those activities on the training day, so we felt more confident in using those activities when doing research as well. Had we not have experienced those activities we wouldn't have known that was a good way to collect information from people.

I think we even did some activities at our selection interviews, so it was like we were learning from day one.

Training isn't just about what you learn. It gives you ownership of your job as well. I am sure I wasn't the only person who found it odd working with adults, not just working with adults but being considered an equal. I found it really hard to get my head round that. So having the training and feeling like you are all on the same step, makes your confidence just soar up and you can do all the things so much better than if you hadn't had the training.

The training was really important to us being able to do the job we were employed to do. It prepared us well for what we had to do and it would have been much more difficult to do the research without it. It helped us think about lots of things and the role play helped us practise things before we actually went on site visits and to interview people and put our plans into action.

Some people say that involving young people will compromise the academic quality of the research. They say it can compromise the academic rigour, the thoroughness, the depth of analysis, these kinds of things. What do you think about this?

I disagree, just having the young people's opinions and the young people-led research alongside adult research would make the data more holistic, rather than compromising it. I think it will add to it. Because you have got both perspectives.

It depends who the audience is. If the audience are adults, then adults may not be willing to take young people seriously. But from what my experience is that's not happened yet, adults have taken us seriously.

If by academic rigour it means perhaps an out of touch, horrifically complicated and unhelpful piece of research that people might not use because they can't understand it, then perhaps us being involved does compromise the academic rigour in that sense! But in terms of a piece of research actually being useful and contributing to service improvement and contributing to better lifes for young people then our involvement can do that.

It's also linked with the question about the training you've had, isn't it? We have all had training to be able to do research. We might not know as much about the field as you two but I think if young people-led research is coupled with academic professionals I don't see why it shouldn't be just as good if not better. Because you have a different perspective, different people collect information in different ways and remember things in different ways and the greater variety of people you have the better your information is going to be.

I think young people's interpretation is a lot different to adults' interpretation. The way we interpret what people said can be different from what adults think they are saying, this is because we may have a better understanding of the things being researched.

It is not just the way it's interpreted, but also the emphasis put on certain things we find out. Adults might think that one opinion was really important, whereas the young people might think that another opinion was.

I can't remember the exact example when we were doing analysis, but … .

I can remember an example, tell me if it's not the one you want to use. We had the same information in front of us, but you gave the young people being involved in creating the environment, the physical environment, a greater importance than we did.

It may affect the status of the research if people regard research undertaken by young people as having a lesser standing as a result of the young people being involved. Talking about the quality, the quality will probably be there but the problem might be people regard it as being a lesser piece of research because young people have been involved. They think young people lack the knowledge or experience, and then link that to the research being poor quality. If that happens then yes it would compromise the academic outcome because it's it would not be taken seriously and not be as prestigious as it should be perhaps.

I think working with young people on research projects does mean things are done differently. An example might be when we thought about all the things people needed to know before they could understand enough to decide if they wanted to take part in the research or not. You didn't necessarily use the same language that might be used in more academic stuff, but you covered the same things. Then instead of producing a conventional information leaflet you said 'Let's do it on a film and let's send the link to them'. It contained all the same information that would have traditionally been in there.

With the young people I would say as young people ourselves it's less formal for them as well in a way. They just feel like they can relate to them and talk to them.

Do you think that the working at the Centre and the things you have done has had an impact on other aspects of your life elsewhere?

Yes it's helped me with applying to university. I have got a lot more to talk about at an interview. The skills we have learnt here can be applied to other situations like in the workplace, a party or something like that. The confidence and the way you are talking to an adult can apply to real life too. It has given me that confidence to talk to an adult, whereas before I would not have approached adults at all.

It's definitely been a benefit in lots of ways. I have definitely used some of the skills we have learnt from the training sessions, and the more direct research skills. For example, during campaigns I have been involved in we have identified a problem: How are we going to capture data? How are we to get recommendations? Being an ARA has certainly changed my way of thinking and changed my way of engaging with young people. For the campaigning work I do, I think it's also helped us to engage young people who perhaps are more vulnerable, because the way we do things in our research I think was very accessible and so it's really helped to inform change from people who would never have had the opportunity to do that before.

It's made a big impact on my life. I have been involved in some training for junior doctors to be counsellors. I was the only young person there and there were three adults. They all gave little speeches; but I had organised a workshop and I used a lot of the skills I have learnt here to help do that. All the doctors said it was really refreshing and good to be able to be a part of something like that.

I think being part of the research breaks down prejudices that you didn't realise were there. Not big things, but the way you relate to people, it really improves that. Day-to-day things like the verbal and non-verbal communication, it makes you much more aware of what you are doing, of how you listen to people. Especially making sure that people's opinions are heard, and that's one of the main things I have learnt and has come out of being a researcher for me.

I can think of three things it has changed. I have spoken to a few adults about the work I do and they are interested and kind of shocked that we are doing this. So it's changing the representation of the uni and how people see the uni, and it's showing the uni is being innovative and doing new things. Secondly, talking to other young people about it, it's good to let them know that it is possible to get into things that young people might not have considered as a young person's role before. And finally I am proud of the job, and it's nice to feel that.

Young people don't actually get this sort of opportunity often. The opportunity to actually plan a group session, and then be able to say 'this is how we are going to get our information', and then for it to actually happen is great. That sense of trust from the university that we can do research as young people and that it would be valued.

You value yourself more. To find out that our piece of research was actually used for something and not just done for the sake of it and it did have a purpose behind it. It makes you feel more valued as a person and that self-value makes you more confident outside of the workplace I think.

Based on your experience, if you were to give advice to others wanting to work in this way with young people as research colleagues, what advice would you give them?

Make us feel welcome, be positive about our involvement.

Treat us young people as equals. A lot of young people have had experiences where they have had a patronising and tokenising role in something, so being treated as really equal will put us at ease.

Make sure we have real responsibilities that will impact on the research – make sure we *can* make a difference to what is being done.

I think that means you have to trust us. Trust us to design young people interviews or sessions. Show you trust us. We will do our jobs better if we know that what we are doing makes a difference. That links with giving us responsibility.

But adults have responsibility too. They are responsible for making sure we are involved in as much as possible. It shouldn't be like we design the workshop, but you'll do the rest of it without us.

It is best if we have a part in all parts of the research. Deciding on the focus, the issue we are going to address. Young people involved from beginning to end – involve us from the ideas stage where possible. It would be good if that can happen more.

Of course, young people would like to be involved from stage 1, but people should not to be afraid to give us the opportunity to do stuff with more limited involvement. You have to start somewhere and, whilst not the best, some involvement might be better than none. For example, maybe we have had limited exposure to the planning stage but we can still get involved later on – it still allows us to learn new things and make a difference.

It can be OK to have a small bit in a project with people who have not involved young people before. If it goes well, they might consider more involvement for young people. So young people's involvement in research grows. Some people are cautious and may feel there is an element of risk. We are not suggesting everyone puts young people in charge of the whole project now – it happens in small stages – as long as it is not tokenistic and we are clear about what we can influence.

Yes but if that happens we must know about what is happening in the other bits – not just work on 'our bit' not knowing what else is going on.

20 Conclusion

Emerging processes to maximize the involvement of children and young people in research

Thilo Boeck and Jennie Fleming

Whilst these themes are overarching, the accounts of them are distinctive. This volume has shown the variety of ways in which children and young people have been involved in health and social care research. The authors have all drawn on their experiences of involving children and young people in research to discuss how they are doing it and how they are facing and overcoming the challenges. The contributions in this volume are diverse, highlighting that people work and research in a range of settings with different young people. Despite these differences, the chapters describe and address similar issues and raise similar questions, including ethical practice, relationships between young people and adults, and the valuable contribution of young people to the whole research process, amongst others. Such commonality indicates that there is much we can learn from work in other settings. In this final chapter we will identify some important themes arising from this volume.

The 'Why?' chapters in Part 2 of this volume set out three main arguments as to *why* we should involve children and young people in research. The first one can be considered to be the cornerstone – the recognition of children's rights based on the United Nations Convention on the Rights of the Child (UNCRC). The second argument for *why* we should involve children and young people in research, is the acknowledgement of children's and young people's agency, focusing on them as social actors. The third argument is that their involvement is not only a matter of principle, but is also a significant element of improved research quality. To a greater or lesser degree, all the chapters underline the significance of these three rationales and they are integral to them all.

Shaped by these rationales, three interconnected processes in research arise from the chapters: (i) *working with and enhancing the critical and creative capabilities* of young people in the research process, (ii) *enhancing power and control* and (iii) *research leading to change*. These processes which inevitably overlap and intertwine, need consideration from the very start of a research project. We will explore these processes using the same headings as in Chapter 1:

- Seeking young people's perspectives and for their voice to be heard: working with and enhancing the critical and creative capabilities of young people

- Young people being active in the process of research: enhancing power and control
- Participation for change: research leading to change.

In the following section, we attempt to disentangle them to be able to consider each one in turn; however, naturally, some intermingling remains.

Seeking young people's perspectives and for their voice to be heard: Enhancing the critical creative capabilities of young people

As already highlighted in Chapter 2, the status accorded to young people's agency is central to this volume. All the chapters show children and young people to be critical, creative and able to challenge and change the dominant structures of research and practice, to a greater or lesser degree. In considering the roles young people take in research, this volume stresses that agency is seen as the input from young people to a research process that needs to be dynamic and flexible. It would be naive to pretend that such a research approach does not have challenges; not only for the adult researcher, but also for organizations, especially those with more traditional work and research environments.

Contributors show that researchers and evaluators who are committed to enhancing the critical creative capabilities of young people are making constant judgments, such as between facilitation and paternalism, the right to autonomy against the principle of justice in seeking service user involvement, and concerns about potential harm (Chapter 13; see also Smith 2008). Adults in positions of power might, in some cases, start by providing leadership and give some structure to the research process, whilst at the same time being ready to follow ideas generated by the children and young people (Chapter 13). This recognizes that both adults and young people are agents in research involving children and young people, each bringing different skills to the research process (Chapters 18 and 19).

Young people and adults in this volume have talked about how the creativity of young people enhances the research process making it more innovative thus challenging more rigid frameworks developed by adult researchers. Young people have the ability to innovate particularly in the development and application of research methods. Thomas and Mackie stressed that the right research environments encourage young people to be spontaneous within the data collection phase, making the research process more flexible to respond to the needs of the young people. Traditional research methods were reconsidered and changed in several research projects, especially those in health research. Newman et al., for example, worked with young people to redesign medical research methods to those that would be more acceptable to young participants. Pickering et al.

adapted their communication style in response to the needs of disabled children and young people. Radford and Ellis acted on the opinions of young people about ethical issues in a research project about abuse.

The area of children and young people's involvement in analysis fits both within the process of enhancing creativity and within enhancing power and control. Analysis and interpretation of data lead to alternative insights which, it is argued in several accounts, enhance the quality of the research and value of what is found (Chapters 14, 15, 18 and 19). This builds on young people's critical insights and their expertise. The chapters show that when analyzing data adult researchers needed to be aware that their interpretation of young people's accounts of their worlds, might not always adequately reflect young people's own experience.

Developing this creative and more spontaneous approach to research that enhances young people's power and control, has a substantial impact on ethical considerations throughout the research process (Chapters 6, 7, 10 and 11). These need to be situational, contextual and relational (Mauthner et al. 2002), within a research environment that is based on respect for what children and young people themselves have to say (Thomas 2002). Butler and Radford and Ellis give deep consideration to informed consent processes, and how to enable participants to give their full consent and so be able to contribute to knowledge and understanding about issues that affect their lives (in line with Article 12 of the UNCRC). Protection and participation should not be in opposition, and researchers should be wary of paternalistic protectionism (Chapter 11). Within an empowering process, ethics need to take into account that young people might want to take part and express views about their own experiences, even though this might make them upset.

An awareness of how power is exercised and redressed is necessary for dialogue to occur and, particularly, for young people's understandings of their own experiences to emerge (Chapter 18). It is important to promote constant reflection, while acknowledging the power differentials between adults and young people (Chapter 13). Boeck and Collin recommend building cycles of reflection and evaluation into each research project. This will ensure that critical reflection is not a one-off activity at the end of the project, but an on-going process of critical examination of each stage of the research.

Young people being active in the process of research: Enhancing power and control

Several chapters shed light on power relationships in specific research environments, including the behaviors and practices of privilege and power that often are overlooked in non-participatory research projects. There is recognition that young people can encounter restrictive, but also enabling, power relationships within research projects. Within a participatory research framework, researchers have to be aware that young people will take full advantage of the opportunities available to them (Chapters 18 and 19). They will also use their adaptability and resourcefulness to grapple with oppressive attitudes of adults (Chapter 9). In Chapter 1 we highlighted that some researchers and research institutions have responded to the challenge of young people's empowerment in and through research. This recognizes that involving children and young people in research and evaluation has to be rooted within an empowering agentic process. However, it is important to remember, as Smith points out, that though equality and justice are inherent features of participation, this does not guarantee fair and non-exploitative outcomes, as inequality and oppression are deeply embedded in human relationships. This means that often, researchers have to negotiate the tensions between competing principles and between ideals and reality.

A rights-based approach is intended to empower children and young people. Empowerment requires 'the appropriation of power by young people beyond just knowledge of the source of their disempowerment to opportunities to engage in activities to change their situation' (Chawla and Malone 2002: 129). Integral to this is the creation of opportunities, and the opening up of new spaces where they can participate in the whole research process – as demonstrated in the chapters in this volume. Staples (1990: 30) identifies three key themes in empowerment: 'participation of people in their own empowerment', 'the importance of recognizing existing competencies' and 'building on individual and collective strengths'. Empowerment is the process by which power is developed or gained by children and young people themselves. It has been argued that this would mean that young people get the opportunity to break 'the internal bridles and perceived powerlessness which underpin their sense of self and guide their actions in the world' (Young 1990: 88). Such empowerment is evident in the chapters in this volume – most particularly in the contributions by young people themselves (Chapters 9 and 19) and those that include significant contributions from young people (Chapters 5, 15 and 18).

Participation for change: Research leading to change

Research interests do not stand in a political or ideological vacuum; they are embedded in agendas that tend to shape and put demands on academic and practice communities. There is a need to acknowledge that both research topics and the current promotion in some circles of participatory research are dominated by specific paradigms and discourses with their own values, questions and categories – which are informed by political ideologies and policy agendas (Bourdieu 1977). Without acknowledgement of this, involving young people in research could face the danger of contributing to the maintenance of the dominant political discourses. Research that is promoted as participatory whilst in practice restricting young people's voices is tokenistic (Chapter 1). The increasing popularity of participatory research with young people in both academic and social policy arenas could create the danger of such tokenistic practice as more researchers and funders jump on the participatory bandwagon as a means of securing funding or of raising interest in their work, with little understanding of the wider issues at stake. Smith (Chapter 3) makes us aware that the distinction between 'participation' and 'participatory' approaches is blurred, and that involving children and young people does not guarantee that young people will be able to exert any degree of control on how the research is undertaken nor the outcomes of the research process.

Children are some of the highest users of health and social care services, and traditionally have had little or no input into national and local policies (Hill et al. 2004: 77–78). Whilst this is slowly changing (Burke 2008), there is still much to be done in creating more spaces for young people's participation directly in the development and delivery of services. Their involvement in research and evaluation is an important means of increasing their influence in such matters. Research involving children and young people seeks to offer them the opportunity to try out and experience new ways of influencing their lives through transforming power relationships, looking to share power between workers and service users, and challenging both to use it non-oppressively (Mullender and Ward 1991). This calls for the need to listen and nurture children and young people's critical voices, questioning who is the 'knower' and the 'questioner' within relationships (Chapter 8). Carter et al. (Chapter 19) state very clearly: 'Treat us young people as equals. Make sure we have real responsibilities that ... make sure we *can* make a difference to what is being done. I think that means you have to trust us'. Gaffney and Munro (Chapter 13) highlight that this can be achieved when young people are supported by adults in their involvement and have their voices heard. An ethic of reciprocity allows this trust and respect to be built over time. Fletcher and Stamp (Chapter 9) say they are not inclined to accept that the world is as it is, and nothing can be done about it. Smith (Chapter 3) suggests an important test of the level of participation achieved is, quite simply, whether or not children and young people got what they wanted out of the exercise.

Policy can be informed by children and young people's understandings of issues that affect them (such as poverty, discrimination, unemployment, abuse), and young people can have fundamental roles in the evaluation of services that are designed to create change in their lives by addressing such issues. The involvement of children in an evaluation of the Children's Commissioner in Wales is an example of this (Chapter 14), as are Chapters 9, 11, 13, 15 and 16. Policies or services developed with the express purpose of making young people's lives better, need to be based on evidence from young people and evaluated with their involvement. As Sabo Flores (Chapter 8) points out, asking those individuals who are most affected what their questions are regarding their life, their world, or the project they are involved in gives them a chance to present a framework that is authentic, real and useful as a benchmark against which to measure change. The challenge made by Skeels and Lewis (Chapter 4) is important when they ask whether participation in research is solely a means of understanding young people's lives better, or if it changes outcomes for young people more broadly.

There is a view that young people experience vulnerability (Young 1990). However, by defining young people as vulnerable, adults might be in danger of taking away young people's agency and constructing power relations with adults as the stronger protectors (Liamputtong 2007: 27). The overlap between the three themes of creative agency, power and change comes together in the accounts of young people and adults in this volume, showing that children and young people can perceive themselves to have strong agency, seeking to influence decisions that affect their lives. This challenges notions of young people being passive consumers of civic life (Ginwright et al. 2005) and powerless. Research involving young people is based on optimistic views of young people, which might sometimes be at odds with restrictions they actually face in other aspects of their lives due to their social and economic circumstances (Furlong and Cartmel 2006; Holland 2008). This should not diminish young people's belief in their capacity to act and have a voice, but needs to recognize the potential barriers they may face within the research process and when trying to pursue change. Sharing power is a form of reciprocity and an important means of equalizing power relations, which then supports the development of relational respect (Holland et al. 2000; Chapter 13).

In conclusion, we recognize that this volume is an unusual but exciting combination of accounts. It includes contributions from young people, academic researchers and practitioner-researchers. It includes those seeking to gain understanding of children and young people's experiences and perspectives, and those striving to create greater equality between young people and adults in the research process and young people undertaking their own research. We wanted to listen to the different voices and different players seeking to involve children and young people in research – all have a contribution to make. This volume is a testimony to how traditional ways of doing research can be challenged or changed. Whilst it is an optimistic volume, illustrating a range of ways of involving children and young people in health and social care research, it is not an entirely positive picture. This is for two main reasons: first, the examples are often isolated examples of good research practice in health and social care, not necessarily providing evidence of systemic change in the world of academic research or policy development or service delivery. Second, the contributors also recognize that many challenges still need to be addressed. The above considerations have major policy and practice implications. Based on researchers' and children and young people's experience, more can be done to create environments and structures that would better support the involvement of children and young people in research.

Apart from the obvious messages and recommendations that are set out in the chapters themselves, we believe there is a need for stronger alliances and partnerships between young people, practitioners and academics to influence policy and service provision. Therefore, it is important to build on the resourceful and creative ways in which many children and young people can be involved in research and overcome constraints and exert their agency. Young people need to have the resources, possibilities and the freedom to create, change and influence events within their lives. Involving children and young people in health and social care research can contribute to creating an environment in which agency is nurtured and children and young people can act upon their rights as creators and critical citizens, being able to have their voices heard and to have a part in decisions that affect their lives.

References

Agar, J. (2005) 'Before critical realism: Kantian empirical metaphysics'. *New Formations*, 56, 27–29.

Allaggia, R. (2004) 'Many ways of telling: expanding conceptualizations of child sexual abuse disclosure'. *Child Abuse and Neglect*, 28(11), 1213–27.

Alanen, L. (2001) 'Explorations in generational analysis'. In Alanen, L. and Mayall, B. (eds), *Conceptualizing Child–Adult Relations*. London: Routledge (pp.11–22).

Alanen, L. and Mayall, B. (eds) (2001) *Conceptualizing Child–Adult Relations*. London: Routledge.

Alderson, P. and Morrow, V. (2004) *Ethics, Social Research and Consulting with Children and Young People*. Ilford: Barnardos.

Alderson, P. and Morrow, V. (2011) *The Ethics of Research with Children and Young People. A Practical Handbook*. London: Sage.

Arches, J. and Fleming, J. (2007) '"Building our own monument": A social action group revisited'. *Practice*, 19(1), 33–45.

Ariès, P. (1979). *Centuries of Childhood: A Social History of Family Life*. London: Penguin.

Badham, B. (2009) *Involving Children and Young People – An Introduction*. Leicester: The National Youth Agency.

Badham, B. and Wade, H. (2005) *Hear by Right: Standards Framework for the Participation of Children and Young People*. Leicester: The National Youth Agency/LGA.

Barker, C. and Renold, E. (2000) '"I wanna tell you a story": Exploring the application of vignettes in qualitative research with children and young people'. *International Journal of Social Research Methodology*, 3(4), 207–27.

Barnardo's (2008) *Statement on Ethical Research Practice*, unpublished. Ilford: Barnardo's.

Barnes, C. (2003) 'What a difference a decade makes: Reflections on doing "emancipatory" disability research'. *Disability and Society*, 18, 3–17.

Barnes, P. and Sharp, B. (2004) *The RHP Companion to Outdoor Education*. University of Strathclyde, Russell House Publishing.

Beazley, H. et al. (2009) 'The twentieth anniversary of the UNCRC: Reflections on the rights based approach for research with children and young people in the south'. *Children's Geographies: Advancing Interdisciplinary Understanding of Younger People's Lives*, Issue No. 4.

Becker, H. (1963) *Outsiders: Studies in the Sociology of Deviance*. New York: Free Press. 1973 edn.

Becker, S. and Bryman, A. (2004) *Understanding Research for Social Policy and Practice: themes, methods and approaches*. Bristol: Policy Press.

Belbin, R.M. (2010) *The Management of Teams: Why they Succeed or Fail*. 3rd edn. Oxford: Butterworth-Heinemann.

Bennett, F. with Roberts, M. (2004) *From Input to Influence. Participatory Approaches to Research and Inquiry into Poverty*. York: Joseph Rowntree Trust.

Beresford, P. and Evans, C. (1999) 'Research note: Research and empowerment'. *British Journal of Social Work*, 29(5), 671–77.

Bevan Foundation (2011) 'Fair play for disabled children and young people in Wales'. www.bevanfoundation.org [accessed 8/4/2011].

Bevan, J., Butler, V. and Gibson, G. (2006) *St. Helen's School and Vincent Street Homezone Feasibility Study*. Cardiff: Barnardo's Cymru.

Big Lottery Fund (2010) *How to Involve Young People in your Project*. London: Big Lottery Fund.

Blackburn, H., Hanley, B. and Staley, K. (2010) *Turning the Pyramid upside Down: Examples of Public Involvement in Social Care Research*. Eastleigh: INVOLVE.

Bland, D., Carrington, S. and Brady, K. (2009) 'Young people, imagination and re-engagement in the middle years'. *Improving Schools*, 12, 237–48.

Boeck, T. et al. (2009) The impact of volunteering on social capital and community cohesion. Final Project Report for Project Re:Action. http://www.dmu.ac.uk/Images/Project%20Reaction%20final%20report_tcm6–61977.pdf [accessed 20/3/2011].

Boman, J. and Jevne, R. (2000) 'Ethical evaluation in qualitative research'. *Qualitative Health Research*, 10, 547–55.

Boote, J., Telford, R. and Cooper, C. (2002) 'Consumer involvement in health research: a review and research agenda'. *Health Policy*, 61, 213–36.

Booth, T. and Booth, W. (1996) 'Sounds of silence: Narrative research with inarticulate subjects'. *Disability and Society*, 11(1), 55–70.

Bourdieu, P. (1977) *Outline of a Theory of Practice*. Cambridge: Cambridge University Press.

Boyden, J. and Ennew, J. (1997) *Children in Focus – A Manual for Participatory Research with Children*. Stockholm, Sweden: Radda Barnen.

Boylan, J. and Dalrymple, J. (2009) *Understanding Advocacy for Children and Young People*. Maidenhead: Open University Press.

Briere J. (1996) *Trauma Symptom Checklist for Children* (TSCC). Professional Manual. Odessa, FL: Psychological Assessment Resources.

Briere J. et al. (2001) 'The trauma symptom checklist for young children (TSCYC): Reliability and association with abuse exposure in a multi-site study'. *Child Abuse and Neglect*, 25(8), 1001–14.

Brownlie, J., Anderson, S. and Ormston, R. (2006) *Children as Researchers*. Edinburgh: Scottish Executive Social Research.

Bruns, E.J. et al. and National Wraparound Initiative Advisory Group (2004) *Ten Principles of the Wraparound Process*. Portland, OR: National Wraparound Initiative, Research and Training Center on Family Support and Children's Mental Health, Portland State University. http://www.myd.govt.nz/working-with-young-people/ [accessed 20/6/2010].

Burke, T. (2008) *Listen and Change: A Guide to Children and Young People's Participation Rights*. London: Participation Works.

Butler, V. (2005) *Research Report of Phase One of the Generation 2020 Project*. Cardiff: Barnardo's Cymru.

——(2007) *Young People's Experiences of, and Solutions to, Identity Related Bullying*. Cardiff: Barnardo's Cymru.

CAHRV (2007) 'Perspectives and standards for good practice in data collection on interpersonal violence at European level'. *Co-ordination Action on Human Rights Violations Report* European Commission, 6th Framework Programme, project number 506348.

Cairns, L. (2001) 'Investing in children: Learning how to promote the rights of all children'. *Children and Society*, 15(5), 347–60.

Campbell, J. and Mackie, P.K. (2011) *Improving the System of Services for Vulnerable Young People: Research into an Approach to the Housing, Social Care and Support Needs of Young Homeless People and Young People Leaving Care in Torfaen*. Swansea: Shelter Cymru.

Card, E. et al. (1999). *Fare's Fair. The Investing in Children Transport Report*. Durham: Investing in Children Archive, Durham County Council.

Cawson, P. et al. (2000). *Child Maltreatment in the United Kingdom*. London: NSPCC.

Chambers, R. (1994) 'The origins and practice of participatory rural appraisal'. *World Development*, 22(7), 953–69.

Chartered Society of Physiotherapy (2005) SWOT analysis. http://www.csp.org.uk/documents/swot-analysis [accessed 29/12/2011].

Chawla, L. and Malone, K. (2002) 'Neighbourhood quality in children's eyes'. In Christensen, P. and O'Brien, M. (eds) *Children in the City: Home, Neighborhood, and Community*. London: Routledge (pp.118–41).

Checkoway, B. and Richards-Schuster, K. (2003) 'Youth participation in community evaluation research'. *American Journal of Evaluation*, 24(1), 21–33.

Chester, P., Kennedy, E.D. and Matthews, D.R. (2011) 'A novel approach to providing patients and the public with information about diabetes research'. *Diabetic Medicine*, 28(1), 303.

Child Rights Alliance (2009) UNCRC Articles. http://www.childrensrights.ie/index.php?q=childrens-rights-ireland/un-convention-rights-child [accessed 10/9/2011].

Christensen, P. and James, A. (2000) *Research with Children*. London: Falmer Press.

——(2008) *Research with Children: Perspectives and Practices*. 2nd edn. Abingdon: Routledge.

Christensen, P. and Prout, A. (2002) 'Working with ethical symmetry in social research with children'. *Childhood*, 9, 477–97.

Clacherty, G. and Kistner, J. (2001) 'Evaluating the Zimiseleni Researchers: Participatory research as intervention with "hard-to-reach" boys'. *PLA Notes*, 42, 29–33.

Clapham, D. et al. (2010) *Young People and Housing in 2020: Identifying Key Drivers for Change*. York: Joseph Rowntree Foundation.

Clark, A. and Moss, P. (2001) *Listening to Young Children: The Mosaic Approach*. London: National Children's Bureau.

Clark, A., McQuail, S. and Moss, P. (2003) *Exploring the Field of Listening to and Consulting with Young Children*. London: HMSO.

Cohen, E., Mackenzie, R.G. and Yates, G.L. (1991) 'HEADSS, a psychosocial risk assessment instrument: Implications for designing effective intervention programmes for runaway youth'. *Journal of Adolescent Health*, 12, 539–44.

Connors, C. and Stalker, K. (2003) *The Views and Experiences of Disabled Children and their Siblings: A Positive Outlook*. London: Jessica Kingsley Publishers.

Cooperrider, D. and Whitney, D. (2005) *Appreciative Inquiry: A Positive Revolution in Change*. San Francisco, CA: Berrett-Koehler.

Corsaro, W. (1997) *The Sociology of Childhood*. Thousand Oaks, CA: Pine Forge.

——(2005) *The Sociology of Childhood*. Thousand Oaks, CA: Sage.

Cree, V., Kay, H. and Tisdall, K. (2002) 'Research with children: Sharing the dilemmas'. *Child and Family Social Work*, 7, 47–56.

Creswell, J.W. and Clark, V.L.P. (2007) *Designing and Conducting Mixed Methods Research*. London: Sage.

Crowley, A. and Skeels, A. (2009) 'Getting the measure of children and young people's participation'. In Percy-Smith, B. and Thomas, N. (eds) *A Handbook of Children and Young People's Participation. Perspectives from Theory and Practice*. London: Routledge.

Cullen, D. and Lane, M. (2003) *Child Care Law: A Summary of the Law in England and Wales*. 4th edn. London: British Association of Adoption and Fostering.

Curtis, L. et al. (2004) 'Consulted but not heard: A qualitative study of young people's views of their local health service'. *Health Expectations*, 7(2), 149–56.

Daniels, P. (2011) *Report to the DECIPHer Steering Group on the ALPHA Group*. Unpublished.

Darbyshire, P., MacDougall, C. and Schiller, W. (2005) 'Multiple methods in qualitative research with children: More insight or just more?'. *Qualitative Research*, 5(4), 417–36.

David, M., Edwards, R. and Alldred, P. (2001) 'Children and school-based research: "Informed consent" or "educated consent"?'. *British Educational Research Journal*, 27(3), 347–65.

Davis, J. (2007) *Evaluation Report for Investing in Children*. Edinburgh: University of Edinburgh.

——(2000) 'Methodological and ethical challenges associated with child self-report of maltreatment: solutions implemented by the LongSCAN Consortium'. *Journal of Interpersonal Violence*, 15(7), 760–75.

Davis, J., Watson, N. and Cunningham-Burley, S. (2008) 'Disabled children, ethnography and unspoken understandings: The collaborative construction of diverse identities'. In Christensen, P. and James, A. (eds) *Research with Children: Perspectives and Practices*. Abingdon: Routledge.

Dawes Knight, E. et al. (2006) 'Reporting participants in research studies to child protection services: limited risk to attrition'. *Child Maltreatment*, 11(3), 257–62.

DCSF (2010) *Working Together to Safeguard Children*. 3rd edn. London: DCFS. http://www.dfe.gov.uk.

DECIPHer (2009) *DECIPHer Public Involvement Strategy 2009–2013*. http://www.decipher.uk.net/en/content/cms/about-decipher/public-involvement/ [accessed 15/12/2011].

Delgado, M. (2006) *Designs and Methods for Youth-Led Research*, London: Sage.

Department of Health (1999) *Patient and Public Involvement in the New NHS*. London: HMSO.

——(2005) *Research Governance Framework for Health and Social Care*. 2nd edn. http://www.oncoreuk.org/downloads/DOH.pdf [accessed 10/9/2011].

——(2007) You're welcome quality criteria: making health services young people friendly. http://www.dh.gov.uk/en/Publicationsandstatistics/Publications/PublicationsPolicyAndGuidance/DH_073586 [accessed 10/9/2011].

Devine, D. (2002) 'Children's citizenship and the structuring of adult–child relations in the primary school'. *Childhood*, 9(3), 303–21.

Duncan, R. et al. (2009) 'Is my mum going to hear this?: Methodological and ethical challenges in qualitative health research with young people'. *Social Science and Medicine*, 69, 1691–99.

Durkheim, E. (1979) Childhood: 1911. In Pickering, W.F. (ed.) *Durkheim: Essays on Morals and Education*. London: Routledge.

Dynamix (2002) *Participation: Spice it Up!* Cardiff: Save the Children Fund.

——(2009) *Participation: Young Spice*. Cardiff: Welsh Assembly Government.

Ellis, C. and Flaherty, M.G. (1992) 'An agenda for the interpretation of lived experience'. In Ellis, C. and Flaherty, M.G. (eds) *Investigating Subjectivity*. London: Sage (pp. 1–16).

Ellis, J. (2004) *Preventing Violence against Women and Girls. A Study of Educational Programmes for Children and Young People*. London: WOMANKIND Worldwide.

Ellis, J. (2006) *Children and the Prevention of Domestic Violence through School-Based Work*. Unpublished PhD thesis. Coventry: University of Warwick.

Ennew, J. (2000) 'How can we define citizenship in childhood?'. Harvard Center for Population and Development Studies. Working paper series 10(12). Cambridge, MA: Harvard School of Public Health.

ESRC (2010) *Framework for Research Ethics*. Swindon: ESRC. www.esrc.ac.uk.

EYSIP (2001) *Action Research Toolkit*. Edinburgh: Edinburgh Youth Social Inclusion Partnership.

Farrell, A., Tayler, C. and Tennent, L. (2004) 'Building social capital in early childhood education and care: An Australian study'. *British Educational Research Journal*, 30(5), 623–32.

Faulkner, K. (2009) 'Presentation and representation: Youth participation in ongoing public decision making projects'. *Childhood*, 16, 89–104. DOI:1177/090768208101692.

Fettersman, D.M. and Wandersman, A. (eds) (2005) *Empowerment Evaluation Principles in Practice*. New York: Guilford Press.

Finkelhor, D. (2008) *Childhood Victimization*. Oxford: Oxford University Press.

Finkelhor, D. et al. (2005) 'The juvenile victimization questionnaire: reliability, validity and national norms'. *Child Abuse and Neglect*, 29, 383–412.

——(2009) 'Violence, abuse, and crime exposure in a national sample of children and youth'. *Pediatrics*, 124(5), 1411–23.

Fitzgerald, R. et al. (2010) 'Children's participation as a struggle over recognition'. In Percy-Smith, B. and Thomas, N. (eds) *A Handbook of Children and Young People's Participation: Perspectives From Theory and Practice*. Abingdon: Routledge.

Fleming, J. (2010) 'Young people's involvement in research – still a long way to go?'. *Qualitative Social Work*, 10(2), 207–23.

Fleming, J., Goodman-Chong, H. and Skinner, A. (2009) 'Experiences of peer evaluation of the leicester teenage pregnancy prevention strategy'. *Children and Society*, 23(4), 279–90.

Fleming, J. and Hudson, N. (2009) 'Young people and research: Participation in practice'. In J. Wood and J. Hine (eds) *Work with Young People: Theory and Policy for Practice*. London: Sage (pp.114–27).

Fleming, J. and Ward, D. (2004) 'Methodology and practical application of the social action research model'. In Maggs-Rapport, F. (ed.) *New Qualitative Research Methodologies in Health and Social Care: Putting Ideas into Practice*. London: Routledge.

Foote Whyte, W. (1943) *Street Corner Society*. Chicago, IL: Chicago University Press. 1993 edn.

France, A. (2000) *Involving Young People in Research Projects*. York: Joseph Rowntree Foundation.

Franks, M. (2011) 'Pockets of participation: Revisiting child-centred participation research'. *Children and Society*, 25, 15–25.

Fraser, N. (2000) 'Rethinking recognition'. *New Left Review*, 3, 107–20.

Fraser, S. et al. (2004) *Doing Research with Children and Young People*. London: Sage.

Funky Dragon (2007) *Our Rights, Our Story*. http://www.funkydragon.org/attachments/article/98/Our%20Rights%20Our%20Story.pdf [accessed 14/9/2011].

Furlong, A. and Cartmel, F. (2006) *Young people and social change: Individualism and risk in late modernity*. Buckingham: Open University Press.

——(2011) *Children as Researchers Resource Pack*. Swansea: Funky Dragon.

Gallacher, L. and Gallagher, M. (2008) 'Methodological immaturity in childhood research? Thinking through "participatory methods"'. *Childhood*, 15(4), 499–516.

Gawler, M. (2005) *Useful Tools for Engaging Young People in Participatory Evaluation*. Geneva: UNICEF.

Giddens, A. (1984) *The Constitution of Society: Outline of the Theory of Structuration*. Cambridge: Polity.

Ginwright, S., Cammarota, J. and Noguera, P. (2005) 'Youth, social justice, and communities: Toward a theory of urban youth policy'. *Social Justice*, 32(3), 24–40.

Goffman, E. (1961) *Asylums: Essays on the Social Situation of Mental Patients and Other Inmates*. New York: Anchor Books.

Gong, J. and Wright, D. (2007) 'The context of power: Young people as evaluators'. *American Journal of Evaluation*, 28, 327.

Goode, W.J. and Hatt, P.K. (1952) *Methods in Social Research*. New York: McGraw-Hill.

Govan, H. et al. (1998) *Best Practice for Community Participation for National Parks*. Edinburgh: Scottish Natural Heritage Review (p.107).

Greene, A. (2004) 'Democratic health care and disciplinary closure: Working in a multidisciplinary health-care team with adolescent diabetes'. *Anthropological Journal on European Cultures*, 13, 111–33.

Hallett, C. and Prout, A. (2003) *Hearing the Voices of Children: Social Policy for a New Century*. London: Falmer Press.

Hamby, S. et al. (2004a) *The Comprehensive JVQ Administration and Scoring Manual*. Durham, NH: University of New Hampshire, Crimes Against Children Research Center.

——(2004b) *The Juvenile Victimization Questionnaire (JVQ): Caregiver Version*. Durham, NH: University of New Hampshire, Crimes against Children Research Center.

Hammersley, M. (2009) 'Why critical realism fails to justify critical social research'. *Methodological Innovations Online*, 4(2), 1–11.

Hanley, B., Bradburn, J. and Barnes, M. (2004) *Involving the Public in NHS, Public Health and Social Care Research: Briefing Notes for Researchers*. 2nd edn. Eastleigh: INVOLVE Support Unit.

Harcourt, D., Perry, B. and Waller, T (eds) (2011) *Researching Young Children's Perspectives. Debating the Ethics and Dilemmas of Educational Research with Children*. London: Routledge.

Hardt, J. and Rutter, M. (2004) 'Validity of adult retrospective reports of adverse childhood experiences: review of the evidence'. *Journal of Child Psychology and Psychiatry* 45(2), 260–73.

Hart, R. (1992) *Children's Participation from Tokenism to Citizenship*. Florence, Italy: UNICEF Innocenti Research Centre.

——(1997) *Children's Participation: The Theory and Practice of Involving Young Citizens in Community Development and Environmental Care*. London: Earthscan.

HASCAS (2008) *Quality Standards for Children and Young People's Participation in CAMHS*. http://www.hascas.org.uk/pdf_files/HASCASselfassessCAMHSparticipation.pdf (accessed 15/9/2011].

Heath, S., Brooks, R., Cleaver, E. and Ireland, E. (2009) *Researching Young People's Lives*. London: Sage.

Hicks, C. (2009) *Research Methods for Clinical Therapists*. 5th edn. London: Churchill Livingstone.

Hill, M. (1997) 'Participatory research with children'. *Child and Family Social Work*, 2, 171–83.

Hill, M. (2006) 'Children's voices on ways of having a voice: Children's and young people's perspectives on methods used in research and consultation'. *Childhood*, 13(1), 69–89.

Hill, M. et al. (2004) 'Moving the participation agenda forward'. *Children and Society*, 18(2), 77–97.

Hill, M., Laybourn, A. and Borland, M. (1996) 'Engaging with primary-aged children about their emotions and well-being: methodological considerations'. *Children and Society*, 10, 129–44.

Hodge, S. (2005) 'Participation, discourse and power: a case study in service user involvement'. *Critical Social Policy*, 25:164 DOI: 10.1177/0261018305051324

Holland, J. et al. (2000) 'Catching on, wising up and learning from your mistakes: Young people's accounts of moral development'. *International Journal of Children's Rights*, 8, 271–94.

Holland, S., Renold, E., Ross, N. and Hillman, A. (2008) *Rights, 'right on' or the right thing to do? A critical exploration of young people's engagement in participative social work research*. ESRC National Centre for Research Methods Working Paper series.

Honneth, A. (2004) 'Recognition and respect'. *Acta Sociologica*, 47(4), 351–64.

Hood, S., Kelley, P., Mayall, B. (1996) 'Children as research subjects: a risky enterprise'. *Children and Society*, 10, 117–128.

Horwath, J. et al. (2011) *You Respond*. Sheffield: University of Sheffield.

Howard, C. (2011) *Pupils should be involved in interviewing teachers*. http://osiriseducational.co.uk/osirisblog/pupils-should-be-involved-in-interviewing-teachers [accessed 22 July 2011].

HMSO (2004) *The Children Act 1989*. London: HMSO.

——(2006) *Employment Equality (Age) Regulations (2006)*. London: HMSO.

Hunleth, J. (2011) 'Beyond on or with: Questioning power dynamics and knowledge production in "child-oriented" research methodology'. *Childhood*, 18(1), 81–93.

Hunt, L. (2011) 'Welsh children want fair play'. *Physiotherapy Frontline*, 17(3). London: Elsevier.

IDeA (2010) *Involving Young People in the Recruitment of Social Care Staff*. http://www.idea.gov.uk/idk/core/page.do?pageId=22019574 [accessed 22/7/2011].

Improve Encylopedia. http://improvencyclopedia.org [accessed 16/1/2012].

Integrated Research System. https://www.myresearchproject.org.uk [accessed 20/12/2010].

James, A. (2007) 'Giving voice to children's voices: Practices and problems, pitfalls and potentials'. *American Anthropologist*, 1009(2), 261–72.

James, A. and James, A. (2008) *Key Concepts in Childhood Studies*. London: Sage.

James, A. and Prout, A. (eds). (1997) *Constructing and Reconstructing Childhood: Contemporary Issues in the Sociological Study of Childhood*. London: Falmer Press.

James, A., Jenks, C. and Prout, A. (1998) *Theorising Childhood*. Cambridge: Polity Press.

Jelsma, J. and Scott, D. (2011) 'Impact of using the ICF framework as an assessment tool for students in paediatric physiotherapy: a preliminary study'. *Physiotherapy*, 97, 47–54.

Johnson, V. (2010) 'Rights through evaluation and understanding children's realities'. In Percy-Smith, B. and Thomas, N. (eds) *A Handbook of Children and Young People's Participation: Perspectives from Theory and Practice*. London: Routledge.

Jones, A. (2000) 'Exploring young people's experience of immigration controls: The search for an appropriate methodology'. In Humphries, B. (ed.) *Research in Social Care and Social Welfare*. London: Jessica Kingsley.

Jones, A. (2004) 'Involving children and young people as researchers'. In Fraser, S. et al. (eds) (2004) *Doing Research with Children and Young People*. London: Sage (pp. 113–31).

Kellet, M. (2005a) *Children as Active Researchers: A New Research Paradigm for the 21st Century?* Southampton: ESRC National Centre for Research Methods: NCRM Methods Review Papers.

——(2005b) *How to Develop Children as Researchers: A Step by Step Guide to Teaching the Research Process*. London: Sage.

——(2009a) 'Children and young people's participation'. In Montgomery, H. and Kellet, M. (eds) *Children and Young People's Worlds*. Milton Keynes: Open University Press.

——(2009b) 'Children as researchers: What can we learn from them about the impact of poverty on literacy opportunities?'. *International Journal of Inclusive Education*, 13(4), 395–408.

——(2010) *Rethinking Children and Research – Attitudes in Contemporary Society*. London: Continuum.

Kellett, M. et al. (2004) 'Just teach us the skills please, we'll do the rest: Empowering ten-year-olds as active researchers'. *Children and Society*, 18, 329–43.

Kilpatrick, R. et al. (2007) 'If I am brutally honest, research has never appealed to me ... The problems and successes of a peer research project'. *Educational Action Research*, 15(3), 351–69.

King, P.E. et al. (2005) 'Positive youth development (PYD): Is there a nomological network of concepts used in the developmental literature?'. *Applied Developmental Science*, 9(4), 216–28.

Kirby, P. (1999) *Involving Young Researchers. How to Enable Young People to Design and Conduct Research*. London: Joseph Rowntree Foundation and Save the Children.

Kirby, P. (2004) *A Guide to Actively Involving Young People in Research: For Researchers, Research Commissioners and Managers*. Eastleigh: INVOLVE.

Kirby, P. et al. (2003) *Building a Culture of Participation: Involving Children and Young People in Policy, Service Planning, Delivery and Evaluation*. Research Report. London: DFES.

Kitzinger, J. (1995) 'Introducing focus groups'. *British Medical Journal*, 311, 299–302.

Kitzinger, J. and Barbour, R. (1999) 'The challenge and promise of focus groups'. In Barbour, R. and Kitzinger, J. (eds) *Developing Focus Group Research: Politics, Theory and Practice*. London: Sage (pp.1–20).

Kodish, E. (2005) *Ethics and Research with Children*. Oxford: Open University Press.

Lansdown, G. (2001) *Promoting Children's Participation in Democratic Decision-Making*. Innocenti Insight Report. Florence, Italy: UNICEF.

Lawton, J. et al. (2003) 'Participating in the United Kingdom Prospective Diabetes Study (UKPDS): A qualitative study of patient's experiences'. *British Journal of General Practice*, 53, 394–98.

Learner, R. (2007) *The Good Teen: Rescuing Adolescence from the Myths of the Storm and Stress Years*. New York: Three Rivers Press.

Lewis, S. Ding, Kellet, M. and Robinson, C. (eds) (2004) *Doing Research with Children and Young People*. London: Sage.

Liamputtong, P. (2007) *Researching the Vulnerable: A Guide to Sensitive Research Methods*. London: Sage.

Lightfoot, J. and Sloper, P. (2002) 'Involving young people in health service development'. *Research Works*, Vol. 4. York: University of York.

Local Government Association (2007) *Get in on the Act: The Local Government and Public Involvement in Health Act 2007*. London: LGA.

Lowes, L. and Hulatt, I. (eds) (2005) *Involving Service Users in Health and Social Care Research*. London: Routledge.

Mackie, P.K. (2008) *Room for Improvement: Research into the Accommodation and Support Needs of Vulnerable Young People in Cardiff*. Cardiff: Cardiff Children and Young People's Partnership.

Mackie, P.K. and Russell, A. (2009) *Developing Temporary Accommodation Standards for Homeless Young People: A Youth-Centred Approach*. Swansea: Shelter Cymru.

Mahon A. et al. (1996) 'Researching children: Methods and ethics'. *Children and Society*, 10, 145–54.

Matthews, D, Kennedy, E. and Chester, P. (2008) 'Giving patients a voice'. *Clinical Discovery*, 16 June.

Matthews, D.R. et al. (2009) 'Clinical research in diabetes: A practical resource to assist with participant understanding and recruitment'. *Practical Diabetes International*, 26(6), 1–2

Mauthner, M. (1997) 'Methodological aspects of collecting data from children: lessons from three research projects'. *Children and Society*, 11, 16–28.

Mauthner, M. et al. (2002) *Ethics in Qualitative Research*. London: Sage.

Mayall, B. (2002) *Towards a Sociology for Childhood: Thinking from Children's Lives*. London: Open University Press.

——(ed.) (1994) *Children's Childhoods: Observed and Experienced*. London: Falmer Press.

McBurney, H. et al. (2003) 'A qualitative analysis of the benefits of strength training for young people with Cerebral Palsy'. *Developmental Medicine and Child Neurology*, 45, 658–63.

McDermott, L. et al. (2006) 'International food advertising, pester power and its effects'. *International Journal of Advertising*, 25(4), 513–40.

McLaughlin, H. (2005) 'Young service users as co-researchers: Methodological problems and possibilities'. *Qualitative Social Work*, 4, 211.

——(2006) 'Involving young service users as co-researchers: Possibilities, benefits and costs'. *British Journal of Social Work*, 36, 1395–1410.

Medical Research Council (2004, revised 2007) *MRC Ethics Guide: Medical Research Involving Children*. London: Medical Research Council.

Mertens, D.M. (2009) *Transformative Research and Evaluation*. New York: Guildford Press.

Ministry of Youth Affairs (2002) *Youth Development Strategy Aotearoa: Action for Child and Youth Development*. Wellington, NZ: Ministry of Youth Affairs. http://www.pcc.govt.nz/DownloadFile/Community/Youth-Development/National-Youth-Development-Strategy-Aotearoa [accessed 28/9/2010].

Mirlees-Black, C. (1995) *Estimating the Extent of Domestic Violence: Findings from the 1992 British Crime Survey*. London: Home Office.

Molina, G. et al. (2009) 'Child-friendly participatory research tools'. *Participatory Learning and Action*, 60(1), 160–66.

Morris, J. (1998) *Don't Leave Us Out: Involving Disabled Children and Young People with Communication Impairments*. York: Joseph Rowntree Foundation.

Morrow, V. (2002) 'Improving the neighbourhood for children'. In Christensen, P. and O'Brien, M. (eds) *Children in the City: Home, Neighbourhood and Community*. London: Routledge.

——(2009) 'The ethics of social research with children and families in young lives: Practical experiences'. Working Paper 53, *Young Lives: An International Study of Child Poverty*. Oxford: DID.

Morrow, V. and Richards, M. (1996) 'The ethics of social research with children: An overview'. *Children and Society*, 10, 90–105.

Morse, J.M. (2007) 'Ethics in action: Ethical principles for doing qualitative health research'. *Qualitative Health Research*, 17, 1003–5.

Mudaly, N. and Goddard, C. (2009) 'The ethics of involving children who have been abused in child abuse research'. *International Journal of Children's Rights*, 12, 261–81.

Mullender, A. and Ward, D. (1991) *Self-Directed Groupwork: users take action for empowerment*. London: Whiting and Birch.

Murray, C. (2006) 'Peer led focus groups and young people'. *Children and Society*, 20, 273–86.

National Assembly for Wales (2004) *Children and Young People's Policy*. http://www.assemblywales.org/tb-07-005.pdf [accessed 13/9/2011].

National Children's Bureau (2003) *Guidelines for Research: National Children's Bureau*. London: National Children's Bureau. http://www.ncb.org.uk/media/434791/guidelines_for_research_with_cyp.pdf [accessed 11/1/2012].

National Evaluation of the Children's Fund (2010) *The Evaluator's Cookbook*. Birmingham: NECF.

National Institute for Social Care and Health Research. https://www.nischr.org.uk [accessed 8/4/2011].

Newman, K. (2007) *Understanding Children's Communication of Their Emotional and Psychological Well Being*. Cardiff: Ifanc.

Nunn, A.J. (2003) 'Making medicines that children will take'. *Archive of Disability in Childhood*, 88, 369–71.

Oakley, A. (1974). *Housewife*. London: Allen Lane.

Oakley, A. (1994) *Women and Children First and Last: Parallels and Differences Between Childhoods Observed and Experienced*. London: Falmer Press.

——(1981) 'Interviewing women: A contradiction in terms'. In Roberts, H. (ed.) *Doing Feminist Research*. London: Routledge (pp.30–61).

Office for National Statistics (2010) 'Internet Access 2010. Households and individuals'. *Statistical Bulletin*, 27 August.

Office for Public Management (2010) *Creative Influence: Research Led by Young People*. London: OPM.

Office of the Children's Commissioner for England (2007) *Pushed into the Shadows. Young People's Experience of Adult Mental Health Facilities*. www.childrenscommissioner.gov.uk [accessed 31/3/2011].

——(2008) *Out of the Shadows?* (A review of the Responses to Recommendations made in *Pushed into the Shadows: Young People's Experience of Adult Mental Health Facilities*). www.childrenscommissioner.gov.uk [accessed 31/3/2011].

Office of the United Nations High Commissioner for Human Rights (OHCHR), *Convention on the Rights of the Child* (1989). http://www2.ohchr.org/english/law/pdf/crc.pdf [accessed 12/7/2011].

O'Kane, C. (2008) 'The development of participatory techniques: facilitating children's views about decisions which affect them. Research with children: perspectives and practices'. In Christensen, P. and James, A. (eds), *Research With Children: Perspectives and Practice*. London, Falmer Press: 136–159.

Okely, J. (1992) 'Participatory experience and embodied knowledge'. In Okely, J. and Callaway, H. (eds) *Anthropology and Autobiography*. London: Routledge.

Ortiz, N. (2007) 'Speaking out in the 21st century'. *SCILife Archives*, 4(3), 7. http://issuu.com/scilife/docs/scilife16/ [accessed 4/12/2012].

——(2008) Foreword. In Sabo Flores, K. *Youth Participatory Evaluation: Strategies for Engaging Youth*. San Francisco, CA: John Wiley.

Packham, C. (2000) 'Community auditing: Appropriate research methods for effective youth and community work intervention'. In Humphries, B. (ed.) *Research in Social Care and Social Welfare*. London: Jessica Kingsley.

Pain, R. et al. (2002) '"Hard to reach" young people and community safety: A model for participatory research and consultation'. http://www.geography.dur.ac.uk/information/staff/personal/pain/word%20documents/The%20very%20final%20report.doc [accessed 30/8/2011].

Partnerships against Domestic Violence (2000) *Working with Children and Young People: Key Findings*. Barton, ACT: Office for the Status of Women. http://ofw.facs.gov.au/downloads/pdfs/d_v/work_with_children_young.pdf [accessed 12/6/2004].

Parton, N. (1985) *The Politics of Child Abuse*. Basingstoke: Macmillan.

Patton, M.Q. (2011) *Developmental Evaluation: Applying Complexity Concepts to Enhance Innovation and Use*. New York: Guilford Press.

Pedal Power. www.cardiffpedalpower.org.uk [accessed 11/4/11].

Percy-Smith, B. and Thomas, N. (eds) (2010) *A Handbook of Children and Young People's Participation*. Abingdon: Routledge.

Petrie, S., Fiorelli, L. and O'Donell, K. (2006) 'If we help you what will change? Participatory research with young people'. *Journal of Social Welfare and Family Law*, 28(1), 31–46.

Pickering, D.M. and Busse, M.E. (2010) 'An audit of disabled children's services – What value is MPOC-SP?'. *Clinical Audit*, 2, 13–22.

Pittman, K., Irby, M. and Ferber, T. (2000) 'Unfinished business: Further reflections on a decade of promoting youth development'. International Youth Foundation. In Public/Private Ventures (2000) *Youth Development: Issues, Challenges and Directions*.

Postman, N. (1982). *The Disappearance of Childhood*. New York: Delacorte Press.

Pountney, T. (2007) *Physiotherapy for Children*. Philadelphia, PA: Elsevier, Butterworth Heinemann.

Powell, M. (2011) *International Literature Review: Ethical Issues in Undertaking Research with Children and Young People*. Coffs Harbour, NSW, Australia: Southern Cross University. http://epubs.scu.edu.au/ccyp_pubs/40 [accessed 30/8/2011].

Price, K. (2011) '"KICk-OFF": A structured education programme for children with diabetes based on the adult DAFNE course'. www.kick-off.org.uk [accessed 22/7/2011].

Prout, A. (2005) *The Future of Childhood: Towards the Interdisciplinary Study of Children*. London: Falmer Press.

Prout, A. and James, A. (1990) 'A new paradigm for the sociology of childhood? Provenance, promise and problems'. In James, A. and Prout, A. (eds) *Constructing and Reconstructing Childhood: Contemporary Issues in the Sociological Study of Childhood*. London: Falmer Press (pp.7–33).

Prout, A. and Tisdall, E.K.M. (2006) 'Conclusion: Social inclusion, the welfare state and understanding children's participation'. In Tisdall, E., Davis, J., Hill, M. and

Prout, A. (eds) *Children, Young People and Social Inclusion*. Bristol: Policy Press (pp.235–46).

Pryse, S. (2009) *How to: Remunerate and Reward Children and Young People's Involvement*. London: Participation Works, National Children's Bureau.

Punch, S. (2002) 'Research with children: The same or different from research with adults?' *Childhood*, 9(3), 321–41.

Qvortrup, J. (1985) 'Placing children in the division of labour'. In Close, P. and Collins, P. (eds) *Family and Economy in Modern Society*. London: Macmillan (pp.129–45).

——(1987) Introduction. *International Journal of Sociology*, 17(1), 1–26.

Qvortrup, J. et al. (eds) (1994) *Childhood Matters: Social Theory, Practice and Politics*. Aldershot: Avebury.

Radcliffe, J. and Campbell, J.A. (2010) *Living in Wales: The Housing and Homelessness Experiences of Central and East European Migrant Workers*. Cardiff: Shelter Cymru.

Radford, L. et al. (2011) *Child Abuse and Neglect in the UK Today*. London: NSPCC. http://www.nspcc.org.uk/childstudy [accessed 16/12/2011].

Royal College of Nursing (2007) *Research Ethics: RCN Guidance for Nurses*. London: RCN.

Read, J., Clements, L. and Ruebain, D. (2006) *Disabled Children and the Law: Research and Good Practice*. London: Jessica Kingsley.

Reinharz, S. (1992) *Feminist Methods in Social Research*. New York: Oxford University Press.

Renold, E., Holland, S., Ross, N.J. and Hillman, A. (2008) 'Becoming participant: Problematising "informed consent" in participatory research with young people in care'. *Qualitative Social Work*, &(4), 427–47.

Research and Development Directorate, DoH (2005) *Best Research for Best Health: A New National Health Research Strategy*. London: DH Publications.

Ribbens, J. (1989) 'Interviewing – An "unnatural situation"?'. *Women's Studies International Forum*, 12(6): 579–92.

Roberts, H. (2008) 'Listening to children: and hearing them'. In Christensen, P. and James, A. (eds) *Research with Children: Perspectives and Practices*. Abingdon: Routledge.

Rosenfeld, S. et al. (1996) 'Primary care experiences and preferences of urban youth'. *Journal of Pediatric Health Care*, 10, 151–60.

Russell, C., Touchard, D. and Porter, M. (2002) 'What's rapport got to do with it? The practical accomplishment of fieldwork relations between young female researchers and socially marginalised older men'. *The Qualitative Report*, 7(1). http://www.nova.edu/ssss/QR/QR7–1/russell.html [accessed 3/7/2011].

Sabo Flores, K. (2008) *Youth Participatory Evaluation: Strategies for Engaging Youth*. San Fransisco, CA: John Wiley.

Saleebey, D. (1996) 'The strengths perspective in social work practice: Extensions and cautions'. *Social Work*, 41(3), 296–305.

Sayer, A. (2003) *Method in Social Science: a Realist Approach*. Taylor & Francis e-library. http://books.google.co.uk/books/about/Method_in_social_science.html?id=q31fv7rFujgC&redir_esc=y [accessed 29/12/2011].

Save the Children (2007) National Children and Young People's Participation Standards for Wales. http://www.participationworkerswales.org.uk/resources.aspx [accessed 19/9/2011].

——(2009) 'Making child rights a reality'. Policy Brief, Save the Children. http://www.savethechildren.net/alliance/what_we_do/child_rights/20anniversary.html [accessed 14/9/2011].

——(2009) *Your Health, Your Rights* (leaflet). http://www.savethechildren.org.uk/en/docs/PDF_Health_Leaflet.pdf [accessed 19/9/2011].

Schäfer, N. and Yarwood, R. (2008) 'Involving young people as researchers: Uncovering multiple power relations among youths'. *Children's Geographies*, 6(2), 121–35.

Sharpe, D. (2009) The value of young people doing research: Where do young people's voices count? *Research, Policy and Planning: The Journal of the Social Services Research Group*, 27(2), 97–106.

Sharpe, D. (2012) 'Methodological challenges of youth-led research'. In Heath, S. and Walker, C. (eds) *Innovations in Youth Research*. London: Palgrave.

Sharpe, D., Jessiman, T. and Long, A. (2010) *Young Researcher Network Toolkit*. 2nd edn. Leicester, LGA & NYA.

Shaw, C., Brady, L.-M. and Davey, C. (2011) *Guidelines for Research with Children and Young People*. London: NCB Research Centre. http://www.ncb.org.uk/media/434791/guidelines_for_research_with_cyp.pdf [accessed 28/12/2011].

Sheffield Hallam University (2011) *Peer Research Methodology*. http://www.shu.ac.uk/_assets/pdf/hccj-ResearchMethodology.pdf [accessed 3/5/2011].

Shemmings, D. (2000) '"Professionals"' attitudes to children's participation in decision-making: Dichotomous accounts and doctrinal contests'. *Child and Family Social Work*, 5, 235–43.

Shenton, F. (1999) *Evaluation of County Durham 'Investing in Children' Initiative*. Durham: University of Durham.

Shier, H. (2001) 'Pathways to participation: openings, opportunities and obligations A new model for enhancing children's particpation in decision-making, in line with Article 12.1 of the United Nations Convention on the Rights of the Child.' *Children and Society*, 15(2): 107–117.

Shufflebeam, D.L. and Shinkfield, A.J. (1985) *Systematic Evaluation*. Boston: Kluwer-Nijhoff.

Silverman, D. (2006) *Interpreting Qualitative data*. London: Sage publications.

Sinclair, R. (2004) 'Participation in practice: Making it meaningful, effective and sustainable'. *Children and Society*, 18, 106–18.

Sinha, S., Uppal, S. and Pryce, A. (2006) *Exploring Sexual Health Needs amongst Unaccompanied Asylum-Seekers in Hackney*. London: Hackney Children and Young People's Services and City University.

Skelton, T. (2008) 'Research with children and young people: Exploring the tensions between ethics, competence and participation'. *Children's Geographies*, 6(1), 21–36.

Sloper, P. and Lightfoot, J. (2003) 'Involving disabled and chronically ill children and young people in health service development'. *Child Care, Health Development*, 29(1), 15–20.

Smith, L.J. (2008) 'How ethical is ethical research? Recruiting marginalized, vulnerable groups into health services research'. *Journal of Advanced Nursing*, 62(2), 248–57.

Smith, R. (2010) *A Universal Child*. Basingstoke: Palgrave.

Smith, R., Monaghan, M. and Broad, B. (2002) 'Involving young people as co-researchers'. *Qualitative Social Work*, 1(2), 191–207.

Spicer, N. and Evans, R. (2005) 'Developing children and young people's participation in strategic processes: The experience of the Children's Fund Initiative'. *Social Policy and Society*, 5(2), 177–88.

Spyrou, S. (2011) 'The limits of children's voices: From authenticity to critical, reflexive representation'. *Childhood*, 18(2), 151–65.

Staples, L.(1990) 'Powerful ideas about empowerment'. *Administration in Social Work*, 14(2), 29–41.

Tay, R. (2010) *Involving Young People in Recruitment and Selection Devon* CAMHS. http://www.vik.org.uk/wp-content/uploads/2010/12/Devon-case-study-recruitment-Robin-Tay-new.pdf [acessed 22/7/2011].

Taylor, C. (1995) *Philosophical Arguments*. London: Harvard University Press.

Taylor, N.F., Dodd, K.J. and Graham H.K. (2004) 'Test-re-test reliability of hand-held dynamometric strength testing in young people with cerebral palsy'. *Archives of Physical Medicine and Rehabilitation*, 1, 77–80.

Telford, R., Boote, J.D. and Cooper, C.L. (2004) 'What does it mean to involve consumers successfully in NHS research? A consensus study'. *Health Expectations*, 7, 209–20.

Thiara, R.K. and Ellis, J. (2005) *WDVF London-Wide Schools' Domestic Violence Prevention Project: An Evaluation. Final Report*. London: Westminster Domestic Violence Forum.

Thomas, N. (2002) *Children, Family and the State: Decision-Making and Child Participation*. Bristol: Policy Press.

Thomas, N. et al. (2008a) *Evaluating the Children's Commissioner for Wales: Final Report*. University of Central Lancashire and Swansea University.

——(2008b) *Promoting the Rights of Children and Young People: The Evaluation of the Children's Commissioner for Wales*. Paper presented at the International Forum for Child Welfare, Cardiff, 29 September 2008.

——(2010) 'Evaluating the Children's Commissioner for Wales: Report of a participatory research study'. *International Journal of Children's Rights*, 18(1), 19–52.

Thorne, B. (1987) 'Re-visioning women and social change: Where are the children?'. *Gender and Society*, 1(1), 85–109.

——(1990) 'Children and gender: Constructions of difference'. In Rhode, D. (ed.) *Theoretical Perspectives on Sexual Difference*. New Haven, CT: Yale University Press.

——(1993) *Gender Play: Girls and Boys in School*. Buckingham: Open University Press.

Twycross, A. (2009) 'An inter-professional approach to the ethics of undertaking research with children'. *Nurse Researcher*, 16(3), 7–20. http://*www.nurseresearcher.co.uk* [accessed 10/1/2011].

United Nations (UN) (1989) *Convention on the Rights of the Child*. New York: UN.

Uppal, S. et al. (2005) 'Asking back: Dilemmas posed when young people ask questions *to* interviewers when researching sex and relationships'. Paper presented at the British Sociological Association: Medical Sociology Group Annual Conference, University of York, 16 September 2005.

——(2009) *Cardiff Young People's Substance Misuse Needs Assessment*. London: Cordis Bright Consulting (in partnership with Cardiff Substance Misuse Action Team and Cardiff Children and Young People's Partnership). http://www.ifanc.org.uk/files/RG1CordSubMis09.pdf [accessed 3/7/2011].

Uprichard, E. (2010) 'Questioning research with children: Discrepancy between theory and practice?'. *Children and Society*, 24, 3–13.

Van Krieken, R. (2010) 'Childhood in Australian sociology and society'. *Current Sociology*, 58(2), 232–49.

Vygotsky, L.S. (1978) *Mind in Society*. Cambridge, MA: Harvard University Press.

Waksler, F.C. (1991) *Studying the Social Worlds of Children: Sociological Readings*. London: Falmer Press.

Walby, S. and Allen, J. (2004) *Domestic Violence, Sexual Assault and Stalking: Findings from the British Crime Survey*. Research Study 276. London: Home Office.

Walker, K. (2009) 'Youth empowerment evaluation: Learning voice'. *American Journal of Evaluation*, 28(3), 321–26.

Webb E. et al. (2009) 'Using the UN Convention on the Rights of Children to improve the health of children'. *Paediatrics and Child Health*, 19(9), 430–34.

Welsh Assembly Government (2007) *National Participation Standards for Wales*. Cardiff: Department of Children, Education, Lifelong Learning and Skills.

——(2005) *Healthcare Standards for Wales*.

——(2006) *National Service Framework*.

——(2008) *All Wales Universal Standards for Children and Young People Specialised Health Services*.

——(2009) *Our Healthy Future: A Public Health Strategic Framework for Wales. Thematic Paper 4: Enhancing Participation*. http://www.wales.nhs.uk/sitesplus/862/page/47916 [accessed 29/12/2011].

——(2010) *Children and Families (Wales) Measure*

——(2010) *Child Poverty Strategy for Wales: Delivery Plan*. http://wales.gov.uk/consultations/childrenandyoungpeople/cpstrategy/?lang=en [accessed 19/8/2011].

——(2011) *Proposed Rights of Children and Young Persons (Wales) Measure*. http://www.assemblywales.org/ms-ld8085-e.pdf [accessed 15/9/2011].

——(February 2011) *Child Poverty Strategy for Wales: Information Document No: 095/2011*. http://wales.gov.uk/topics/childrenyoungpeople/poverty/newcpstrategy/?lang=en [accessed 10/9/2011].

——(21 January 2011) News Article – *Children's Rights Measure Moves Forward in Wales*. http://wales.gov.uk/newsroom/childrenandyoungpeople/2011/110121children/?lang=en [accessed 15/9/2011].

Wessells, M. et al. (2010) *Community-Based Reintegration of War-Affected Young Mothers: Participatory Action Research (PAR) in Liberia, Sierra Leone and Northern Uganda*. http://www.uwyo.edu/girlmotherspar/_files/pubs-final-report.pdf [accessed 16/12/2011].

Wiles, R., Crow, G., Heath, S. and Charles, V. (2008) 'The management of confidentiality and anonymity in social research'. *International Journal Social Research Methodology*, 11(5), 417–28.

Wilkins, P. (2000) 'Collaborative approaches to research'. In Humphries, B. (ed.) *Research in Social Care and Social Welfare Issues and Debates for Practice*. London and Philadelphia: Jessica Kingsley (pp.16–30).

Williams, C. (2009) *The New NHS and the Third Sector*. Paper prepared for the National Advisory Board meeting of the National Assembly for Wales, 21 September 2009.

Williamson, B. (2003) *Grit in the Oyster. Evaluation Report on Investing in Children*. Durham: University of Durham.

Willamson, E. et al. (2005) 'Conducting research with children: The limits of confidentiality and child protection protocols'. *Children and Society* 19(5), 397–409.

Winter, R. and Munn-Giddings, C. (2001) *A Handbook for Action Research in Health and Social Care*. London: Routledge.

Wolitzsky-Taylor, K. (2008) 'Prevalence and correlates of dating violence in a national sample of adolescents'. *Journal of the American Academy of Child and Adolescent Psychiatry*, 47(7), 755–62.

Wood, J. and Hine, J. (eds) (2009) *Working with Young People*. London: Sage.

Woodhead, M. (1990/1997) 'Psychology and the cultural construction of children's needs'. In James, A. and Prout, A. (eds) *Constructing and Reconstructing Childhood: Contemporary Issues in the Sociological Study of Childhood*. London: Falmer Press.

Woodhead, M. and Faulkener, D. (2008) 'Subjects, objects or participants? Dilemmas of psychological research with children'. In Christensen, P. and James, A. (eds) *Research with Children: Perspectives and Practices*. Abingdon: Routledge.

World Health Organisation (2001) *International Classification of Functioning*. http://www.WHO.ICF.

——(2007) *International Classification of Functioning, Disability and Health for Children and Youth*. Geneva: World Health Organisation.

Wright, N. and Reid, J. (2003) 'Keeping ourselves honest: Research relations in data collection'. Paper prepared for the Australian Association for Research in Education Annual Conference, Auckland, December 2003. http://www.aare.edu.au/03pap/wri03286.pdf [accessed 3/7/2011].

Wyness, M. (2009) 'Adult's involvement in children's participation: Juggling children's places and spaces'. *Children and Society*, 23(6), 395–406.

Young, I.M. (1990) *Justice and the Politics of Difference*. Princeton, NJ: Princeton University Press.

Zolotor, A. et al. (2009) 'ISPCAN child abuse screening tool: children's version (ICAST-L) instrument development and multinational pilot testing'. *Child Abuse and Neglect*, 33(11), 833–41.

Author index

Subject index

www.ingramcontent.com/pod-product-compliance
Ingram Content Group UK Ltd.
Pitfield, Milton Keynes, MK11 3LW, UK
UKHW022021180926
475701UK00005B/968

* 9 7 8 0 4 1 5 5 2 3 0 3 5 *